SOCIOLOGICAL THEORY: WHAT WENT WRONG?

Theorizing in the social sciences today is in disarray. A disarray marked by the relative disconnection between theory and empirical research, the subordination of sociological to philosophical theorizing, the abolition of boundaries between social science disciplines and subdisciplines and the conflation of their internal logics. *Sociological Theory: What Went Wrong?* is a compelling analysis of the central problems of sociological theory today and the means to resolve them.

By examining critically a variety of developments in post-Parsonian theorizing (various micro-sociological approaches, Giddens' structuration theory, Elias's figurational sociology, Bourdieu's theory of practice, neo-functionalism, post-structuralism), the author both attempts to provide a diagnosis of what went wrong in the development of sociological theory and to offer suggestions of how to overcome the present impasse. The latter is done by the elaboration of a set of concepts which help us to view under a new light on-going debates on the nature of functionalist explanations, the agency/structure distinction, micro-macro linkages, the social versus sociological theory controversy and so on.

Sociological Theory: What Went Wrong? will be essential reading for all concerned with the state of theorizing in the social sciences today.

Nicos Mouzelis is Professor of Sociology at the London School of Economics.

SOCIOLOGICAL THEORY: WHAT WENT WRONG?

Diagnosis and Remedies

Nicos Mouzelis

London and New York

First published 1995
by Routledge
11 New Fetter Lane, London EC4P 4EE

Simultaneously published in the USA and Canada
by Routledge
29 West 35th Street, New York, NY 10001

Typeset in Bembo by
Michael Mepham, Frome, Somerset

Printed and bound in Great Britain by
Mackays of Chatham PLC, Chatham, Kent

British Library Cataloguing in Publication Data
A catalogue record for this book is available from the
British Library

Library of Congress Cataloguing in Publication Data
A catalogue record for this book has been requested

ISBN 0–415–12720–3 (hbk)
ISBN 0–415–07694–3 (pbk)

For Euphrosyne

CONTENTS

CONTENTS

ACKNOWLEDGEMENTS

I would like to thank the following people who, either through reading parts of the manuscript or through discussing various theoretical problems with me, have greatly helped me in my work: Jean-Karim Challaby, Percy Cohen, José Domingues, Costas Douzinas, Alexis Krokidas, Akis Leledakis, Joe Llobera, Akis Papataxiarchis, Leslie Sklair, Anthony Smith, Alain Swingewood, Tony Woodiwiss.

Particular thanks are owed to my friend John Hall who, in reading an early version of the text, stressed that it is not enough to show what went wrong in sociological theory. It is more important to show ways in which the present impasse can be overcome.

Finally I want to thank Ellen Sutton for her insightful remarks and her excellent editing.

INTRODUCTION

This book is quite deliberately Janus-faced, simultaneously looking forwards and backwards. It attempts selectively to appropriate certain
anti-essentialist and anti-foundationalist insights developed by post-structuralism and other versions of modern social theory, in order to come to
the rescue of sociological theory – a mode of analysis neither very popular
in the 1960s and 1970s when sociology was under the sway of Althusserian
Marxism, nor very fashionable today when sociology is mesmerized by
anti-Marxist versions of structuralist and post-structuralist thought.

1 THEORY AS TOOL AND THEORY AS END-PRODUCT

In order to explain the gist of my argument I shall begin with an
old-fashioned distinction between two types of theory: (i) theory as a set
of interrelated substantive statements trying to tell us something new,
something we do not know about the social world, which statements can
be tentatively proved or disproved by empirical investigation; and (ii)
theory as a set of tools that simply facilitate, or prepare the ground for, the
construction of substantive theory.[1] In non-Marxist sociology, the type (ii)
theory is designated by various terms such as conceptual framework,
paradigm, metatheory or heuristic device. Since none of the above are
entirely unambiguous nor do they overlap completely, I prefer the terms
Generalities II and Generalities III, coined by Althusser when he set out
to distinguish theory as a tool/means (Gen. II), and theory as a provisional
end-product (Gen. III).[2]

The distinction between conceptual framework and substantive theory,
between Gen. II and Gen. III, is not, of course, entirely clear cut. All actual
theories contain within them both types of theoretical statements. In most

1

cases the admixture is such, however, that it is quite easy to decide whether a specific work belongs predominantly to (i) or (ii). So for instance Parsons' *The Social System*,[3] irrespective of what the author claimed to be doing, is clearly a Gen. II book.[4] It tries to elaborate a set of conceptual tools which, rather than telling us anything substantive about social systems, simply suggest ways of looking at them. It provides conceptual means that allow us, for instance, to ask systematic, comparatively-oriented questions about social wholes, ranging from work groups to formal organizations or whole communities.

N. Smelser's *Social Change in the Industrial Revolution*,[5] on the other hand, is mainly a Generalities III book. Although it quite systematically uses Parsonian tools (Gen. II), its primary purpose is to provide a substantive theory of how the Industrial Revolution in England came about and what its impact was on kinship and work arrangements.[6]

Given the above differences between these two works, the appropriate mode of assessing them is also different. In the case of Smelser's theory it is the issue of empirical evidence (in the light of the available primary and secondary sources) that is crucial. In the case of Parsons' *Social System*, empirical testing is of less importance than the conceptual adequacy or the heuristic utility of the tools he offers. To be more precise: when Parsons (or functionalists in general) suggests that groups or formal organizations can be viewed as wholes of interrelated parts, and that the degree of the interrelatedness of parts is an open, empirical question, this does not give us a great deal that can be empirically tested. What we can do is to assess the utility of this conceptualization for generating interesting questions and for generally facilitating empirically-oriented research.

I find the distinction between these two types of theory absolutely essential. In fact, very frequently neglecting or refusing to distinguish between theory as tool/resource and theory as end-product/topic has social scientists talking at cross purposes. So the anti-foundationalist attack against law-like, universal, transhistorical social theories is more relevant and effective when applied to Generalities III than Generalities II. For instance, Parsons' analysis of the concepts of role or institution, Giddens' development of his duality-of-structure schema, Bourdieu's notion of *habitus* – all these are obviously transhistorical conceptualizations. They are supposed to be useful in the analysis of different types of society or social situation, regardless of time and space. The contextless, universal character of the above conceptual tools is not, however, as problematical as that of substantive theories that try, for example, in a highly positivistic manner, to establish universal connections or laws between such variables as communication, innovation, literacy,[7] or between the need for achievement and economic growth.[8] In the first case the universal conceptual tools may lead to context-sensitive, historically-oriented comparative investigations that can throw much light on how social wholes are constituted, reproduced and transformed. In the second case the theory's lack of context invariably leads to substantive conclusions that are either trivial or wrong (wrong in the sense that the connection between variables is valid only in certain conditions which, due to the theory's universal character, are not and cannot be specified).

2 THE RISE AND FALL OF MODERN SOCIOLOGICAL THEORY

An important feature of classical sociology was its relative non-differentiation between the two types of theory outlined above. In so far as the founding fathers attempted to understand the unique social arrangements that had emerged in the aftermath of the Industrial and French Revolutions, there were very close connections in their writings between their analyses of industrial societies on the one hand, and their conceptual/methodological insights on the other. The work of Marx, for example, when seen a whole, contains extensive analyses of other scholars' theories (that were to become part of his major raw material – what Althusser calls Generalities I); an emphasis on such basic conceptual tools as mode of production, forces and relations of production, etc. (Gen. II); and a fully developed substantive theory on the genesis and basic 'laws of motion' of the capitalist mode of production (Gen. III).

This fine balance between conceptual framework and substantive theory was upset during this century when sociological theory grew into a distinct subfield or branch of sociological enquiry (which focuses predominantly on the construction of Gen. II rather than Gen. III). It is generally accepted that the sociologist who contributed most to this type of division of labour was Talcott Parsons.

Some observers consider the relative divorce or rather differentiation between Gen. II and Gen. III an unfortunate development that could not help but lead to the highly abstract, 'vacuous', 'untestable' kind of theorizing that is exemplified by Parsons' work.[9] Others (including myself) do not believe this development to be as regrettable as critics of Parsonian theory imply, and see it rather as an unavoidable and irreversible result of the growing division of labour within sociology. In any case, the charge of non-verifiability is ill-placed – since the chief aim of modern sociological theory is not to fashion substantive theories (Gen. III) but to construct sets of conceptual tools (Gen. II) for looking at social phenomena in such a way that interesting questions are generated and methodologically proper linkages established between different levels of analysis. Therefore, while empirical verifiability is the crucial mode of assessment for Generalities III, heuristic utility is that for Generalities II.

Moreover, it is worth emphasizing that while the emergence of modern sociological theory has meant a break with the great classical syntheses, it has not led to a disconnection from empirical research. On the contrary, the work of the first generation of sociological theorists (Parsons, Merton, Gouldner, Lockwood, etc.) expresses a clear concern with providing conceptual tools for empirical investigation. This is apparent from both the conceptual frameworks elaborated and from the fact that such frameworks were systematically applied in practice (either by the theorists themselves and/or by their disciples) as a means of generating empirically-oriented accounts of the social world. Using an evolutionary vocabulary, one can say that the differentiation between sociological theory and the more empirically-oriented subdisciplines was accompanied by integrative mechanisms that ensured a minimum of linkages between theory and empirical research.

It seems to me that it is in the light of the above considerations that one should assess Parsons' complex work, which has contributed so much to establishing sociological theory as a specialized subdiscipline. Despite its serious shortcomings (on which more below), the Parsonian framework could and did lead to considerable empirical research on both the micro and macro levels of analysis.[10] However, although Parsonian sociological theory successfully advanced the intellectual division of labour within sociology without breaking the link between theory and research, it has done less well in terms of the conceptual tools offered. Applied to empirical issues, these tools systematically neglect the voluntaristic dimensions of social life, and this has led more or less directly to a reified, positivistic and often teleological treatment of social phenomena.

As numerous critics have pointed out, Parsons – especially when his analysis progressed from his early theory of social action to a theorization of social systems and their long-term evolution – overemphasized the systemic/functionalist dimensions of social systems at the expense of agency. His theory either portrays agents as passive outcomes of a system of core values or ignores them altogether.

On the level of micro action, Parsons fails to develop a theory of interaction, his analysis moving abruptly from a theorization of unit-acts to a theorization of social systems.[11] As a result of this omission, Parsons' role-players seem to be guided exclusively by normative considerations, as core values are institutionalized into role expectations and internalized into need depositions.[12] On the macro level of analysis, on the other hand, agents tend to disappear entirely, given that Parsons conceptualizes society in terms of four subsystems, each consisting of a set of institutionalized norms geared to the solution of society's four functional problems (adaptation, goal achievement, integration and latency – AGIL for short). Since each subsystem is further divided according to the same AGIL logic into four subsystems, social reality ultimately becomes a complex of systems within systems. In this onion-like construct, macro actors such as interest groups, social movements, etc. do not seem to have a theoretically worked out place. (This is not to say that Parsons and those influenced by him never refer to macro or collective actors in their empirical writings. It simply means that when they do portray macro actors as relatively autonomous agents, it is despite, not because of their conceptual framework.)[13]

In this book I shall focus particularly (though not exclusively) on the agency–structure and the micro–macro issues, and argue that post-Parsonian sociological theory took several different directions, all of them problematical.

Those interpretatively-oriented sociologists who have continued in the Parsonian tradition have, in overreaction to the ultra-systemic and reifying features of structural functionalism, overemphasized agency, and theorized action and interaction in a manner that creates serious obstacles to the study of how micro situations (on which they focus exclusively) link up with macro-institutional structures and actors.

Similar difficulties (as far as the agency–structure and micro–macro issues are concerned) were encountered by rational-choice theory, another influential approach, and one that tried to combat the reifying and teleological tendencies of both Parsonian and Marxist macro theories. Rational-choice theorists endeavour, among other things, to bridge the micro–macro gap by providing 'micro foundations', by showing how macro phenomena (such as state institutions, social movements or revolutionary transformations) have at their roots the decision-making activities of concrete utility-maximizing/optimizing actors.

However, rational-choice theory tends to link micro with macro levels of analysis via logico-deductive methods that result in the neglect of 'emergent' phenomena and/or the various socio-historical contexts within which rationality takes its specific forms. In that sense it comes up against the following dilemma: in so far as its mainly logico-deductive theorizing refuses to take into account 'emergence', history and context, its statements (like all transhistorical, universalistic statements) tend to be either wrong or trivial. On the other hand, when rational-choice theory does seriously consider institutional context, it loses its distinctive profile and its logico-deductive elegance.[14]

Another major reaction to Parsonian functionalism (initially led by politically radical sociologists, incensed by Parsons' neglect of collective action and struggles) turned its attention first to conflict theory, then to Marxism, and finally, after the relative demise of Marxism in the 1980s, to post-structuralist/postmodernist approaches to the social. What is interesting about postmodern social theory is that it rejects not only Parsons' specific conceptualizations of system and action, but also his attempt (quite positive, as I see it) at establishing sociological theory as a specialized subdiscipline of sociology – i.e. as an intellectual activity portraying a specific logic of analysis quite distinct from that of philosophy or of theorizing in other, neighbouring disciplines.

Post-structuralists, by rejecting the crude positivism and theoretical provincialism of Parsonian-influenced sociology, as well as the economistic holism of Marxism, turned their attention to philosophical issues and/or theoretical developments in fields such as linguistics, semiotics, psycho-analysis, etc. The desire to break through entrenched barriers and to broaden the horizons of a hitherto inward-looking discipline is reflected in the fact that philosophers like Foucault and Derrida, or luminaries in neighbouring disciplines like Lacan, have now become central figures in social theory discourse.

However, as I shall argue below, this broader outlook was not accompanied by any theoretically coherent and systematic attempt to translate insights derived from philosophy and other disciplines into the framework of sociological theory proper. Instead, sociological theorizing gave way to amateur discussions on ontological/epistemological issues, and to attempts at reducing the study of complex societies to that of language, discourse, texts, the unconscious and suchlike. Moreover, the poststructuralists' total rejection of the agency–structure and micro–macro distinctions, as well as their failure to show how discourses or texts are hierarchized via unequally empowered agents, has led to a systematic neglect of the hierarchial features of complex societies, as well as to the disconnection, or very tenuous connection, between theory and empirical research.[15] Such disconnection is not found in either historically-oriented Marxist sociology or in Parsonian functionalism, nor for that matter in the micro-sociological writings of the hermeneutically-oriented critics of Parsons.

If post-structuralism has turned its back on both the substance and the type of division of labour that Parsonian theory has brought about, there are a number of very influential theorists who, while distancing themselves from the basic assumptions of post-structuralism, agree with its rejection of all forms of functionalist theorizing. In their attempts to go beyond the subjectivist-versus-objectivist divide in sociology, theorists like Giddens, Elias and Bourdieu endeavour to transcend rather than restructure Parsonian functionalism by elaborating conceptual tools that are to take us beyond the misleading dichotomies of subject–object, action–system and micro–macro. Looking critically at aspects of N. Elias's figurational sociology, Giddens' structuration theory and Bourdieu's notion of the *habitus*, I shall argue that (the utility of these conceptualizations aside) they have failed to transcend functionalism in general, and Parsonian functionalism in particular. They have simply avoided the by now unfashionable functionalist vocabulary (as well as that of agency–structure, micro–macro) while retaining its fundamental logic – with the result that crypto-functionalist elements and related distinctions are clandestinely reintroduced into their writings.

Finally, in a more modest way, several old and new disciples of Parsons have tried not to transcend but to restructure Parsonian functionalism in such a way as to overcome some of its oversystemic features. Without being a Parsonian, my own theoretical strategy also aims more at restructuring rather than transcending functionalism. In that sense I feel very sympathetic to the type of neo-functionalist analysis that J. Alexander, P. Colomy or N. Smelser are producing in an effort to retrieve the useful features of Parsonian functionalism and evolutionism.

My main objection to their work is that their restructuring has not yet gone far enough. With a few exceptions,[16] the concepts that are supposed to render Parsonian theory more dynamic (such as group strategies or class conflict) are introjected *ad hoc* into the Parsonian corpus – without, that is, assessing the theoretical consequences these new elements have for the basic features of Parsonian theory, particularly for his fundamental AGIL scheme. In that sense these attempts seem to bring changes to the Parsonian edifice that are cosmetic rather than substantial.

All in all, if, following Habermas,[17] we must relate what is happening in theoretical sociology today to the Parsonian 'constitutive' contribution, one can maintain that most current tendencies fail to appropriate creatively what is positive and useful in Parsons' *oeuvre*.

First, those who have tried to continue the research-oriented, specialized theorizing initiated by Parsons have either dealt exclusively and one-sidedly with Parsons' underemphasis of micro interaction (interpretative micro sociologies) or accepted the Parsonian edifice in its entirety and embellished it further, or introduced voluntaristic elements (neo-functionalism) into it in an *ad hoc* manner.

Second, those who have opted for a logico-deductive solution to the agency–structure and micro–macro issues posed (but not solved) by Parsonian theory have been able to provide only reductive solutions to these issues (rational-choice theories).

Third, those post-structuralists who reject not only Parsonian functionalism but also the type of division of labour sociological theory entails, as well as all conventional distinctions and boundaries within and between the social sciences, have ended up with theorizations that are of little use to empirically-oriented sociologists.

Fourth, those who have tried to 'transcend' Parsonian functionalism/evolutionism, while to some extent continuing the specialized and empirically-oriented theorizing that Parsons initiated, have managed to transcend functionalism only in form rather than substance.

Concerning now the specific organization of the book, *Part I* is primarily diagnostic. It tries to show in what ways interpretative sociologies (Chapter 1) as well as rational-choice theories (Chapter 2) have failed to find adequate solutions to the micro–macro and agency–structure issues. It also tries to show that post-structuralist theories, by following a strategy of theoretical dedifferentiation (i.e. the abolition of boundaries between disciplines), have ended up with extremely crude conceptualizations that hinder rather than facilitate the empirical exploration of how complex societies are constituted and transformed (Chapter 3).

In *Part II* the focus shifts from diagnosis to tentative remedies. By looking critically at theories that purport to transcend Parsonian functionalism (Elias's theory in Chapter 4, and Bourdieu's and Giddens' in Chapter 6), and by trying to show how the Marxist notions of technology, appropriation and ideology can, via a more adequate handling of the agency–structure issue, contribute to an effective restructuring of Parsonian theory (Chapter 5), I try to formulate a set of conceptual tools which try both to solve certain puzzles related to functionalist theorizing and to help the empirically-oriented sociologist to move from micro to meso and macro levels of analysis – while avoiding both the reductive and reificatory treatment of social phenomena (Chapter 7, Appendix to the Conclusion, Appendix).

3 CONCEPTUAL PRAGMATISM

The basic orientation underlying both this and my two previous theoretically-oriented works could, for want of a better term, be called 'conceptual pragmatism'.[18] Viewing pragmatism in the manner of C. S. Pierce – i.e. as a method for the clarification of concepts by showing how they are or can be used [19] – one might argue that sociological theory, as developed by Parsons and others, has as its major task to clarify current conceptual tools and to construct new ones by following criteria of utility rather than truth. Adhering to this orientation, I have kept clear of the type of ambitious theorizing that purposes to provide substantive universal propositions (Gen. III) either in the form of 'laws' and contextless generalizations, or in the form of philosophical analysis of the ontological nature of the social, the possibility of social knowledge, the constitution of the subject, and so on.

Broadly accepting the intellectual division of labour as this has been established by Parsonian theory, I view sociological theory as a specialized subdisipline of sociology, the chief objective of which is the critical assessment of existing conceptual tools/frameworks and the construction of new ones. To say it again: the *raison d'être* of such tools is, negatively, to solve puzzles that hinder the open-ended, dialogic communication between social scientists; and, more positively, to facilitate the empirical investigation of the social world via asking theoretically interesting questions, providing conceptual means for comparative work, for moving from one level of analysis to another, etc.

As I shall explain in detail in Chapter 3, I think that this perhaps somewhat narrow definition of sociological theory need not make sociologists turn their backs on philosophy or other relevant disciplines within and outside the social sciences. If successful, it leads not to isolation, but rather to an effective *rapprochement* with other disciplines – but a *rapprochement* from an autonomous position that does not dissolve the specific identity and logic of sociological theorizing, and does not turn it into an adjunct of philosophy, linguistics or psychoanalysis. In other words, sociological theory as here defined combats both dedifferentiation and compartmentalization, both the total abolition of disciplinary boundaries as well as the erection of insurmountable barriers between disciplines and subdisciplines.

It is precisely in this area that sociological theory can and should play a very crucial, strategic role today. By maintaining its specialized logic and orientation it is capable of providing a set of conceptual tools that can operate as a theoretical *lingua franca*, as a flexible vocabulary with no foundationalist pretensions, which can help sociologists establish bridges between their own and other disciplines, as well as between competing social science paradigms. This is to say that sociological theory should not aim at the establishment of some sort of monolithic paradigmatic unity, but at strengthening the present pluralism by removing the obstacles that are a hindrance to open-ended communication between the differentiated subdisciplines or paradigms. While boundaries and distinctions should not be rejected dogmatically or mindlessly, sociological theory should also make sure that boundaries are not turned into impregnable barriers, and that distinctions do not become dichotomic essences.

Lastly, a few words about the limitations of this study. This is neither a book on the history nor on the sociology of sociological theory. I neither try to establish historical linkages or influences between the various approaches or theories I examine, nor do I try to relate their authors' writings to the broader socio-cultural context in which they are rooted. Assuming that theoretical traditions have an internal logic and relative autonomy *vis-à-vis* broader socio-political and cultural developments, I have limited myself to a critique and restructuring from the 'inside out', so to speak. Therefore, although the problem of (for instance) why post-structuralism has had and still has such an important influence among Anglo-Saxon theoretically-oriented sociologists is very interesting, it is beyond the scope of this book. What does lie within its range is to consider to what extent the major conceptual tools of post-structuralism help or hinder the development of empirical research and the advancement of our knowledge of the social world. There can be no doubt, of course, that the two problems are related: a better knowledge of the 'social context' can help the exploration of the 'internal logic'. But there is equally no doubt that there are also breaks or discontinuities between the two problematics, and that for practical purposes it is possible to bracket the one while investigating the other.

Another qualification of the book is that it does not pretend to be systematic or exhaustive in analysis of the major approaches and/or issues in sociological theory. For instance, despite their phenomenal growth during the last decade, I did not consider it necessary to deal at all systematically with cultural studies or feminist theory.[20] Neither is it particularly scholastic or scholarly in its treatment of major writers. Instead, focusing on the micro–macro and agency–structure issues, I have tried to show how various theorists have actually put them to use in practice rather than in rhetoric. I have tried to find out what they actually do with their conceptual tools, rather than what they claim they do.[21] Furthermore, I have tried to rework some of the concepts available in the literature, so as to suggest some new ways of bringing micro and macro sociologies closer together, as well as agency– and systemically-oriented approaches.

Another way of putting all this is to say that this book sets out to express in a rather eclectic and/or idiosyncratic manner some tentative views (based on a long-term involvement with theory in teaching and research) on what has gone wrong in the development of sociological theory and whether or not we can do anything about it today.

Finally, concerning stylistic matters, I do not believe (contrary to some post-structuralists) that to insist on clarity of exposition is a form of intellectual terrorism. Accordingly, I have tried to make the major points of the book as clear as possible by avoiding neo-logisms, by providing concrete and straightforward examples to illustrate abstract arguments, by summarizing the major themes at several points in the book and by putting more technical points into the Notes section.

Part I
DIAGNOSIS

1

IMPASSES OF MICRO-SOCIOLOGICAL THEORIZING
Overreaction to Parsons

With the middle and late periods of Parsons' *oeuvre* marked by an under-emphasis of both micro and macro actors, the various interpretative sociologies that mushroomed from the 1960s onwards have almost entirely focused on the former. This disregard of macro actors has had grave consequences for the further development of sociological theory as such.

There are several explanations for this surprising neglect by theorists, whose avowed purpose had been to redress Parsons' overly systemic analysis and to 'bring back people' into sociological studies.

One obvious reason is the excessive fear of reification that haunts hermeneutically- and ethnomethodologically-oriented sociologists. For them, any reference to organizations or larger collectivities as having goals, taking decisions, implementing policies, etc., smacks of anthropomorphism, of endowing collectivities with characteristics proper only to individual human actors. For several reasons this excessive fear of reification (often exacerbated by the crude manner in which macro sociologists, especially Marxists, refer to whole classes as having projects, strategies, etc.) is quite unjustified. The ascription of anthropomorphic, decision-making capacities to formal organizations and other collectivities is mostly no more than a convenient shorthand to avoid long-winded descriptions of complex processes of representation and of group decision-making. In so far as verbal abridgements can readily be translated into detailed action terms, there is no reification. The stenographic assertion that, for instance, the trade union movement has adopted such-and-such a policy entails no reification because one can, when asked, give a blow-by-blow account of the actual interactive, decision-making processes the trade union leaders, cadres, etc. were involved in.[1]

Another reason that partly explains the reluctance of interpretative sociologists to deal with macro actors is their populistic predilection for

15

'lay persons', 'ordinary members of society', 'mundane' encounters, etc. Partly in overreaction to the explanations by conventional historians of long-term developments as the doings of kings and 'great men', micro sociologists have concentrated their energies on micro actors' contributions to the construction of social reality. As a result they ignore not only collective actors but also what for convenience one may call 'mega' actors – i.e. individual actors in control of considerable resources, whose decisions stretch widely in space and time.

In other words, micro sociologists tend to forget that actors, because of their very unequal access to the economic, political and cultural means of production,[2] contribute just as unequally to the construction of social reality. Attempting, however, to explain the symbolic construction of social wholes by exclusive reference to 'lay persons' or 'ordinary' members is like trying to account for the construction of a complex edifice by reference only to bricklayers, completely ignoring the contribution of architects, managers, foremen, accountants, lawyers, etc.[3]

A third reason for the neglect of macro actors by interpretatively-oriented sociologists is the all-pervasive 'individual–society' schema, which one finds in the Durkheim–Parsons tradition. Despite significant alterations by micro sociologists, this schema has survived in its fundamental logic up to the very present. Being highly misleading, it has driven micro-sociological theorizing into a fatal cul-de-sac. Nowadays, of course, given the phenomenological shift from Weber's focus on the subjective orientations of individual actors to intersubjectivity as the basic unit of analysis, one no longer speaks of the 'individual'. Moreover, given the micro sociologists' fear of reification, Society (capital S) is also considered a highly suspect concept. But the macro-society/micro-individual distinction has survived in various new guises, such as the contrast between institutional or social structures on the one hand and interactions or encounters on the other – the former being always linked with the macro, and the latter with the micro level of analysis.

This association of action with micro makes itself felt particularly strongly in respect of face-to-face interactions which, as a matter of course, are invariably considered as micro phenomena, as the building blocks out of which macro institutional orders are constructed. Whether one looks at the writings of Garfinkel, Cicourel, Goffman, or their numerous disciples, one always comes up against the ubiquitous idea that to study face-to-face interaction is to study micro phenomena, and given this, the problem then becomes one of linking face-to-face encounters on the micro level with social or institutional structures on the macro level.

1 THE DEBATE ON THE NATURE OF GOFFMAN'S 'INTERACTION ORDER'

I shall try to make the above point more concrete by taking a look at the recent debate on the nature of Goffman's idea that interaction is an order *sui generis*, quite distinct from both individual agents and macro social structures.[4] The major contributors to the debate take it for granted that the interaction order is micro and quite distinct from macro phenomena. Their only point of serious disagreement is over which aspect of micro-social reality the interaction order refers to. So Ann Rawls tries to establish its specificity by reference to moral 'ground rules' emanating from the interaction situation itself, and particularly from the 'presentational' needs of the social self.[5] Stephen Fuchs rejects this, and attempts a definition of the interaction order based on Luhmann's distinction between interactional, organizational and societal systems. The interaction system, which emerges 'as soon as copresent interactants perceive mutual perceptions and select their communications accordingly',[6] is less encompassing than the organizational and societal systems.

What is interesting in the arguments of Rawls and Fuchs is that both conceive of the interaction order as micro, with Rawls focusing on micro rules specifically linked to the logic of encounters, and Fuchs on micro-social systems. Moreover, they both contrast interaction with a macro state of affairs: for her this being 'social structure' or 'institutional order', for him the more encompassing organizational and societal systems.[7]

The identification of institutional and social structures with the macro level, and 'free' agency of interaction with the micro level, is not limited to micro sociologists. It is equally accepted by those interested, whether positivistically or non-positivistically, in the analysis of macro phenomena. So Peter Blau, in his attempt to differentiate between micro and macro sociology, says that the macro-structural approach is not interested in 'social interactions between individuals', and analyses instead 'the rates of social interaction between social positions'. He argues further that

> the macro-sociological focus is appropriate for the study of entire societies or other large-scale collectivities, because it is impossible to trace and dissect the interpersonal relations of many thousands or millions of people, and neither would it be meaningful if all were described.[8]

But if macro sociology focuses on large collectivities and micro sociology on 'relations between individuals', where does an interaction fit in between a few individuals (mega actors) who happen to be heads of state and whose decisions may have world-wide repercussions?

To give an obvious example: the face-to-face encounter between Churchill, Roosevelt and Stalin at Yalta in 1945 led to crucial decisions which, among other things, shaped the post-war map of Europe and profoundly affected the lives of millions of people. In what sense could that interaction between these three men be seen as a micro event?

There appears to be no place in the schemes of Rawls, Fuchs, Blau or Goffman for interactions of this kind, i.e. face-to-face encounters whose intended or unintended consequences, to use Giddens' formulation, stretch very widely in time and/or space. The broad, macro impact of face-to-face interactions may be due to the fact that the interacting individuals occupy a powerful institutionalized social position (as in the example given above); or it may be due to dispositional (e.g. personal charisma) or situational factors (e.g. an assassin who kills a head of state).

The key distinction between the positional, dispositional and interactive-situational dimensions of social games will be developed extensively in Chapter 6; here it is enough to emphasize that, for whatever reason, face-to-face interactions are not always micro phenomena. Often the face-to-face interactions of a few individuals who – for positional, dispositional or situational reasons – have a lot of power, are absolutely crucial for understanding how whole societal orders are constructed, reproduced or transformed. To repeat, it is the micro-interaction/macro-structure distinction that is responsible for this obvious fact not being taken seriously among sociologists.

The misleading distinction between macro-institutional structures and micro interaction disregards not only the fact that face-to-face interactions can be macro, but also that institutional structures can take a 'micro' form. Consider, for instance, the banal example of a national business organization which has a number of local branches. One can view the local organization as a social system related to a more encompassing social system at the national level. The local business organization like the national one can be viewed, to use Giddens' terminology, both in terms of 'strategic conduct' and in terms of 'institutional analysis' (see Chapter 6, Section 2). That is to say, one can view it as a figuration of interrelated actors (managers, employees, blue-collar workers, etc.) as well as an interrelated ensemble of institutionalized rules/norms. To focus on the latter, and to use Parsonian terminology, the local organization's social structure can be viewed in terms of four institutional subsystems: adaptation (A), goal achievement (G), integration (I), latency (L). These, as I will explain in Chapter 5, do not refer directly to actors but to institutions – in our example, to micro institutions. For instance, the adaptation subsystem (A) refers to all institutionalized norms which deal with the 'economic', i.e. the 'acquisition of resources' problem of the local firm, such as rules about how to recruit personnel, how to buy raw materials, how to borrow money, etc. Such institutionalized rules can be strictly local (i.e. one might find them only in this local system or only in local social systems); or they may be rules which are more widely used (for instance, basic rules about property, contract, etc.). But in so far as the latter rules are embodied within the social positions of our local social system, and in so far as they contribute together with the 'local' rules, to the constitution and reproduction of local micro games, then they can be viewed as the economic micro institutions of the local firm. And as we can talk about the economic institutions of the local firm, we can as well talk about its political institutions (G), legal institutions (I), etc. Despite the fact that Parsons' AGIL scheme presents serious difficulties (see Chapter 5), I think it is useful in reminding us that one can analyse not only whole societies in terms of institutionalized subwholes, but also less encompassing social systems like a formal organization.[9]

2 NEGLECT OF SOCIAL HIERARCHIES: BRIDGING THE MICRO–MACRO GAP VIA THE LOGIC OF AGGREGATION OR REPRESENTATION

Another important point to emphasize here is that the identification of interaction with micro, and of institutions with macro, leads to an under-emphasis of social hierarchies, of the fact that institutionalized positions/roles and actors are often related not only horizontally but also vertically. For instance, actors, being part of a multiplicity of hierarchically organized wholes (corporations, trade unions, political parties, etc.) deal routinely with other actors both hierarchically subordinate and superordinate. (The same can be said, of course, when the focus is not on actors and interactions but on hierarchically organized positions.)

The acute importance of the above emerges beyond any doubt when one takes into account that, ever since the development of state societies, hierarchies have played the crucial role in 'caging' human beings in authoritatively organized social systems[10] – this caging being dramatically accentuated by the spread of bureaucratic forms of organization in most spheres of modern life. Even if in 'postmodern' or post-industrial societies there has been a certain amount of debureaucratization, in the long run bureaucratic structures (though perhaps of a more flexible nature) will remain the major mode by which social members relate to the increasingly centralized economic, political and cultural arenas of nation-states.

In view of the above, one cannot properly consider the passage from the micro to meso[11] and macro levels of analysis without seriously taking into consideration how modern societies are hierarchically organized, and particularly how micro actors are hierarchically related (through formal organization or otherwise) to meso and macro actors.

Micro sociology ignores all of this by insisting that actors and face-to-face interactions belong to the micro, and institutional structures to the macro level. This absurd but strongly rooted misconception precludes any study of how micro, meso and macro actors relate to each other within specific hierarchically organized contexts. It is not at all surprising, therefore, that the present debate on the links between micro and macro sociology, as well as the older, related debate on methodological individualism versus holism, has led precisely nowhere. Not only do neither of these debates theorize the concept of social hierarchies, they both leave it out of account altogether as though it did not exist.[12] Trying, however, to investigate how micro actors and encounters relate to the constitution, reproduction and transformation of larger collectivities without taking into serious consideration the hierarchical aspects of social wholes, is like trying to swim in a pool that has been drained of water.

In the absence of a concept of macro interaction, and of the notion of hierarchically organized positions linking micro, meso and macro actors, how do micro sociologists relate micro to macro phenomena? The short answer is that they try to do so through the direct or indirect use of a logic of aggregation. Randall Collins' theory of 'methodological situationalism' is a typical recent attempt at bridging the micro–macro gap in this manner.[13]

For Collins, the micro–macro debate in modern sociology was infused with new vigour by such empirically-oriented branches of micro sociology as ethnomethodology, conversational analysis and cognitive sociology. The earlier philosophical and more abstract debates of macro sociology have had to give way to criticism from a perspective that is both theoretically sophisticated (ethnomethodology, for instance, is based on Husserlian phenomenology) and founded on very detailed empirical research. The purpose of the new approach is not to reject what macro sociology is doing, but on the contrary to improve its exploratory potential by reconstituting it on radically empirical, micro foundations. It is believed that only in this way can we move 'towards a more successful sociological science'.[14]

Collins' own chief goal is to fashion a conceptual apparatus for translating such macro concepts as society, community, class or state into empirically observable or accessible interactions between real people. For this purpose, and contrary to mainstream methodological individualism, his basic unit of analysis is not the individual actor, but the encounter or micro-interactional situation (hence his label 'methodological situationalism'). Whether applied to the examination of Churches, schools, factories or social movements, methodological situationalism always sees human beings at the root of such phenomena – human beings interacting with each other in specific situations and investing their encounters with varying degrees of emotional energy and cultural resources.

Although Collins' methodological situationalism is quite complex, based as it is on the central role of conversation and of interaction ritual chains in the construction of the social world, the basic assumption underlying his theory is the idea that all macro phenomena 'are made up of aggregations and repetitions of many similar micro-events'.[15] For instance, what we usually call social structure (of an organization, say, or of society as a whole) is 'nothing more than large numbers of micro-encounters repeated (or sometimes changing) over time and actors' space'.[16]

Collins' approach is flawed, of course, by his contention that macro phenomena are simply aggregates of micro encounters. The concept of aggregation does not imply any analysis of the actual relationship between one micro situation (or micro encounter) and another. Neither does Collins consider the hierarchical relationships between micro and macro encounters or games. For instance, meso encounters or games between junior managers of some particular corporation may be hierarchically connected with games or encounters of employees lower down in the organizational hierarchy, as well as with the macro games of senior managers nearer the top. The latter games (which, to say it once more, do not necessarily entail many actors but rather powerful ones) are certainly no mere aggregates of those played lower down in the organizational hierarchy. The relationship between micro, meso and macro games is not one of aggregation at all, but one of subsumption: decisions taken at the top tend to become the value premises that those in subordinate positions have to consider when they take their own, more limited decisions.[17]

Because Collins ignores both the horizontal and vertical relations between encounters, he can deal only with 'aggregative' social wholes: those that consist of a mere addition of myriad, relatively disconnected micro events. He is unable to deal seriously with what Piaget has called Gestalt or configurational social wholes, whose parts are related horizontally and/or vertically in specific ways.[18] In so far as methodological situationalism considers micro situations to be discrete and commensurable units, and that one can easily pass from the micro to the macro level by simply aggregating a great number of these units, its position is not so very different from that of methodological individualism. Just as the latter, in its more extreme form, reduces macro phenomena to a heap of isolated individuals, so methodological situationalism reduces them to an assembly of encounters. In the first case the *monad* is the individual, in the second the micro encounter.

While Collins tries to move from micro to macro by means of a simple logic of aggregation, Karin Knorr-Cetina adopts a somewhat different strategy which, however, is equally impervious to macro actors and social hierarchies.

Although Knorr-Cetina sees Collins' methodological situationalism as a major improvement over the methodological individualism that preceded it, she disagrees with his aggregation thesis. Her criticism uses more systematically ethnomethodological insights (especially Cicourel's). She does not consider macro structures as either aggregations of micro events, nor – as implied by conventional sociology – as a distinct layer superimposed on that of micro situations and encounters. For her, macro phenomena are summary representations of micro events, these representations being 'actively constructed and pursued within micro situations'.[19]

In other words, Knorr-Cetina contends that when actors try to make sense of the complex macro situations in which they are involved, they use various techniques of inference, interpretation and summary representation to construct for themselves an intelligible model of the social world. Such abstract typifications, instead of being perceived as the shorthand representations of micro situations that they are, are often wrongly taken (by their creators or by investigating social scientists) for actual macro structures subsuming, controlling or generating micro situations. In other words, historians, scientists or mere participants, in their endeavour to make sense of complex macro events (such as wars or revolutions) construct summary representations of the event in question, and then ascribe to that representation specific causal powers.

For Knorr-Cetina what often leads to the wrong conception of how micro events are related to macro representations is the 'fallacy of unwarranted subsumption': the erroneous belief in a homogeneous social space where micro phenomena are subsumed and controlled by macro structures. In support of her point she quotes Braudel's work on the development of pre-industrial Europe, and more particularly his identification of three types or systems of economic transaction: (i) transactions regulated by national markets, (ii) those which took place within the large-scale subsistence economies of those countries, and (iii) transactions related to the international market.

Now Knorr-Cetina is fully aware of the temptation to view the international market as related, through subsumption, to the national one, and that in turn to the subsistence economy – in the sense that the most encompassing (i.e. international) transactions control or affect transactions on the level of the national market, and so on, Braudel leaves no doubt, however, that even though the three economies did interlink, they stood in no relation of subsumption. The international economy did not fully control the national one, and the national markets for their part developed in relative independence from the subsistence economies. Instead of one subsuming the other, these three types of economy evolved as quite separate provinces of transaction: they simply coexisted.[20]

A critical evaluation of Knorr-Cetina's representation thesis must straightaway note her tendency, *pace* R. Collins, to view all encounters as micro events. Macro events such as revolutions or wars are held to be aggregations of micro encounters. Cases that are more than aggregations are simply mere representations by participants or observers, and incorrect ones at that; they are second-order theories wrongly representing the participants' first-order theorizations and actions.

So the historians' view that the famous Battle of Borodino was primarily decided by the macro strategies of Kutuzov and Napoleon is something of a misrepresentation of what happened. It ignores the interactional complexity of the myriad micro encounters between the men who did the actual fighting, which had its own autonomous dynamic and was only tenuously related to the orders issued by the military leaders.[21] Second-order theorizations (such as historians' macro representations) do not, therefore, reflect accurately first-order theorizations or actions. Or, in other words, the first-order macro strategies and decisions at Borodino were ineffective and ultimately beside the point; the only real events were the encounters of fighting micro actors.

There is no doubt that nominalism of the kind Knorr-Cetina mentions does occur, and frequently. On the other hand, it is absurd to claim that all macro phenomena consist of nothing more than summary representations of micro events. It may well be, for example, that with regard to the Battle of Borodino, Knorr-Cetina, who adopts Tolstoy's version of the events, might be right; that neither the French nor the Russian leadership was capable of co-ordinating and effectively monitoring micro events. But one can hardly elevate this into a general principle. The first atom bomb being dropped on Hiroshima, for instance – an event that played a crucial role in the termination of the Second World War – was not a historian's faulty representation of unco-ordinated micro events. It was due to a weighty decision taken by macro actors (primarily by those controlling the means of domination and coercion in the United States) and effectively transmitted downwards via a network of hierarchically organized decision-makers.

In similar vein, to take Braudel's example, if economic transactions in pre-industrial Europe on the level of national markets did not subsume transactions on the level of the more localized subsistence economies (since the space where these two types of transaction took place was not homogeneous), this does not justify the elevation of this insight into a general principle regulating all macro–micro connections. Granted that national-market transactions in sixteenth-century Europe did not subsume but ran parallel with transactions in the local subsistence economy, this is much less the case in the Europe of the twentieth century. The development and consolidation of nation-states, the relative decline of local and regional subsistence economies, and the establishment of national economic, political and cultural arenas mean that today's relation between national and local markets and transactions is very much more a matter of subsumption and much less of parallel development. It is hardly necessary to add that the actual degree of subsumption (like the degree of falsity in macro representations) is always a question for empirical investigation.

3 THE DISCONNECTION BETWEEN MICRO AND MACRO ANALYSIS

I think that Collins' and Knorr-Cetina's attempts to bridge the micro–macro gap in sociology are a truthful reflection of the overall failure of theoretically-oriented micro sociologists to deal satisfactorily with the major flaws of Parsons' middle and late work, particularly with its under-emphasis on macro actors. As the above analysis has shown, this failure is not due primarily to political conservatism or to inadequate epistemological/ontological presuppositions. It is due rather to not taking into serious account (i) macro actors, whose unequal access to the major economic, political and cultural means of social construction enables them to take decisions stretching very widely in time and space; and (ii) the complex social hierarchies which, via formal organizations or otherwise, link micro, meso and macro actors and encounters.[22]

In the absence of any concern with (i) and (ii), micro sociologists either attempt to bridge the micro–macro gap via aggregative or 'representational' techniques, or they adopt the more defeatist strategy of turning their backs altogether on macro issues of societal reproduction and transformation.

Their rationale for ignoring macro issues is either that such issues are so complex that they are not amenable to any effective analysis, or that macro and micro sociology have radically different concerns and that efforts at integration are premature. As J. Turner argues in a recent book that attempts to produce a synthesis of various approaches to social interaction,

> Perhaps too much effort and attention has been devoted to reconciling micro and macro before we have adequate models and theories of either.[23]

Focusing for a moment on Turner's position, his advocacy of a strict division between micro and macro sociology is based on the typical fallacy that interaction implies micro:

> micro sociology examines the properties of social interaction, whereas macro sociology studies the properties of populations of individuals.[24]

Given this position, it is not surprising that Turner's attempt to build a general theory of social interaction fails to take seriously into account that the micro interactions he tries to theorize are invariably embedded in complex hierarchical networks very intricately linking micro, meso and macro actors, and that such networks are indispensable for grasping the specific meaning, logic and dynamics of micro-interactional games. How is it possible, for instance, to understand the games white-collar employees play at the bottom of a multinational corporation's hierarchy without linking them to games played by actors whose more elevated hierarchical positions enable them to take decisions stretching widely in time and space and affecting directly the fortunes and decisions of thousands of people inside and outside the organization? [25]

When interactions among micro actors are studied in a hierarchical vacuum, when hierarchical contexts are ignored, one easily succumbs to the positivistic temptation of searching for 'laws' of interaction that are supposed to apply at all times and in all places in a transhistorical and transcultural manner. This is precisely what Turner has done in his ambitious attempt to bring together the insights of Weber, Schutz, Mead, Garfinkel, Goffman, Collins and others in such a way that one has a body of universal generalizations about the nature and structure of interactive processes. Like all universal, i.e. contextless, generalizations in the social sciences, Turner's propositions end up by being either trivial or wrong – wrong in the sense that they hold true only in certain conditions, which are not and cannot be specified by a theory that ignores social contexts in general and hierarchical ones in particular.[26]

4 CONCLUSION

In conclusion, both the strategy of ignoring micro–macro linkages, and the one of trying to bridge the micro–macro gap via aggregative techniques have, in different ways, contributed to the impoverishment of both micro and macro sociology. Particularly with regard to the latter, as long as micro sociologists neglect social hierarchies linking micro, meso and macro actors, and view macro phenomena as mere additions of micro events, they will not provide micro foundations, but simply a false, reductive picture of the social world. Moreover, as long as systemically-oriented macro sociologists neglect actors, they provide an equally false reified picture of the social world, since any reference to macro structures that does not systematically link them to macro actors simply hypostasizes a virtual order of institutionalized rules.[27] In other words, *reification or reductionism* – that is the price present-day sociology is paying for failing to deal properly with Parsons' underemphasis of macro actors.

The way to get out of this reification–reductionism impasse is to reject resolutely the macro-institutional/micro-interaction distinction by emphasizing that institutional structures *and* interactions can be viewed on micro, meso and macro levels of analysis. Whether it is a small group, a communal organization, a multinational corporation or a whole nation-state that is under investigation, all four social wholes can be examined from both an institutional and an agency point of view. This being so, the micro–macro imbalances that have plagued sociological discourse for so long can be avoided. It must at last be realized that no amount of theorizing or rather philosophizing about the ontology of the subject and the nature of interaction can help to bridge the micro–macro gap as long as human interaction continues to be conceptualized in a hierarchical vacuum. The micro–macro issue can only be solved properly by taking into account seriously the hierarchical and onion-like systems-within-systems nature of all complex, differentiated social wholes.

Looking at the subject in more detail, there are two fundamental rules on how to study hierarchized, configurational wholes in relation to the micro–macro issue.

First, all hierarchized social wholes, micro as well as macro, must be viewed from both a systemic/institutional and an agency perspective. From a systemic or, to use Lockwood's expression, from a system-integration point of view,[28] such wholes can be understood as a set of hierarchically organized roles or positions that are more or less compatible with each other. Such roles or social positions are *virtual* in the sense that the institutionalized rules and norms they consist of are only 'instantiated' when actors draw upon them in the course of relating to and playing games with each other. From an agency or social-integration perspective, social hierarchies consist of hierarchically related actors involved in complex games of a conflictual or co-operative nature.[29]

Second, not only is it necessary to view hierarchized social wholes from both a system- and a social-integration point of view; it is equally vital to do so in balanced manner. So if it is the constitution, reproduction and transformation of societal macro-institutional structures that is at issue, we must start by looking at macro actors and their modes of connecting with such structures; only then can we move 'down' to consider meso or micro actors. Another way of putting this (and paraphrasing Durkheim's rule that social facts must be explained by other social facts) is that 'macro facts' must in the first instance be explained by other 'macro facts'.

If, for instance, one wants to understand the constitution, reproduction or transformation of a whole political order, one should start with those macro actors (political parties, trade unions and other pressure groups, political leaders, etc.) whose privileged access to the overall means of domination and coercion enables them to contribute considerably to the construction of the polity. That does not mean, of course, that establishing macro–micro linkages and providing micro foundations is a useless activity. It simply means that explanations will be more effective, and the provision of micro foundations more successful, if one starts by exploring the dialectical relationships between macro institutions and macro actors before moving 'downwards'.

2

RATIONAL-CHOICE THEORIES
From micro foundations to reductionism

While interpretative sociologies have reacted to the holistic orientation of functionalism by emphasizing the complex ways in which actors, via the application of various social skills, achieve day-to-day interaction, rational-choice (or game-theoretic) approaches, in an equally anti-functionalist mood, try to show that at the basis of all social phenomena are real, purposive actors pursuing their interests in more or less rational manner. Both orientations being hostile to systemic/'externalist' concepts, they try to combat reification by resorting to more or less crude or sophisticated versions of methodological individualism. They both insist that the focus of social analysis should properly be on agents and their strategies, rather than on systemic wholes and their alleged functional needs or requirements. The basic difference between the two sides lies in the way in which they study agents and their interactions. Unlike interpretative sociologists, rational-choice theorists tend to adopt a logico-deductive, 'armchair' orientation in their attempts to explain social phenomena and to establish linkages between micro and macro levels of analysis.

Rational-choice theory has been gaining considerable ground during the last decade among both Marxist[1] and non-Marxist[2] social theorists. Evidently both sides wish to put an end to teleological analysis as exemplified by Parsonian and Althusserian functionalism; both are attempting to build up a body of generalizations solidly based on actors pursuing strategies of maximum utility. In doing so they aim to combat the vague, totalizing theorizing that is all too ready to resort to such macro concepts as society, societal system, social structure, etc., without making any serious attempt at showing how these concepts link up with specific actors who, within limits, are able to choose rationally between alternative courses of action.

1 MICRO–MACRO LINKAGES

Game-theoretic approaches typically have as their starting point not systemic wholes but specific decision-makers trying to follow in their choices rational criteria of maximum/optimum utility. Whether the focus is on players involved in 'prisoner's dilemma' type of games, in 'free-riding' issues, or in free-market situations, the basic logic is much the same. Rational-choice theorists start by making a number of basic assumptions about the purposiveness and rationality of social action – assumptions such as that actors have clearly formulated goals, that in the light of such goals they evaluate alternative courses of action, that they apply rational criteria when choosing the courses of action for obtaining their ultimate goals, and so on. Micro models of rational decision-making are built up on the basis of such assumptions so that, via aggregative procedures or other logico-deductive means, social phenomena can then be explained on a more concrete, macro-historical level of analysis.

A standard critique against such an analysis is that the basic assumptions on which game models are constructed are unrealistic.[3] In real life situations, micro actors do not conduct themselves in the manner assumed by rational-choice theorists, so that theories trying to explain concrete macro phenomena in terms of the ideal-typical rational behaviour of actors are inevitably flawed. For example, to base a macro-economic theory on assumptions derived from a *homo economicus* model of individual consumers or entrepreneurs will show that they do not operate perfectly rationally, and that there are a great many factors that weaken or completely destroy their capacity for acting in an even moderately rational manner.

The reply to this from rational-choice theorists is that they are perfectly well aware that models of micro-economic rational action are ideal-typical, and as such never to be found in pure form in actual micro situations.[4] But what appears to be a gross distortion of reality on the micro level might be less so when, with the help of ideal-typical models, one questions and tries to explain phenomena at a more aggregate, macro level. Assumptions about the rationality of consumers or entrepreneurs may seem totally unrealistic to the social psychologist studying the actual conduct of specific entrepreneurs or consumers, but they may be extremely useful for the macro economist who wants to explain why, for instance, when the state raises corporation taxes, entrepreneurs tend to disinvest;[5] or why, in a perfectly competitive market, an increase in the demand of a commodity raises its price and vice versa.[6]

The above argument in defense of rational-choice ideal-typical models seems to me perfectly acceptable – with one very crucial proviso: it is valid only for aggregative rather than figurational,[7] hierarchically organized wholes. With respect, for instance, to the examples above, in many actual cases a hike in corporation taxes may raise rather than lower productive investments (for example when there is a very favourable international conjuncture).[8] Moreover, an increase in the demand for a commodity does not necessarily raise its price if powerful consumer organizations succeed in persuading the government to impose price controls. In that case, the assumption of market competition does not obtain, and it is impossible to predict price fluctuations by means of purely logico-deductive operations based on the ideal-typical conduct of consumers or entrepreneurs. Here armchair reasoning is not enough, and the examination of *emergent* configurations, of hierarchical relationships, of power struggles among competing groups becomes necessary.

One can still argue, of course, that even in the case of figurational wholes, ideal-typical constructions of the rational-choice pattern continue to be useful: they indicate tendencies rather than iron laws. The fact that in actual situations such tendencies can be neutralized by counter-tendencies not incorporated into the model (e.g. power struggles among interest groups leading to state intervention) only indicates that the logico-deductive methodology underlying rational-choice theory must be complemented by a more 'historico-genetic' approach geared to grasping the specificity of particular contexts.[9] The difficulty with this argument, however, is that rational-choice theorists have failed to show us how the two approaches are to be brought together on the level either of theory or of empirical analysis.[10] Instead of attempting such an integration (which would, of course, dilute the distinctiveness of the approach), rational-choice theorists continue singlemindedly in the pursuit of their logico-deductive operations, and defend themselves against empirical refutation by such escape clauses as 'other things being equal' (as in: other things being equal, a change in x will bring about a change in y). But given that in most real situations other things are not equal, the end result of such exercises is the production of dubious generalizations. These generalizations are either true and trivial, or wrong in that they are valid only in certain conditions which, given the ahistorical, contextless nature of logico-deductive reasoning, are left unspecified.

2 COLEMAN'S CONTRIBUTION

A rational-choice theory that tries to overcome some of the difficulties discussed above (particularly that of the automatic jumping of levels) is James Coleman's *Foundations of Social Theory* (1990).

In this voluminous work the author has constructed a theory of social action and society that is based on purposive actors striving at utility maximization, but which avoids the type of reductionism to be found in the cruder forms of methodological individualism. Coleman states at the very outset of the book that macro phenomena are not mere aggregates of micro ones, and that the micro-to-macro transition entails complex methodological as well as substantive problems. These are related to the fact that moving from a study of individual decision-makers to that of social systems brings to light phenomena that are not mere additions to purposive activities or interactions viewed in isolated fashion.[11] Moreover, Coleman devotes a large part of his book to corporate actors (such as business corporations, trade unions, political parties, etc.) which, unlike primordial groupings, are constituted in a highly purposive manner and form the dominant part of the 'constructed' environment in which modern men and women are living.[12]

Despite all this, however, neither Coleman's emphasis on emergent phenomena nor his focus on corporate actors allows him to correct the major shortcomings of the rational-choice approach. With respect to reductionism, when Coleman leaves his general programmatic statements for the actual analysis of specific problem areas, the idea of 'emergence' as one moves from micro to macro is not given any serious consideration. Let us see what he has to say, for instance, about the macro phenomenon of revolution.

He starts by criticizing the highly reductive nature of what he labels 'frustration' theories of revolution. These are theories purporting to explain the well-known fact that revolutionary outbreaks tend to occur when a society's economic conditions are improving by declaring that the amelioration of material conditions at the macro level creates frustration among individuals at the micro level (through generating, for instance, exaggerated expectations or feelings of relative deprivation); these frustrated individuals are then assumed to be directly involved in revolutionary outbreaks. Coleman points out, and rightly so, that the micro-to-macro transition in such a theory is grossly reductive, because the theory implies that the existence of a lot of frustrated individuals in a given society will more or less automatically bring about revolutionary insurgence. This means that a macro state of affairs (the revolutionary outbreak) is equated with an aggregate of individuals expressing a particular state of mind:

> If the action of individuals is merely expressive, then there is no macro-level purpose. The overthrowing of authorities is merely an outcome of these actions taken together and nothing more.[13]

31

According to Coleman, a non-reductive explanation of revolutionary phenomena should start by emphasizing purposive rather than expressive action. It should start by asking questions about the cost/benefit analysis made by individuals when they are deciding whether or not to join the revolutionary movement, or – more circumspectly – whether or not to 'divest authority', that is, withdraw their support from the government.

Looking at the question from this angle shows that an improvement in economic conditions frequently strengthens the opposition forces, and so may lead individuals to think that the chances of overthrowing the regime are quite good, and that the benefits from participating in revolutionary activities or of divesting authority are likely to be substantial. Given that the core of the theory centres around these two crucial decisions (of participating in the revolutionary movement and of divesting authority), Coleman goes on to consider how various macro factors – such as the increase in the social and economic power of the government's opponents, the vacillation of governmental policies *vis-à-vis* the opposition, the existence of a utopian ideology – affect the way in which individuals arrive at their chosen decision.

For the author of *Foundations of Social Theory*, such an approach allows an effective linking of macro to micro, since

some of the factors that affect the decision on participation and the decision on divesting are conditions that exist at the level of the system in question;

it also helps the transition from micro to macro, since the emphasis on purposive rather than expressive action allows tracing the 'effects of various actors' actions on other actors' action'.[14]

While this is all very well, it does not seem to me to be of much use for overcoming reductionism. If the existence of a lot of frustrated individuals is not enough to bring about a revolution, neither is the existence of a lot of purposive actors willing to participate in the revolutionary movement or to divest authority. Whether or not these decisions (to participate or to divest) will lead to a revolutionary outbreak depends on how they are related to such macro phenomena as the organizational structure of the revolutionary movement and its broad strategies *vis-à-vis* the government and the populace, the hold that governmental elites have over the means of coercion, the internal divisions within the armed forces, and more generally the complex power games that political, cultural and economic elites or macro actors are playing at the time on local, regional, national and even international levels. Consideration of all of the above entails much more than a socio-psychological exercise of showing how various macro factors influence the decisional environment of single individuals.

To be more specific, it is one thing to show how a revolutionary/utopian ideology affects an individual's decision to participate in the revolutionary movement; it is quite another to study the ideology itself, to see how it articulates with other belief systems in that particular society, how various antagonistic groups use certain of its themes in the complex games they play with one another in a variety of institutional contexts, etc. Attempting to filter all macro-structural analysis through the narrow funnel of cost/benefit analysis by individual decision-makers simply won't work.

3 NEGLECT OF THE SOCIO-CULTURAL AND HISTORICAL CONTEXT

There are similar difficulties with Coleman's emphasis on purposive (rather than expressive) action as facilitating the transition from micro to macro via the establishment of linkages between the decisions of simple citizens and those of revolutionary elites, the authorities, etc. Nowhere in his book does Coleman show how these linkages are actually constituted and reproduced. The reason for this failure is quite obvious: once one seriously and systematically links the actions and cost/benefit analysis of simple participants with those of elites or macro actors at different levels of analysis (local, regional, national, international) and in different institutional contexts (political, economic, religious, educational, etc.), the neat contextlessness of Coleman's cost/benefit analysis is lost. To understand the more or less rational strategies of various interest groups at different levels and in different institutional settings requires that one abandons the contextless, logico-deductive theorizing that characterizes Coleman's approach: it requires that context, in terms of both time and space, is seriously taken into account.

To find out, for instance, what type of rationality makes peasants available for mobilization by revolutionary activists, as well as how such rationality relates to the specific rationalities of other relevant actors such as landlords, merchants, usurpers, bandits, state officials, etc., needs a careful appraisal of history and culture. This means that the fruitless search for transhistorical propositions about 'revolution in general' must give way to context-bound generalizations. If Coleman had taken context into serious account, his analysis of revolution would look very much more like the kind of analysis of revolutionary phenomena that is found in the works of Barrington Moore, Theda Skocpol and Eric Wolf.[15] In these seminal and highly illuminating works, rationality and interests are taken very seriously.

But, unlike Coleman's thesis, they are not studied in a contextless, transhistorical manner; they are firmly located within historically specific institutional contexts. Therefore, the greater rigour and universality of Coleman's theory has been won at the price of not telling us anything really interesting. Like all universal generalizations in the social sciences, those concerned with revolution tend to be either inconclusive (holding only in certain conditions not specified by the theory) or trivial. Although this triviality can be concealed by the use of jargon or by attempts at formalization, it cannot be eliminated.

What I have just said is not, of course, an argument against the construction of generalizations in the social sciences. It is an argument against transhistorical, transcultural, universal generalizations. In so far as one refers not to conceptual tools that have a predominantly heuristic character, but to substantive generalizations that are supposed to say something not already known about the social world, the interesting generalizations in sociology are invariably those that give proper consideration to context – those that strike a balance between in-depth analysis of a single case and analysis so widely spread that it becomes vacuous. This admittedly very difficult balance between context and generality is not infrequently met within works of historical and comparative sociology. It is precisely this kind of generalization that rescues sociology from the otherwise justified layperson's conception of it as a discipline specializing in the production of trivialities and of pompous, pseudo-scientific 'laws'.

In brief, it is not possible when dealing with problems entailing *not aggregative but figurational wholes* to move from micro to macro analysis by purely logico-deductive theorizing. In order to obtain non-trivial, substantive statements about macro phenomena there is no substitute for the painstaking effort of examining what happens to 'human rationality' when real living micro actors operate in a multiplicity of social hierarchies that link them to meso and macro actors. With such a focus, generalizations lose their transhistorical character and invariably become more context-bound in terms of time and space. Those generalizations (found neither in the various forms of micro sociology nor in rational-choice theory) take fully into account the specific historical trajectories of societies and the projects of macro actors, as well as the fact that, as one moves from micro to macro analysis, new figurations emerge that cannot be derived from, or explained by focusing exclusively on, social phenomena at lower levels of analysis.

4 NEGLECT OF THEORETICAL CONTEXT

Rational-choice theories tend to neglect context not only when they deal directly with first-order social phenomena (i.e. with the social constructs and theorizations laypersons generate in their everyday interactions); they are equally neglectful of context with second-order constructs or theories. This is the case when they deal with another theorist's work by extracting from it some isolated points or statements, without making any serious attempt to see how these interrelate with each other or with the structure and objectives of the work as a whole. This means that in the same way that rational-choice theories tend to see social wholes as aggregates of individual decisions, they tend to see theoretical wholes as aggregates of statements or propositions that can be 'tested' in isolation from the theoretical framework in which they are embedded.

There are examples of this in the way in which rational-choice theorists deal with classical texts, particularly those of Marx and Weber. A good illustration is Coleman's maltreatment of Weber's work. For instance, in a critique of the Protestant ethic thesis, Coleman argues that Weber's theory is greatly defective because it tries to establish causal linkages between Protestantism and the development of Western capitalism without exploring either macro→micro linkages (to see by means of which specific mechanisms the Protestant creed had an impact on the daily practices of individual believers), or micro→macro ones (how changes in the practices of individual believers led to the constitution of capitalist enterprises and the overall development of a capitalist economy).[16]

Now while it is perfectly true that Weber's thesis does not deal systematically with macro→micro or micro→macro connections, a more careful reading of his work will show very clearly that it was not at all his intention to establish causal linkages between Protestantism and Western capitalism. His purpose was (i) to establish something of an 'elective affinity' between the Calvinist ethic and the spirit of Western capitalism, both conceptualized in ideal-typical terms; and (ii) to ask why Western capitalism (in so far as it portrayed certain uniquely rational elements) originated in Western Europe rather than in China, India, or elsewhere on the globe. Weber thought he could answer this question by demonstrating, with the help of his highly erudite comparative studies, the uniqueness of the Protestant work ethic, as well as of some other features of Western European societies (such as the relative autonomy, commercial orientation, and early *Gesellschaft* character of some West European cities).[17] One may well be critical of Weber and remain unconvinced by his findings concerning the 'uniqueness of the West' but one cannot and should not criticize

35

him for not tackling, or tackling badly, a problem not set by him, but by Coleman a good many years later.

Coleman indulges in similarly reductive treatment and misinterpretation of Weber's work when he deals with Weber's ideal type of bureaucracy. Ignoring Weber's methodological point that ideal types are not theories but constructs that can be more or less useful in the generation of theories, Coleman treats the ideal type of bureaucracy as a substantive theory to be tested by direct reference to the structure and functioning of actual bureaucratic organizations. On that count Coleman finds Weber's construct wanting, since in his theory

> only the central authority is treated as a purposive actor. The fact that the persons who are employed to fill the positions in the organisations are purposive actors as well is overlooked. That oversight has never been wholly rectified.[18]

As in the case of the Protestant ethic critique, here again Weber's methodological orientations are brushed aside, and no attempt is made to see what actual use he makes of the ideal type of bureaucracy. If Coleman had taken the trouble, he would have realized that Weber's intention was not to construct a substantive theory of modern bureaucratic organizations, but to utilize the ideal type of bureaucracy as a conceptual tool – helpful, among other things, in the macro comparative analysis of different types of domination characterized by specific administrative apparatuses (patrimonial, feudal, legal-bureaucratic, and so on). It is only when the ideal type of bureaucracy is placed within this larger theoretical context that an effective criticism can be launched. Because, contrary to the belief of empiricists, the mode of refutation or empirical testing of a theory is provided by the theory itself. It is only after comprehending a theory in its entirety that the meaning of a particular statement can be properly understood, and its mode of empirical validation properly established.[19]

5 NORMS AND INTERESTS

If the reductive treatment of classical texts is an unintended result of the excessive zeal of rational-choice theorists for rigour and formalization, some of their own key notions are based on an extremely sloppy, *ad hoc* empiricist form of conceptualization. By way of illustration I shall examine how Coleman and Elster use two concepts that are at the very heart of their work, namely interests and norms.

For Coleman, the two basic building blocks of a theory of social order are actors, and resources or events. Now actors have interests, and in the light of these interests they try to control events or resources.[20] As regards norms, these are derived from interests. Whereas the starting point of analysis should be purposive, 'norm-free, self-interested' action, norms are generated as the actors relinquish some of the control over their actions to others.[21]

An evident objection to Coleman's conceptualization of the linkages between interests and norms is that he portrays the former as a taken-for-granted, 'natural', pre-constituted state of affairs. So for instance he argues that, unlike interests, norms cannot be taken for granted, in the sense that one cannot *a priori* assume that individuals will comply with norms:

> To assume adherence to norms would impose a determinism that would reduce the theory to a description of automata, not persons engaged in voluntary action. To assume that persons come equipped with a moral code would exclude all processes of socialization from theoretical examination.[22]

Yet the self-same argument could be put forward concerning interests. Because (and using Coleman's own phrasing) to assume that persons come equipped with a set of interests would exclude from theoretical examination all processes related to the social construction, reproduction and transformation of such interests – which is, of course, precisely what Coleman does exclude from theoretical examination.

Despite the centrality of interests in his overall theory, there is very little discussion about how they are constructed or how they relate to other major features of societies (such as institutions, social structures, roles, etc.). Given the absence of such theorization, it is not surprising that Coleman has no real answer to the objection that interests are socially constructed, with norms and normative orientations being central to their constitution.

In fact, the absurdity of the notion of 'norm-free' interests becomes obvious when one considers that actors' conceptions of what constitute their self-interests vary widely in time and space. With respect to direct agricultural producers, for example, the ideas Peruvian peasants hold of their interests are radically different from the views of Vietnamese plantation workers, Ghanean petty-commodity producers, or farmers in the United States. The difference is greater still if the comparison is with Spartan helots, Roman slaves, or medieval serfs. This being so, it is quite impossible to account for that enormous variation without taking into consideration the specific institutional contexts – i.e. the sets of institutionalized norms and roles – within which the direct agricultural producers operate. In other words, an adequate conceptualization of the notion of interests must seriously examine context, both on the level of conceptual tools (one has to show how 'interests', as a sensitizing concept, relates to other sensitizing concepts), and on the level of first-order social phenomena (one has to relate interests to specific historical and socio-cultural contexts). If such contexts are ignored, the notion of interests remains *ad hoc* and/or trivial.

While Coleman reduces norms to interests, Elster is opposed to such a practice. For him,

> social norms provide an important kind of motivation for action that is irreducible to rationality or indeed to any other form of optimizing mechanism.[23]

Rationality, as a minimalist notion, is seen as 'consistent, future-oriented, and instrumentally efficient behaviour', whereas 'the operation of norms is to a large extent blind, compulsive, mechanical or even unconscious'.[24] For Elster, motivation in terms of interests, and motivation in terms of norms relate in zero-sum manner. Although a varied mix of both types of motivation are at the basis of actual behaviour, the more actors follow their self-interest, the less they follow social norms and vice versa.

It seems to me that this is misleading, because an activity being predominantly interest-oriented need not at all entail the eclipse or even the partial displacement of normative considerations; instrumental as well as non-instrumental actions can both be strongly motivated by norms.

Consider for example the case of a medical practitioner who violates professional norms and deals with patients in strictly 'commercial' terms. Now this self-interested, utility-maximizing behaviour is not devoid of norms; it is simply based on norms that emphasize – to use the Parsonian pattern variables, which incidentally are properly theorized and not *ad hoc* notions[25] – role specificity rather than diffuseness, self rather than community orientation. Such norms, although highly inappropriate and reprehensible in the doctor–patient context, are perfectly appropriate in the context of business transactions. Here, to apply the norms proper to the medical profession would result in both ridicule and material penalties.

Even with respect to Elster's own and extreme example of a Sicilian vendetta, whatever the choice made by the actor concerned, norms are always present. Elster suggests that an actor involved in a vendetta must choose between following the social norms that dictate vengeance (as a means of saving his/her honour), and not taking action so as to avoid the risk of being killed.[26] In my view, the latter and more instrumental or self-interested course of action is as normative as the first. Being instrumental or self-interested in the vendetta case simply means applying the norms of self-preservation (or for that matter of family preservation) in a context where they are supposed to be suspended and superseded by 'honour-saving' norms.[27]

Elster might defend himself by stressing that interests are not reducible to norms. To the argument that rationality is simply a Western norm, he retorts with the counter-proposition that rationality in its more general features is universal:

> there can be no society where people as a rule knowingly refuse to choose the best means to realise their goals.[28]

Still, it is one thing to argue that rationality or interests cannot be reduced to a culturally specific norm and quite another to say that rationality does not entail norms at all. For if it is true that rationality in the minimalist definition provided by Elster exists in all societies, it is equally true that it takes different forms in different societies, and in different institutional contexts within a particular society. To use the previous example of agricultural producers again, if rationality entails 'optimizing mechanisms', such mechanisms take different forms in the case of a medieval serf, a Peruvian peasant and a United States farmer. It is quite impossible to account for such differences without bringing in norms. If, on the other hand, these differences are ignored in an attempt to develop 'universal' propositions about rationality, then (as already noted) this invariably results in generalizations that are either wrong or trivial – like the platitude that in all societies, as a rule, people choose the best means to realize their goals.

In short, the dichotomy between norms and interests is misleading; interests being socially constructed,[29] they always entail norms. The reason why both Coleman and Elster have failed to demonstrate satisfactorily how these two notions interrelate (notions that are central to their work) is that, despite the overall rigour of their analyses, their basic conceptual framework is founded not only on unrealistic assumptions but also on *ad hoc* empiricist improvisations.

In fact, the profoundly atheoretical treatment of other theorists' work and of key sociological concepts (such as is found in the rational-choice literature) is the clearest possible indication of the need for sociological theory proper; an activity that aims at demolishing misleading conceptualizations and elaborating logically coherent conceptual tools, with the help of which students of society can ask interesting questions and pursue empirically related research projects.

6 CONCLUSION

In their attempt to avoid the reification and teleology that functionalism often entails, rational-choice theorists have opted for a logico-deductive strategy that takes as its starting point the assumption that at the basis of all social phenomena are specific actors striving for utility maximization. While this approach may be useful when linking ideal-typical, micro, decision-making models with macro phenomena of an aggregate nature, it is much less useful when it is applied to macro phenomena of a figurational character. Given that the relational, often hierarchized nature of figurational wholes entails emergent phenomena that cannot be reduced to their constituent parts, the transition from micro to macro via purely logico-deductive processes is simply not possible.

Moreover, when rational-choice theorists focus directly on macro actors (rather than on micro–macro linkages), their formalistic, ahistorical and transcultural orientations lead them to construct generalizations that neglect context in terms of both time and space. Like all contextless generalizations in the social sciences, their propositions tend to be merely trivial or wrong.

Finally, when rational-choice theorists try seriously to take context into account by reasoning that their logico-deductive approach must be complemented by a 'historico-genetic', context-sensitive orientation, they fail to show the connections between the two. They are therefore faced with the following dilemma: they can either maintain their formalistic elegance at the cost of producing reductive generalizations or they have seriously to consider emergence and context, in which case they are bound to lose their distinctive logico-deductive rigour.

In consequence, if for different reasons, game-theoretic approaches have been as unsuccessful as interpretative micro sociologies in establishing effective linkages between the micro and macro levels of analysis. While the interpretative sociologies (for reasons I have explained in the previous chapter) tend to ignore collective action, game-theoretical approaches deal with macro/collective actors in a way that underemphasizes the various historical and socio-cultural contexts within which human rationality takes its specific forms.

3

POST-STRUCTURALISM
The demise of boundaries

In the preceding sections some of the reasons were examined why sociological theory has not succeeded in overcoming the major weaknesses of the Parsonian paradigm and in creating more effective linkages between micro and macro approaches, or between approaches primarily emphasizing agency and those emphasizing institutional structures. This failure has created a void within sociological theory proper, and part of the space has been filled by a marked preoccupation with philosophical issues and theoretical developments in disciplines like linguistics and psychoanalysis.

This is particularly true of theoretical approaches influenced by post-structuralist/postmodernist orientations to the social sciences. Here the reaction to sociological theory is rather radical, in that it rejects not only such distinctions as agency–structure or micro–macro, but equally all conventional boundaries between social science disciplines and subdisciplines. To use evolutionary terminology again, if the emergence of sociological theory as a specialized subdiscipline indicates a process of differentiation on the level of social knowledge, the new trends in theory point to a process of *dedifferentiation*, to a deliberate attempt to weaken or abolish the established boundaries between philosophy, linguistics, psychoanalysis, and the various social science disciplines and subdisciplines.

Although in France post-structuralism is now in decline, teachers of sociological theory in the Anglo-Saxon countries know all too well that its basic orientations still exercise a profound influence in several spheres of sociological enquiry. This being so, the present chapter will focus on the specific forms taken by the post-structuralist critique of conventional sociological theory[1] – with particular attention to the implications of such a critique for the micro–macro and agency–structure issues. In broad terms, post-structuralism opposes conventional theory on three fronts: it is against foundationalism, against the notion of the centred subject, and against the notion of representation and empirical reference.

1 ANTI-FOUNDATIONALISM

Postmodern writers reject all and any theoretical effort at finding universal criteria that could provide unshakeable foundations for a theory of the social. They consider any attempt at epistemological grounding, any effort to establish first principles, as utopian; and they consider as equally utopian any theory that tries to formulate general laws or general propositions that might help to explain society or social development holistically. They argue that, given the fragile, chaotic, transient and discontinuous character of the social, any holistic theory imposes an order and a systemness on the social world that, in fact, exists only in the confused minds of social scientists.[2]

If we now look critically at the anti-foundationalist thesis, we can start by agreeing with postmodernists that the interminable efforts of social scientists to elaborate some first principles that would provide incontrovertible foundations for the social sciences have not been very fruitful. One can also agree that not only the search for evolutionary 'laws' but equally, as I argued in the previous chapters, any attempt at constructing universal transhistorical generalizations will never be successful because, in as far as universal generalizations fail to take into serious account the historical and cultural context of social phenomena, they are doomed to be either wrong or trivial.

Even so, the above need not necessarily lead to a root-and-branch rejection of all holistic approaches. For, to repeat a point already made, we should distinguish between substantive generalizations and generalizations that are predominantly methodological/heuristic – in the sense that their aim is less to tell us things we do not know about the social, than to provide us with conceptual tools for asking interesting questions and preparing the ground for the empirical investigation of the social world. Keeping this distinction in mind, there is nothing wrong with building up holistic conceptual frameworks, with the help of which one can put questions about the construction, reproduction or transformation of social wholes in their entirety.

To give an example from my own research: in my study of modern Greek society I have examined the way in which economic, political and social changes in late-nineteenth-century Greece related to each other as well as to more global transformations on the international scale.[3] I think this is as legitimate a problem as a more restricted investigation that might focus, say, on the disciplinary practices of nineteenth-century Greek hospitals or prisons. Now, if examination of the first problem is indeed as legitimate and as useful as the second, then the methodological construction of a holistic framework which, without providing ready-made answers, helps me investigate global transformations in a theoretically interesting and at the same time empirically open-ended manner, is a perfectly acceptable and worthwhile exercise. There are some holistic methodologies, of course (such as certain versions of Marxism), that automatically lead to closed substantive theories, and as such they do result in authoritarian dogma. But not all holistic conceptual frameworks are of this type.

For instance, the flexible and extremely perceptive manner in which sociologically-oriented historians like Braudel, or historically-oriented social scientists like Barrington Moore, have used holistic, 'political-economy' tools has helped them produce theories that throw a great deal of light on the constitution and transformation of capitalist societies. Why should we totally reject such theories? If we do, what is there to put in their place? Postmodernists have nothing to offer instead, and as long as this remains the case, their crude anti-holism is at best mere rhetorical posturing, and at worst a serious obstacle to the painstaking task of studying the hierarchical aspects of social life, and of showing how micro encounters and games are systematically linked to meso and macro ones (and vice versa).

Not only have postmodernists a rather negative attitude towards conventional political economy approaches but, in their indiscriminate attacks against all holistic theories they show an inflexibility that contradicts their supposed anti-foundationalist open-mindedness. Moreover, on the one hand, their anti-foundationalism stresses the importance of cautious, limited, tentative, 'regional' theorizing; but on the other, their own positions and tools lead them to theorizations that have a globalizing, overgeneralizing character.

Consider for instance Foucault's work, which has had such an important impact on postmodern social scientists. On a rhetorical level Foucault is all for caution, for modesty, for the particular rather than the general, for 'regionalist' rather than universal types of knowledge, etc. But all this is false modesty. His rhetorical, programmatic statements are constantly contradicted by the overgeneralizing style of his theorizing. To give a specific example: Foucault's oversimplified account of the Renaissance episteme systematically neglects crucial differences between various types of discipline. Historians with an in-depth knowledge of the subject and the period have pointed out that Foucault not only commits the error of considering as central a rather marginal group of thinkers with a predominantly 'magical' view of the world, but by stressing the peaceful coexistence between magical and proto-scientific thinking, he completely ignores the deep rift between the two and the profound hostility of the natural scientists for the magicians. Other critics have similarly pointed out the crude oversimplification and distortions in Foucault's theories on the classical and modern episteme.[4]

Foucault's answer to the above has been to argue that, 'In *The Order of Things*, the absence of methodological sign-posting may have given the impression that my analyses were being conducted in terms of cultural totality'[5] – whereas in fact, he says, his aim was to stress the 'regional', the 'local'.

But why should one consider Foucault's discourse on Renaissance learning as 'local' when, as he himself admits, there is a total absence of methodological 'sign-posting', a refusal to specify boundaries, to spell out the conditions in which what he is saying holds true? After all, setting methodological sign-posts is not some casual little affair one may or may not happen to do; it is a very serious business, requiring a profound knowledge of the subject matter and of the relevant literature – such as Foucault never bothers to acquire.[6]

The same vagueness and overgeneralization are seen in Foucault's less substantive, more methodological/heuristic conceptualizations. In this area too the systematic neglect of the relevant literature, in combination with his predilection for sweeping statements, leads to results that are anything but cautious, regional, anti-foundationalist.

Take his key concept of power, for instance. What strikes one straight away is his dismissal or caricaturing of all previous approaches to the subject. In the same way that he mounted an indiscriminately dismissive critique of modern psychiatry on the basis of some early writings that have since been completely bypassed by subsequent theoretical developments,[7] so in the field of power relations the type of reference he makes to the work of others clearly shows a total disregard for or ignorance of (or both) contributions that are directly relevant to his theme. So he comes up with the incredible statement that before the 1968 events power was analysed either in terms of the 'sovereign' and his rights or, as in some Marxist texts, in terms of the state – both approaches proceeding from the top to the bottom of the social order, rather than, as Foucault would prefer, the other way round.[8]

As to his general concept of bio-power, this is constructed in so vague, globalizing and 'exclusionist' a manner that it is never clear how the micro processes of power deployment that Foucault examines link up with other types of power,[9] with the state or with the type of macro technologies that Weber, for instance, has studied (such as administrative apparatuses, military means of destruction, techniques of mass conscription, of taxation, etc.). The only hint of micro–macro linkages Foucault offers is the highly dubious proposition that power should be studied from the bottom upwards rather than the other way round. At best this is a half-truth, and at worst (given that Foucault never bothered to spell out how one moves from micro to macro modes of analysis) it leads to the reductive idea that macro power structures can be more or less automatically derived from the study of Foucault's micro technologies.

In brief, despite constant statements to the contrary, Foucault's analyses fail to provide the kind of sign-posting that would really render his thesis 'anti-foundationalist'. His systematic neglect and/or caricaturing of works directly relevant to his concerns, his highly abstruse style and his neglect of agency (see below), make it difficult to break away from an overambitious, totalizing, apocalyptic type of discourse that constantly claims the transgression of all limits, the radical questioning of all that has ever been said on the subject, the transcendence of all previous approaches, etc. This rather bombastic and megalomaniacal style often obscures the undeniably brilliant insights Foucault has offered in a variety of areas and makes it difficult to use such insights systematically as tools for the empirical investigation of how modern societies are constituted, reproduced and transformed.

2 DECENTRING THE SUBJECT

A second *bête noir* of postmodernism is the tendency of conventional social theory to view the subject as the foundation of all analysis, or to explain social phenomena in terms of the projects and strategies of individual and collective actors. Contrary to various phenomenological approaches, postmodernism puts at the centre of analysis not the individual subject, but social practices that are, in a manner of speaking, disconnected from the actors who have generated them. This reflects the view that practices do not have any one specific creator, be it a class, an elite or an interest group. In other words, for postmodernism social arrangements have no overall author or ultimate goal. The social consists of systems of differences, and in that sense lacks an overall coherence; it lacks a centre or a unifying will that could endow it with guidelines and overall objectives. So if modern culture gave us the 'death of God', postmodernism gives us the 'death of Man', or rather the 'death of the subject' as this is conceived of by phenomenology and the Kantian philosophy of consciousness.

Looking now critically at the 'decentring the subject' notion one can, of course, agree that actors' practices may have unintended consequences, and that social phenomena are often constructed in a non-conscious manner – i.e. in a manner which does not allow us to identify individual or collective constructors. All this is perfectly acceptable. Equally acceptable is the argument that people's identities are, at least in part, the unintended result of a variety of practices operating in different social spheres.

But all this should not make us ignore the non-passive, conscious dimension of both individual and social development. Towards the end of his life Foucault realized the one-sidedness of his concept of individual subjectivities as the passive product of micro technologies of power. In consequence, in the last two volumes of his *History of Sexuality*, he began to speak not only of 'practices of subjugation', but also of 'practices of freedom' – by which he meant intra-active practices of self-communication and self-construction.[10] Unfortunately, Foucault did not extend this late emphasis on the relative autonomy of the subject to the level of collective action. Social practices continued for him to be presented in a decentred, 'subjectless' manner.

In that respect, therefore, and despite Foucault's categoric denials, his thought is very close to the functionalist type of thinking to be found in Parsons' and Althusser's work. Because, in as far as actors cease to be viewed as at least the partial creators of their world, there is no way of explaining social continuity or change other than by teleological references to social needs or hidden codes. As a result, with the notion of the decentred subject Foucault simply reintroduces by the back door the self-same teleologically-oriented explanations that he was so keen on throwing out in the first place.

Since, from the perspective of this book, Foucault's decentring of the subject and its connection with functionalism is a very fundamental point, I shall proceed to develop it further.

Foucault's insistence that practices of subjugation fulfil specific objectives in a subjectless, disembodied manner comes remarkably close to Parsons' middle-period writings on the social system, where systemic analysis completely displaces agency considerations. Take for instance Foucault's analysis of the disciplining of the working classes in France:

> the moralisation of the working class wasn't imposed by Guizot, through his schools' legislation, nor by Dupin through his books. It wasn't imposed by the employers' union either. And yet it was accomplished because it met the urgent *need* to master a vagabond, floating labor force. So the objective existed and the strategy was developed, with ever growing coherence, but without it being necessary to attribute to it a subject.
>
> (italics mine)[11]

It seems to me that this teleologically-oriented functionalist analysis is very similar to Parsons' way of dealing with social processes and their operation within specific subsystems. According to Parsons, for instance, the integration subsystem consists of all normatively regulated social processes that contribute to the social system's integration objective or requirement. What brings all these processes together is not their connection with specific subjects or groups, but their contribution to a systemic objective (i.e. integration). The same is true about the latency subsystem, which entails the basic problems of 'tension-management' and 'pattern-maintenance'. With society seen as a whole, these twin requirements refer to the societal system's need for motivating its members in such a manner that they go on performing their roles in ways that ensure goal achievement and overall adaptation/survival. All social processes contributing to the requirements of tension-management and pattern-maintenance (e.g. processes referring to the socialization of children, religious practices, educational training, etc.), irrespective of the groups in which they are located, are brought under the latency label, since they all contribute to the same social need.

If instead of 'subjectless practices' one posits subjectless social processes, instead of 'objectives' system requirements, and instead of 'the construction of subjectivities' socializations, the methodological similarities between Foucault and Parsons become quite striking. Both of them underemphasize agency, and as a result both of them have to resort to teleologically-oriented functionalist explanations.[12]

Of course there are also major differences between the two approaches. Parsons' analysis is more 'neutral', in the sense that it assumes a benign societal system that motivates human beings to follow the normative expectations entailed in their roles. Foucault on the other hand views society, and particularly modern society, more critically and negatively, stressing subjugation rather than socialization, resistance rather than deviance, etc. Such substantive differences notwithstanding, there is remarkable similarity in the basic mode of explanation. For despite Foucault's avowed hostility to functionalism, his key notion of subjectless practices fulfilling domination/subjugation 'objectives' unavoidably leads him to teleological forms of functionalist explanation.

Where functionalist explanations are avoided, Foucault by necessity falls back on structuralist ones. As in the case of functionalism, on the rhetorical level he of course denies that he uses structuralist methodologies. Despite his pronouncements, however, a lot of his work focuses on rules of discourse construction and transformation, rules of which actors are not aware.[13]

Needless to say, this oscillation between functionalist-teleological and structuralist explanations is the price one has to pay for neglecting or decentring agency when dealing with issues of social causation.[14] When actors are peripheralized, the only ways of accounting for social phenomena and their transformations is in terms of systemic needs or hidden codes.

Furthermore, Foucault's decentring of the subject not only leads him to teleology, it also prevents him from assessing the different weight or impact of different practices – the fact that certain practices may contribute more than others to the constitution or transformation of specific subjectivities.

By way of example let us look at the construct of the oversensitive Victorian lady prone to fainting. According to Foucault, this type of social construct is the unintended result of innumerable discursive and non-discursive practices located in a variety of dispersed social spheres: medical discourses, literary discourses on 'femininity', social etiquette manuals, confessional practices, boarding-school training, etc. Given the extreme variety of influences, which practices were more influential and which less so in shaping the 'Victorian lady'? Were literary discourses perhaps more important than those of the medical profession? Foucault cannot answer such questions. The reason is that the peripheralization of agency does not allow him to explore how practices or discourses are articulated to form complex wholes.

The absence of any concept of agency that might suggest who questions, or questions about how economic, political or cultural technologies are differentially controlled, means that there is no way of assessing the relative weight of practices (be they practices of freedom or unfreedom), or the way in which struggles between interest groups can intentionally or unintentionally affect the articulation of practices on any specific level of analysis.

To repeat it once more: the only way to show how discourses articulate and form *hierarchically structured wholes*, or the only way to show how and why certain discourses are more powerful than others, is to put at the centre of analysis individual and collective actors. When this is not done, the social world is reduced to a non-hierarchical, 'flat' place, and as such it can neither be described nor explained properly.[15]

3 REJECTION OF THE NOTION OF REPRESENTATION AND EMPIRICAL REFERENCE

Postmodernism rejects not only holistic theories, but is equally opposed to the notions of representation and empirical reference. It scorns the idea that social theory could or should, directly or indirectly, represent a social reality existing 'out there', a reality that is constituted and continues in time separately from, or irrespective of, theory.

One way of understanding the background of this position is to recall Saussure's idea of the arbitrariness of the sign. Saussure argued that in order to comprehend a word, the relation between the word as physical sound (i.e. as signifier) and the word as concept (i.e. as the signified) is less important than the relationship between this signifier and other signifiers within the context of specific linguistic rules. With Saussure, therefore, the focus moved from the empirical referent and the signified, to the links existing between a signifier and other signifiers and the linguistic rules that regulate their differences. Derrida, as is well known, took this process further still, and his emphasis on the signifier, or rather on the differences between signifiers, is so overwhelming that the signified and its empirical referent become peripheral or disappear altogether.

Following this kind of logic, social reality consists of endless chains of signifiers, each specific signifier drawing its meaning from its synchronic and diachronic differences *vis-à-vis* other signifiers. This leads to the postmodern idea of society as language, as text, or rather as a network of texts, whose only referents are other texts. In such a situation the meaning of each signifier or text is inherently unstable, since any solid anchorage to an empirical reality *hors texte* becomes impossible.

Starting from such a basis, social theorists influenced by Derrida's approach (like Laclau[16] and Baudrillard[17]) have set out to 'deconstruct' any theory that either has holistic pretensions or tries to describe and explain in 'representative' fashion the empirical reference we call social reality, and which sociologists naïvely consider to be 'out there', so to speak.

For postmodernists there is nothing 'out there' for a social theory to describe or explain. There is no dualism or any kind of distance between theory and 'empirical reality' since, in the first place, any social phenomenon is a symbolic construction, that is to say a theoretical construction. Conventional social thought is the dupe of essentialism, of a naïve faith in the material, extra-theoretical existence of social phenomena; in actual fact, all social phenomena are nothing more than symbolic constructions derived from the fact that social players, while trying to interact, incessantly build up theories about the others and about themselves.

Looking now critically at the postmodernists' attack on 'representation', here as well their analysis – although it does contain interesting elements – is so exaggerated as to be unacceptable. Their attack on the essentialism and empiricism as found in certain versions of conventional social science is conducive to a relativism so extreme that it hinders rather than helps empirical research. The idea that social phenomena are symbolic constructions (an idea not, of course, invented by postmodernism), and that in consequence there is nothing 'out there' for a sociological theory to reflect or represent, does not necessarily lead to relativism, or to the abolition of all distinctions between theory and its empirical referent. Even if there is no 'material' reference to help us decide the correctness of a theory, there is a reference of a symbolic, discursive type – which can be as empirical and determinate as any material one.

Let me clarify this. If one assumes that at the base of social phenomena are theories generated by lay persons in their attempt to communicate with each other, then sociological theories are simply second-order theoretical constructs: they are theories about theories.[18] This formulation leads neither to relativism nor to the postmodern all-out rejection of any idea of empirical reference. In the same way as conventional social scientists try to test their theories with reference to a 'material reality' out there, so a non-essentialist approach should try to corroborate empirically second-order theories by reference to first-order ones. The vocabulary has changed, but the basic logic is, and should remain, the same.

As a specific example, the statement that during the Thatcher years social inequalities in the United Kingdom increased can be empirically tested by assessing how correctly it 'represents a reality out there'. The fact that this 'reality' is not material but discursively constructed and reproduced does not mean that the statement (a second-order theoretical construct) cannot more or less accurately 'represent' the state of affairs on the level of first-order theoretical constructs. Neither does it mean that the statement about growing inequalities cannot be compared with a conflicting statement, with a view to deciding, on the basis of examining the discursively produced actual relations between subjects (first-order constructs), which of the two statements is empirically closer to the facts.

If instead of 'material reality' the term 'first-order theoretical constructs' is used, or 'discursively produced social reality', this will avoid essentialism as well as the ultra-relativistic idea that there is 'nothing out there' for a sociological theory to describe or explain.

Moreover, if in this book (third-order theoretical construct) I present an account of Foucault's views on the development of the epistemes (second-order theoretical construct), this account of the French philosopher's theory can be empirically tested. There is in fact a 'reality out there' (i.e. Foucault's book *The Archeology of Knowledge*), and on the basis of this reality one can assess how correctly or incorrectly I am interpreting or 'representing' Foucault's theory here. If we hypothesize that my dislike of Foucault's person, style or political convictions have led me to caricature his theory, there is always the possibility of an open debate leading to a rejection of my account and its replacement (by myself or my critics) by a more accurate one.

It can be argued, of course, that an absolutely objective or 'correct' interpretation is an impossibility. Second-order theoretical constructs can only approximate first-order ones, and the same holds true of the relationship between third- and second-order constructs. But this is very different from the absurd contention that it is impossible to compare two interpretations in order to assess which of them 'represents' a certain text more accurately.

Even if we accept Gadamer's 'fusion of horizons' in the process of interpretation, this still leaves room for assessing and comparing two conflicting interpretations in terms of how successful they are in approximating the meaning of a text. To take an obvious example: is it not possible to establish a difference (in terms of the correctness of interpretation) between, say, propagandistic accounts of Marx's historical materialism and accounts by G. A. Cohen[19] or A. Giddens? [20] Is it not true that both Cohen and Giddens, despite their disagreements, give a more correct account of Marx's theory (and in that sense 'represent' more correctly what Marx thought about the subject) than, say, Stalinist or Fascist interpretations?

There is another difficulty worth discussing here. This is the argument that the 'discursivity' of social reality is yet another challenge to the idea of empirical reference and representation. It propounds that the human sciences study a subject matter that not only is not material, but that it is also, at least partly, constructed by the scientists themselves. In that case, the distinction between social theory and a social reality 'out there' – or, to put it in an anti-essentialist mode, the distinction between first- and second-order theoretical discourses – becomes blurred.

Let us take Foucault as an example again. For him, psychoanalysts explore modern sexuality as a subject matter 'out there', existing in its own right and portraying regularities that their discipline is supposed to discover and decipher. This essentialist fallacy conceals that psychoanalytical practices themselves have contributed considerably to the construction of their object of study (e.g. the modern libido), as well as the fact that subjectivities are not pre-constructed entities whose inner nature or truth can be revealed by the analyst once and for all; they are ongoing constructions or inventions that have no specific constructor or inventor.[21]

Here again, an important insight is in danger of being lost by the author's predilection for grandiose overgeneralization. His sweeping assertion fails to specify the conditions in which this phenomenon does and/or does not obtain. It is quite true that, for instance, psychoanalysis explores a subject matter to the construction of which its practices have contributed a great deal – and to a lesser extent this is true also of psychiatry, criminology, etc. But not all social knowledge is so intimately related to its subject matter. As an extreme example, to argue that the discursive and non-discursive practices of scientists in human geography, who are researching the patterns of human settlements in ancient or modern China, are strongly associated with the generation or construction of such patterns, is plainly absurd.

Obviously, Foucault's concept of knowledge/power is more relevant and useful for examining the ways in which psychoanalysis or psychiatry have partly shaped the modern psyche than for examining the relationships between human geography and patterns of human settlement in China. In the former case the relationship between the knower and the object of knowledge is much closer and more 'internalized' than in the latter. In both cases, of course, the object of knowledge is socially constructed, but the mode of construction is radically different.

Moreover, even when the interplay between first- and second-order discourses is close (as in psychoanalysis), one should not exaggerate the degree of interdependence. The idea that the social sciences have pro-foundly shaped the modern and postmodern world says less about the nature of the connection between social reality and social knowledge than about the overinflated, even paranoid views of certain social scientists or philosophers concerning the importance of their discipline.

Finally, since the post-structuralist attack of the notion of representation extends into the realm of politics, it is worth making some comments on that issue also.

For some post-structuralists[22] the idea that a political party can 'repre-sent' the interests of a class leads again to essentialism. The notion assumes that, because of a material reality out there, an 'objective' way exists for assessing such interests, and that by using it an observer can assess to what extent politicians express correctly and/or successfully the interests of those they represent. For post-structuralism such an assumption is misleading, since it does not admit the existence of such things as material or objective interests an observer can use as a means for assessing the performance of political representatives.

Here too the post-structuralists, overreacting to the notion of objective interests, jump from one unacceptable position into another. Granted that there are no iron laws or any other means on the basis of which one can assess the objective interests of a social category or group from a completely detached, 'externalist' position. It should also be granted that the forma-tion/articulation of interests is a discursive construction, partly based on how group members themselves perceive their interests.[23] These anti-es-sentialist points do not undermine the notion of representation. The latter is still useful if we merely substitute for material or objective interests the notion of discursively constructed interests. There is still a reality out there, there are still interests that political representatives can more or less successfully articulate in the political arena.

To conclude: post-structuralism is right to reject the material–ideal distinction which has created so much confusion in the social sciences. For apart from inert cultural objects (e.g. machines) it is misleading to speak of material interests, material base, material relations of production. But the rejection of this false dichotomy need not lead to a rejection of the notions of representation and empirical reference. If the social is discursively constructed, we can still safeguard the Weberian notion of objectivity by translating 'material' into discursively constructed and reproduced phenomena, which are extremely durable and resistant to actors' manipulation.[24] What I am trying to say is that the 'materiality versus discursivity' argument is quite distinct from the empirical reference/representation issue. Post-structuralists tend to conflate the two, and this leads them from their perfectly acceptable anti-essentialism to a totally unacceptable relativism/negativism.

4 DEDIFFERENTIATION

The three theoretical orientations of post-structuralism examined above lead to a view of the social as a set of discourses that cannot be conceptualized in either hierarchical terms, or in terms of such conventional distinctions as micro–macro, agency–structure or, finally, in terms of the institutional differentiation in modern societies between the economic, political and cultural spheres. All such distinctions are dismissed, or rather 'transcended'. It is not surprising, therefore, that post-structuralists completely ignore the boundaries between social science disciplines and subdisciplines.

Here again postmodern theory jumps from one extreme to another. It merely exchanges one undesirable situation – where the micro–macro and agency–institutional-structure distinctions lead to antagonistic theoretical traditions (e.g. macro versus micro sociology, interpretative sociologies versus positivistic approaches) – for another where, instead of building bridges, one simply ignores not only the negative but also the positive points that each tradition entails.

The same shift from one unacceptable extreme to another occurs in the case of boundaries between disciplines and subdisciplines. Post-structuralism exchanges the undesirable situation of lack of communication between the social sciences for the equally undesirable one where the internal logic of each subdiscipline is completely ignored. To be specific, there is little satisfaction with the present *status quo* where the boundaries between economics, political science, sociology and anthropology have become solid blinkers preventing interdisciplinary studies of social phenomena. But such compartmentalization will not be transcended by the facile and mindless abolition of the existing division of labour between disciplines. It can be overcome only by a painstaking process of theoretical labour that aims at building bridges between the various specializations. Such a strategy does not abolish social science boundaries: it simply aims at transforming them from impregnable bulwarks to transmission belts facilitating interdisciplinary research. In other words, the real issue at present is not differentiation versus dedifferentiation. Given the irreversibility of the actual intellectual division of labour, the real issue is between compartmentalized and open-ended, non-compartmentalized, 'dialogical' differentiation.

From this perspective what is badly needed today are more systematic efforts towards the creation of a theoretical discourse that would be able to translate the language of one discipline into that of another. Such an interdisciplinary language would not only facilitate communication among the social science disciplines, it would also make it possible to incorporate effectively into the social sciences insights achieved in philosophy, psychoanalysis or semiotics.

Post-structuralism, by completely side-stepping this difficult but necessary theoretical task, simply proposes the free and indiscriminate mixture of concepts and ideas derived from philosophy, literature, sociology, psychoanalysis, semiotics and elsewhere. This rejection of boundaries, in combination with the neglect of micro, meso and macro levels of analysis, of social hierarchies, and of the agency–structure distinction, quite predictably leads to a hotch-potch that is neither good philosophy nor good literature, nor yet good sociology, psychoanalysis or semiotics. It is precisely this free-for-all strategy of dedifferentiation, and the abolition of distinctions and boundaries, that has led to the present incredible situation where anything goes, and where complex macro phenomena are reductively explained in terms of signs, texts, the unconscious or what have you. As far as I am concerned, such crude exercises constitute a relapse to pre-Durkheimian attempts at explaining social phenomena in terms of instincts, race, climate or geography. The only difference is that today's postmodernists draw their reductive explanations from psychoanalysis and linguistics rather than from biology and geography.

In these circumstances it is not surprising that postmodern theorizing is marked by a relativism that tries to persuade us that any theoretical construction, however bizarre or crude, is just as true or false as any other. It is also not surprising that postmodernist theory tends to adopt a style where the lack of depth and of substantive analysis is concealed by a quasi-poetical language glorying in the obscure, the ambivalent, in plays on words and similar gimmicks.

To conclude, one cannot deny that sometimes boundaries between subdisciplines are based less on rational/'scientific' considerations and more on administrative power struggles or historical accidents. But if it is absurd to accept as rational (i.e. as portraying an autonomous logic) all disciplinary divisions, it is equally absurd to reject in aprioristic fashion *all* boundaries between disciplines and subdisciplines.

5 THE CONSEQUENCES OF DEDIFFERENTIATION

I shall try to illustrate some of the points made in the previous section by examining how social scientists or historians have used post-structuralist ideas in their analysis of actual social situations.

5.1 From political economy to political discourse

If one leaves aside the numerous social analyses that use post-structuralist terminology in purely decorative fashion,[25] those who take post-structuralism's anti-holistic orientations seriously usually try to break out of the by now discredited Marxist or Marxisand political economy approach. Keith Baker's *Inventing the French Revolution*[26] is a good illustration of this tendency. He attempts to use Foucault's insights in order to show that the French Revolution was not an inevitable outcome of 'material', socio-economic forces, but a contingent construction or invention, primarily based on three discourses within the politico-administrative sphere. These relate to three aspects of monarchical sovereignty: justice, reason and will. The first, the judicialist discourse, centred round the relations between the throne and the *parlements*: those in favour of monarchical absolutism wanted to reduce the considerable autonomy of the judicial bodies, whereas their liberal opponents wanted to restrict the king's arbitrary powers and to restore the *parlements* to their pre-absolutist power and prestige.

The second discourse was less about the distribution of power between the king and the judicial nobility, and more about the rationalization of the highly venal and inefficient state apparatus. Those like Turgot who used this administrative discourse were confident about the unlimited possibilities of science and technology to solve not only technical but also

politico-administrative problems. They were advocating a close collaboration between scientists, technocrats, politicians and administrators in an
effort to redress the corrupt features of public administration.

Third, the discourse on will (represented by the writings of Rousseau
and Mably) focused on the revolutionary idea that political legitimation
should not be based on the divine rights of kings or on a body of laws and
legal precedents, but on the people's will.

Now Baker is anxious to stress that, although his analysis of the three
discourses is primarily based on texts of social thinkers and influential public
figures, his intention is not to go back to the type of idealist history that
explains socio-political developments in terms of famous persons and their
ideas. Wanting to dissociate himself from the '*c'est la faute de Rousseau*'
approach, he stresses that his orientation does not entail

> the endless genealogy of revolutionary ideas ... on the contrary, we
> should aim not to write the history of particular unit ideas, but to
> identify a field of political discourse, a set of linguistic patterns and
> relationships that defined possible actions and utterances and gave
> them meaning. We need, in short, to reconstitute the political culture
> within which the creation of the revolutionary language of 1789
> became possible.[27]

But even if this – i.e. the reconstitution of political culture – is the task
we set ourselves, it cannot possibly be accomplished by mere reference to
the kind of texts that Baker offers us. First of all if, as Baker argues, the
three discourses were not merely the ideas of important people but
represented 'something wider', nowhere in his book does he give any
serious indication of precisely how widespread they were. There is no
attempt, for instance, to link the polished ideas and theorizations of political
and intellectual elites with *les mentalités*, with the first-order discourses of
the common people.

What, for example, are the connections between the discourses of
national, regional, local elites and those of peasants? In other words, how
are discourses hierarchically organized in social space? Baker does not even
bother to raise such questions; and if his analysis neglects the vertical
linkages between first- and second-order discourses – or discourses between macro, meso and micro actors – he also neglects to relate
horizontally, so to speak, political discourses to discourses emerging within
other institutional spheres, particularly that of the economy. Yet if, as Baker
contends, all social phenomena are symbolically constructed, then economic discourses are as vital as political ones for a proper understanding of
how the French Revolution was constructed or 'invented'. Moreover, if

one is to understand how first- and second-order discourses articulate with each other within a specific institutional sphere, or between spheres, one has to abandon Foucault's obsession with 'subjectless' practices. It will be necessary to take into account much more seriously than Baker does collective actors (political, economic, religious, etc.) and their intricate games and struggles over the distribution of resources, and over the control of economic, political and cultural technologies.

Baker does none of these things and his approach, notwithstanding his pronouncements, tends to be very much an ideal-typical account of the political ideas of important people. To really break out of the *'c'est la faute de Rousseau'* approach needs a lot more than simply dressing up the conventionally dubbed 'idealist' orientation into discourse terminology. This terminology simply serves as a smoke-screen to conceal the very flimsy empirical foundation for Baker's analysis. Avoiding economism is one thing, but not taking economic phenomena into consideration at all is quite another. An anti-economistic, anti-essentialist orientation does not neces-sarily preclude a more comprehensive, holistic approach – an approach that

(i) tries to see how first- and second-order discourses in the polity are linked with first- and second-order discourses in other institutional spheres;

(ii) tries to explain the manner in which economic, political, religious, educational discourses articulate on a multiplicity of hierarchical levels (local, regional, national) by linking them to the intricate games that relatively autonomous actors play with each other.

A 'holistic'-discourse analysis of the above type leads unavoidably to the difficult and time-consuming kind of research that more conventional, sociologically-oriented historians and historically-oriented social scientists have been and are still doing.[28] It implies that discourse terminology should not be used as a pretext for avoiding painstaking empirical research and opting for 'lazy' solutions – such as pontificating about extremely complex macro-historical transformations on the basis of a casual analysis of a few texts.

5.2 'Transcending' the agency–institutional structure distinction

If Baker's approach completely neglects the complex hierarchization of discourses, as well as how political discourses link with economic ones, Laclau and Mouffe's post-structuralist analysis of modern capitalism goes a step further in the art of dedifferentiation by abolishing (*inter alia*) the fundamental distinction between agency and institutional structure.[29]

Their *Hegemony and Social Strategy*, although influenced by Foucault, is based rather more on Derrida and Lacan. For Foucault 'sign-posting' was (in theory if not in practice) a necessary theoretical activity. For those social scientists, on the other hand, who are influenced by Derrida's deconstructionism, it becomes superfluous. Foucault's distinction between discursive and non-discursive practices, and his attempts, however problematical, to link discourses to a variety of 'institutional contexts', gave to his analyses a degree of concreteness and embeddedness that is completely lacking in the writings of those who categorically reject the discursive–non-discursive dichotomy, and view society as an endless, non-hierarchical chain of discourses, texts or signifiers.

When this type of approach is not limited to the analysis of literary texts but extends to the analysis of complex societies and their transformations, the results are even more unsatisfactory than Levi-Strauss' classical attempt to apply a methodology derived from linguistics to discovering the hidden grammar and syntax of kinship and other institutions. At least in Levi-Strauss' case 'the retreat to the code' was not total; he saw his structuralist approach as *complementing* rather than replacing other approaches to social phenomena. Although he never satisfactorily explained the nature of this complementary relationship, he was quite explicit that a structuralist analysis of myths or kinship systems did not rule out a sociological, psychological or historical analysis of the same phenomena. This type of caution and respect for disciplinary boundaries has disappeared in the writings of those post-structuralists who do not even contemplate the possibility of linking texts or discourses to the institutional contexts within which they are embedded. In this way they completely fuse language and society, the linguistic and the social.

However, except if we speak in wildly metaphorical terms (in which case homologies can be established between anything at all), language and society cannot be conflated. There are two reasons for this. First, the passage from *langue* to *parole* cannot be understood by exclusive reference to language. The social skills and techniques that laypersons use in their attempt to communicate with each other entail not only a practical knowledge of linguistic rules, but also what Garfinkel and his disciples call 'ethnomethods'. Second, the way in which discourses or discursive practices articulate in social space cannot be derived linguistically. Although this articulation always entails language, the way discourses are (for instance) hierarchized has primarily to do with power games, the relatively autonomous logic of which cannot be grasped by a mere study of language rules.

When, therefore, the distinction between language and society is ignored, the result is either reductionism or eclecticism. In the first case one ends up with the production of extremely crude explanations of macro phenomena in terms of simplistic notions derived from linguistics or linguistically informed psychoanalysis, these explanations doing justice neither to the enormous intricacies of institutional arrangements, nor to the complex games actors play at a variety of hierarchical levels. In the case of eclecticism, given the inadequacy of the discourse conceptual apparatus, more conventional sociological tools are introduced into the analysis in an *ad hoc*, atheoretical fashion.

In the light of the above, let us take a closer look at Laclau and Mouffe's work. The two writers have reacted to the 'crisis of Marxist theory' by attempting to replace Marxism with a conceptual framework primarily based on linguistics, semiotics and psychoanalysis. In their critique of Marxist theory they proclaim that it is irretrievably essentialist, since it is based on a necessitarian logic that focuses on deterministic laws, on a linear-evolutionist view of societal development, and on a Messianic faith in the proletariat as mankind's saviour. Whenever Marx and his disciples have attempted to mitigate the teleology and essentialism entailed in the above views, they unavoidably ended up with hybrid theoretical constructions that avoided essentialism only at the price of conceptual 'dualism' or eclecticism.

With this as their starting point, and striving to leave their Althusserian past as far behind as possible,[30] Laclau and Mouffe offer us a set of concepts that stress the inherent discontinuity, openness, fragility and malleability of the social. At the same time they emphasize the fictitious character of the notion of durable institutional structures 'out there', supposedly determining or even setting limits to agents' actions. For Laclau and Mouffe, the very distinction between social and system integration, between subjects' practices and institutional structures, is misleading: the only reality is in discursive practices. Discourses/discursive practices ceaselessly construct and deconstruct self-identities, subject positions, 'nodal' points, social spaces, etc. Given the lack of fixity and necessity in social arrangements, Laclau and Mouffe reject any reference to durable institutional structures as smacking of essentialism. This leads them to examine discursive practices and the subjects that they constitute in an institutional vacuum. If, therefore, in their Althusserian phase agents were more or less passive products of structural/institutional determinations, in their post-Marxist or rather anti-Marxist phase agents' practices operate in a social space where everything is in constant flux, and where relatively durable social arrangements recede into the background or disappear altogether.

What this amounts to is that Laclau and Mouffe, by rejecting the

agency–institutional-structure distinction, and by considering any reference to durable institutional structures as an essentialist attempt to turn
symbolic constructions into things, have ended up with a view of the social
world as consisting of an infinite chain of discursive practices, the meanings
of which are constituted via an ever-changing play of 'differences'. The
way in which such discursive practices are linked with more permanent
institutional arrangements (which latter may be seen as the conditions of
existence of specific discursive practices) is never theorized.

The reasoning behind this unidimensional view of society is that, since
the social is discursively constructed, and since discourses are evanescent
and fragile constructions, any reference to durable institutional structures
as enabling and constraining actors and their practices must unavoidably
lead to essentialism.

The confusion here is due to Laclau and Mouffe's wrong assumption
that the notion of institutional rigidity or durability entails reification/es-
sentialism; that institutions, being symbolic constructions, are by their very
nature infinitely malleable.

One might counter this assumption by pointing out that it is possible
to speak of durable institutional structures without committing the sin of
essentialism. The fact that discursive practices are at the root of social
phenomena does not mean that certain institutional arrangements (such as
the institution of private ownership, or the separation of ownership and
control in corporate capitalism) are not extremely enduring, limiting as
well as enabling for actors' projects. It is precisely because of their durability
that their transformation can be conceived of only in the very long term.
In consequence, core institutions often enter the social space of individual
subjects, not as something that can be negotiated and manipulated at will,
but as an incontrovertible given, as a relatively unchanging terrain that both
delineates and makes possible specific practices – practices of which the
intended or unintended consequences may seriously affect less durable
institutional arrangements.

The degree of fixity or malleability of institutional arrangements is
obviously not given once and for all, but varies widely in historical time
and geographical space. But it can be properly assessed only when one
retains the fundamental agency–institutional-structure distinction, when
one acknowledges the irreducible tension between actors and institutions,
the fact that, despite obvious interconnections, it is impossible to entirely
reduce the one to the other.[31]

Consider institutional arrangements within the educational sphere, for
example. If the focus is on the discursive practices of pupils and teacher in
a specific classroom, 'local' institutionalized rules (such as may have

emerged via the interaction of teacher and pupils) pertaining to the organization of the class are, from the point of view of this specific teacher, much more malleable than institutionalized rules regulating, say, collective agreements between the state and the teaching profession. These latter rules may, on the other hand, appear quite malleable when seen from the point of view of more powerful 'macro' actors such as the education minister or the leader of the teachers' union.

Lastly, there are certain institutional arrangements that are even more durable, in the sense that neither micro nor macro actors can, to all intents and purposes, reverse them. Take for instance the requirement of a minimum level of formal qualifications as a precondition for entering the teaching profession. Although one can raise or slightly lower these requirements, one can hardly reverse the general bureaucratic principle of the need for formal qualifications. Such an 'immovable' institutionalized regulation is, of course, discursively produced and reproduced. Thousands of subjects, by striving to acquire and use qualifications during their professional careers, discursively produce and reproduce on a routine basis the rule about qualifications. But, to say it again, 'discursivity' by no means always entails fragility or malleability; it is compatible with institutionalized arrangements with high degrees of immutability.

If this is accepted, it then becomes necessary to deal with the question of why certain discursively constructed institutions are more durable than others. To answer such a fundamental question requires portraying subjects not simply as the unintended outcome of discursive practices, but as relatively autonomous actors, whose varying control of resources is directly relevant to the durability or fragility of certain core institutional arrangements. In other words, it is impossible to distinguish effectively between different types of discursive practices (in terms, for instance, of their degree of durability or fragility), without using the agency–institutional-structure distinction.

Let me reiterate that it is only when the balance between institutional analysis and analysis in terms of strategic conduct is maintained that one can adopt a perspectivist orientation and assess, for example, the durability of institutionalized rules from the perspective of actors portraying different types and degrees of power. When the balance between agency and institutional structure is ignored and the distinction rejected, one ends up either with the reduction of complex macro-institutional structures to intersubjective understandings of micro actors (as in various interpretative micro sociologies), or, as in Laclau and Mouffe's structuralism, with the portrayal of institutions as 'instant' creations of discursive practices. In the latter case the social world becomes a homogenized, non-hierarchical, 'flat' space, consisting of an endless chain of discursive practices.

To summarize the above: Laclau and Mouffe's fascination with the notion of discursive practices and their rejection of the agency–institutional-structure distinction prevents them from locating such practices within the complex institutional frameworks of modern, highly differentiated societies. Such frameworks are not amenable to serious analysis when the only basic tools at one's disposal are either highly abstract philosophical notions, or the idea of discursive practices and derivatives therefrom such as discursive formations, fields of discursivity, 'nodal' points, etc. This philosophico-linguistic vocabulary is quite incapable of accounting for developments in actual capitalist societies.

In consequence it is not surprising that, as a rule, discourse-oriented post-structuralist theorists avoid the analysis of whole societies and their transformation, and limit their conceptual skills to the analysis of texts, ideologies and other second-order discourses. What is exceptional in the case of Laclau and Mouffe is that they do attempt, however tentatively, a macro analysis of modern capitalism, with the result that they are faced with the reductionism/eclecticism dilemma. Whenever they try to stick to their framework, their analysis becomes extremely reductive – in the sense that it glosses over the enormous complexities of institutional structures and their differentiation in time and space. Whenever, on the other hand, they try to pay greater attention to the complexity of their subject matter than to the simplistic certainties of their methodology, they revert to the use of the more traditional Marxist or Marxisand concepts such as the labour process, civil society, commodification, accumulation of capital and suchlike, which their theoretical analysis has discarded as essentialist.[32] In this way they end up with a conceptual eclecticism which is even more *ad hoc* than the non-deterministic version of historic materialism they have so vehemently rejected.

5.3 Baudrillard: from eclecticism to reductionism

If we now move from Laclau and Mouffe's to Baudrillard's post-structuralism, the tendency towards dedifferentiation reaches its absurd climax. Baudrillard's obsessive determination to transcend all conventional concepts and distinctions has led him to extreme forms of reductionist explanation. Let us take a closer look at his work.

In his early writings Baudrillard set out to extend and complement Marx's analysis of capitalism by shifting the emphasis from production to consumption, from the economy to culture, his chief substantive thesis being that consuming rather than producing commodities becomes the major key for understanding present-day capitalist societies. For Baudrillard, goods in late capitalism become completely interchangeable, impersonal and unidimensional, in the sense that they lose their embeddedness in time and space, and the symbolic meaning and ambivalence they have in traditional societies. They follow less a logic of utility or symbolic significance, than a logic of equivalence (in terms of interchangeability via price mechanisms) or a logic of difference (commodities differentiating consumers in terms of status and prestige). So in as far as consumption constitutes a system of domination, this system manipulates consumers and reduces them to a state of total passivity.[33]

Now these rather banal points about the evils of commodification and capitalist consumption are dressed up in the then fashionable structuralist terminology: the shift from traditional goods to modern commodities is linked to the 'semiological reduction' of symbols to signs (symbols, for Baudrillard, entailing an ambiguity and depth not to be found in signs[34]). Moreover, in so far as commodities entail a logic of equivalence or exchange, they relate to traditional goods (which entail a logic of utility) in the same way as the signifier relates to the signified. Following a logic of equivalence and difference, commodities as signifiers are detached and disconnected in late capitalism from what they signify (i.e. from their use value). They constitute systems of signification the hidden codes of which Baudrillard tries to reveal, and it is precisely these hidden codes or grammars of consumption that determine the passivity and apathy of modern consumers.[35]

This very brief and elliptical exposé of Baudrillard's early work is quite sufficient to show the conceptual incongruity between his linguistically-oriented methodology and the Marxist political-economy approach which, at this stage, he still accepts. In so far as Baudrillard's aim was to provide Marxism with a theory of consumption, this theory is left hanging in the air, so to speak. His 'political economy of the sign', despite its alleged holism, fails to link consumption with the production process, with the type of issues dealt with in Marxist economic analysis – i.e. the labour process, surplus value, forces and relations of production, and so on.[36] In other words, Baudrillard in his early work neither rejected nor did he try to reformulate Marx's theory of production in a way that would allow its effective articulation with a theory of consumption based on structural linguistics. This conceptual dualism was resolved only when Baudrillard, in his later work, rejected Marxism *in toto*, and attempted to make sense of late capitalism by developing further his semiological imagery through incorporating into it the notions of simulation and simulacrum.[37]

At that stage of his work, codes regulate not only consumption but all spheres of social life: all social arrangements are understood in terms of an interminable play of signs which have a life and logic of their own, and whose connections with the 'real', with the empirical referent, is not only tenuous but non-existent:

> from now on signs will exchange among themselves exclusively, without interacting with the real (and they only exchange themselves among themselves smoothly, they only exchange themselves per- fectly on the condition that they no longer exchange themselves with the real). The emancipation of the sign: released from that 'archaic' obligation that it might have to designate something, the sign is at last free for a structural or combinatory play according to indifference and a total indetermination which succeeds the previous role of deterministic equivalence.[38]

This quite extraordinary sign fetishism is further enhanced when Baudrillard tries to develop a theory of simulation – arguing that in late capitalism the frightening proliferation and dominance of simulacra (par- ticularly digital simulacra) has led to a situation where people are no longer able to distinguish the simulacrum (the signifier) from that which it is supposed to simulate (the signified). Hence the 'implosion' of not only the 'real' but also of the 'social', the 'political', etc.

Although since then Baudrillard's work has moved from his concern with simulacra to other related issues (seduction, the 'fateful strategies' of objects, and suchlike),[39] what runs through the whole of his *oeuvre* is an obsession with signs, and a single-minded attempt to reduce the enormous complexity of institutions and of actors' struggles in modern society to some sort of simplistic, linguistically derived formula (the code, the sign, the infinite play of signifiers) which, in some magical fashion, will reveal the inner essence of late capitalism. With Baudrillard the postmodernist tendency towards cultural dedifferentiation[40] reaches its most extreme form, as all boundaries between disciplines, and all conventional distinc- tions (agency–structure, representing–represented, subject–object) are rejected and replaced by a phantasmagoria of signs and simulacra.

Needless to say, this retreat from the complexities of sociological analysis to the simplicities of the code[41] leads unavoidably to extreme forms of reductionism, not dissimilar to the pre-Durkheimian explanations of social phenomena in terms of notions such as climate, geography, instincts, sin, and what not.[42]

Baudrillard has been criticized for identifying an important trend in modern capitalist societies (the growing significance of simulacra) and then exaggerating it to such an extent that it ceases to be trend and becomes an all-embracing, all-dominant actuality.[43] There is no doubt that this is so, to be explained in part by the author's overriding ambition to shock and to 'transcend' whatever is conventional and established. But the tendency towards reductive oversimplifications is not limited to Baudrillard's work, it is a feature common to all those post-structuralists who have tried to apply their methodology to the analysis of complex social institutions (from the French theorists of desire to the deconstructionists).[44] There is therefore, a more general explanation for their cavalier treatment of social complexity. This has to do with the fact that once agents and institutional structures are banned from the analysis, sign-posting (i.e. an attempt to identify the conditions in which generalizations hold true, and those in which they do not) becomes impossible. So it becomes impossible to examine, for instance, whether simulacra are more important in certain institutional spheres than in others, and if so, why their importance varies, or how the dominance of simulations in certain spheres of social life is related to actors' strategies and struggles (and to the unintended consequences of such strategies and struggles).

Once actors as relatively autonomous agents of social transformation are banned from the analysis (via an exclusive emphasis on disembodied or subjectless practices, codes, signs, simulacra, desire, or what have you), one is led to contextless generalizations that are invariably trivial (their triviality often obscured by structuralist jargon) or wrong (in the sense that they only apply in certain conditions which are not and cannot be specified).

To conclude: the postmodern critique of conventional social theory has destroyed a number of myths and has, to some extent, forced social scientists into reconsidering some of their basic presuppositions. On the other hand, the postmodernist emphasis on theoretical dedifferentiation, and on the more relativistic and negatory aspects of modern culture, unavoidably leads to a theoretical impasse that hinders rather than facilitates the advance of social knowledge.

Part II

TENTATIVE REMEDIES

4

INSTITUTIONAL AND FIGURATIONAL STRUCTURES
Parsons and Elias

1 INTRODUCTION

In the second part of the book I shall try to move from diagnosis to remedies. In the light of what was argued above about theoretical pragmatism, the problem cannot be solved by merely drawing up a list of rules on which sort of methodological practices to follow and which to avoid. Although this is useful, what is more important is to demonstrate in practice the utility of certain rules by creating conceptual tools (Generalities II) that can contribute to the promotion of sociologically relevant empirical research. As repeatedly mentioned already, this can be done either by solving the puzzles that create obstacles to interparadigmatic communication or by putting forward interesting questions and indicating new ways of looking at how social wholes are constituted, reproduced and transformed.

In consequence, the following chapters will focus mainly on the distinction that has played such a crucial role in the development of sociological theory – that between agency and structure. In the debates this fundamental dichotomy has shaped, one of the arguments has been that functionalism (both in its Parsonian and Marxist versions) emphasizes institutional structures at the expense of agency; whereas the various interpretative sociologies do the opposite. As to structuralist analysis *à la* Levi-Strauss, this decentres the subject and at the same time uses the notion of structure in a way very different from that of structural functionalisms etc. It is not unreasonable, therefore, to say that what most distinguishes theoretical paradigms in sociology from each other is the way in which they each deal with the notions of agency and structure and the linkages between them.

At the same time there have been various attempts to dismiss the agency–structure distinction as misleading, and as creating more problems than it solves. As is apparent from my criticism of post-structuralism, I do not agree with this position. I consider that any attempt to reject or 'transcend' the distinction – either by conflating the two notions, or by more or less automatically deriving the one from the other – must lead to a theoretical impasse: it leads either to reductionism, or to the reintroduction of the distinction by the back door, so to speak (that is, by keeping the logic of the agency–structure dichotomy while expressing it through a different terminology).

This does not mean, of course, that all is well with the present state of affairs. The reason why many theoretically minded sociologists are looking at the agency–structure distinction with growing suspicion and/or exasperation is (apart from attitudes to fashionable jargon) the fact that there is an enormous confusion over the meaning of the two terms. So structure, for instance, can obviously mean very different things according to the theoretical context in which the term is being used. The way out of this confusion is not, however, to turn our backs on the distinction. It is rather to show,

(i)   the major ways in which the agency–structure distinction is used in the various paradigms;

(ii) the complex linkages between the two notions.

In other words, the solution to the difficulties generated by the agency–structure dichotomy is not at all to reject it outright or to use it in camouflaged form. Instead, I see it in spelling out the different ways in which it is used and then establishing bridges between the various types of logic inherent in these different usages. Or, in evolutionary terminology again, the solution lies not in dedifferentiation, but in the further conceptual differentiation of the notions of agency and structure, and in the more complex theoretical integration between them.

In the three chapters that follow I shall not explore and criticize the use of the agency–structure distinction in an oversystematic, exhaustive manner. Much more modestly and eclectically I shall try to identify the ways in which a small number of theoretically-oriented sociologists, although not sharing the post-structuralists' major assumptions, attempt like them to 'transcend' the agency–structure distinction. In particular I shall examine how agency–structure is handled in Norbert Elias's figurational sociology, in Anthony Giddens' structuration theory and in Pierre Bourdieu's work. By critically looking at this aspect of their writings, and by using the Parsonian paradigm (and its comparison with Marxism) as a steady frame of reference, I shall endeavour:

(i) to show that the strategy of transcending the agency–structure distinction leads either to lopsided accounts of the social world or to the reintroduction of the distinction by the back door;

(ii) to elaborate (via my critiques of Elias, Bourdieu, Giddens and Parsons) a set of interrelated concepts that will, I hope, throw some light on certain key issues entailed by the agency–structure distinction (particularly the issue of functionalist explanations – see Chapter 7);

(iii) to show the utility of these same concepts for empirical research (see Appendix to the Conclusion and Appendix)

A good way to start exploring the notion of structure is to focus on Elias's figurational sociology which, in some respects, provides conceptualizations that are the mirror image of Parsonian ones. In order to show how N. Elias and his growing number of disciples think about the notion of structure,[1] it is necessary to say a few words about Elias's substantive work, particularly about his classical theory of the civilizing process.[2]

2 SUBSTANTIVE ISSUES: SOCIAL INTERDEPENDENCE AND THE CIVILIZING PROCESS

Elias's two-volume work on the civilizing process identifies a long-term trend in West European societies (from the Middle Ages to the present) towards a refinement of social behaviour. He explains this trend mainly by such processes as growing division of labour and social differentiation, state formation and the concentration of the means of violence at the top, and advancing interdependence of individuals leading to increasing equalization of power differentials between various groups. As chains of interdependence become longer and more complex, and as the centralizing power of the state brings the pacification of very large areas, violent or crude forms of social behaviour gradually give way to more controlled, 'civilized' conduct. This in turn entails a type of personality that is characterized by greater individuation, more empathy, stronger internalized controls and a better overall capacity for self-regulation, for mastery of the emotions and deferment of immediate gratification.[3]

A standard criticism of Elias's thesis is that it very much resembles nineteenth-century evolutionist theories stamped by unilinear, deterministic descriptions and explanations of social change. Figurational sociologists rebut that charge (quite correctly, I think) by pointing out that Elias's theory is not marred by the drawbacks of classical evolutionism, since it neither implies progress in any moral sense of the term nor does it claim the civilizing trend to be unilinear or irreversible.

As Chris Rojek has pointed out, the theory allows, for instance, for such 'decivilizing spurts' as the football hooliganism of recent years, as well as for major reversals such as the Nazi atrocities.[4] To this defence I would add that, in contrast to neo-evolutionist modernization theories (which in a sense are also non-deterministic), Elias emphasizes that it is figurations of actors and group struggles that are at the root of processes of differentiation and state formation. This insight enables him to avoid the reification so often encountered in Parsons-influenced writers, who explain structural-functional differentiation in terms of role or institutional 'strains' or, even worse, in terms of the functional requirements of the changing social system.[5]

The above notwithstanding, the civilizing thesis does present serious difficulties. These have to do less with evolutionism than with its sweeping generalizations. Like all such grand theories in the social sciences it comes up against the dilemma of being either trivial or wrong. To allow for minor and major reversals, or to point out that civilizing processes in one area (e.g. table manners) do not rule out decivilizing processes in another (e.g. football hooliganism), makes the overall thesis impregnable, but does so at the price of it not telling us anything either new or interesting. If the various qualifications introduced by Elias and his defenders are accepted, the whole theory boils down to the proposition that sometimes growing division of labour and interdependence leads to growing self-regulation and sometimes it does not. The statement could be strengthened by the argument that, in the long run, the counter-trends (decivilizing spurts, or more radical reversals) are minor, and that the overall current flows in the direction of greater interdependence and greater control over the emotions. However, even in this form this is no more enlightening than are the innumerable attempts to delineate long-term trends in the transition from 'traditional' to 'modern' societies, such as growing urbanization, commercialization, rationalization, individuation, empathy, need for achievement, and so on. All these 'overall' trends, as far as general rather than specific evolution is concerned,[6] can indeed be substantiated, but they do not tell us much that we do not know already.

In view of the above it seems to me that the way ahead for Elias's followers is to abandon the issue of whether or not there has been an 'overall' civilizing trend in Western Europe or the world at large and ask instead the much more interesting question of in what conditions the growing division of labour and interdependence are related to the type of self-regulation Elias is talking about, and in what conditions they are not.

To answer this more limited, context-bound question requires two things. First, it must be conceded that establishing more meaningful linkages between interdependence and 'civilized' conduct necessitates a considerable refinement of these two categories. For instance, it is quite obvious that certain types of interdependence are more conducive to the emotional controls Elias speaks of than others. From this point of view, Eric Dunning's attempt to explain football hooliganism in England by introducing the distinction between functional and segmental types of interdependence is a step in the right direction.[7]

The second requirement for going beyond the 'overall-trend' predicament is for the theory to renounce its universalizing pretensions and to look closely at context in time and space. This seems to be precisely what Elias was doing when he focused on the civilizing process in France, but then he claimed that the connection between interdependence and civilizing conduct applies not to France only, or not even just to Western Europe, but to all and any processes of social differentiation whenever and wherever they may occur (hence his idea that one should 'test' the theory also in India and China). If the aim of the theory is as all-embracing as that, one can safely predict that, like all universal theories in the social sciences, it will end up with propositions that are either trivial or wrong, in that they are true only in conditions that remain unspecifiable as long as the theory adheres to its all-inclusive orientation.

If, therefore, figurational sociologists take history seriously (as they claim they do), they should construct more context-bound subtheories to account for both civilizing and decivilizing processes. Such subtheories should concern themselves with the civilizing/decivilizing dialectic within and between specific institutional spheres (not only sport and leisure, but also those of the economy, politics, religion, family, etc.). To give just one example: the religious figuration of a Catholic Mass is quite different from that of a strictly Calvinist congregation, although both entail much more 'civilized' conduct than a Pentecostal gathering where the emphasis is on deregulation and absence of affective controls. This example should make it quite clear that the conceptual tools Elias has provided for explaining civilizing and decivilizing processes, though useful and relevant, not only need much refinement, but must also be supplemented by notions that are systematically underemphasized in his figurational approach.

The methodological problems raised by the all-pervasive notion of figuration will be discussed later. Here it is sufficient to state that Elias and his disciples overstress the structural/figurational features of societies at the expense of their cultural dimensions. They emphasize division of labour, interdependence, competition and monopolization, but they say very little about specific values, about belief systems and their crucial impact on civilizing/decivilizing processes. To use the previous example again, it is not differences in the degree of either interdependence or any of the other structural/figurational dimensions Elias discusses that can explain why the conduct of people brought up in a strictly Calvinist ethos can be radically different (in terms of self-regulation, for instance) from that of people brought up in a Catholic or Pentecostal milieu.

What I am trying to say is that it is not enough to show how growing social differentiation and interdependence lead to a more differentiated personality structure. It is also necessary to show the reverse: how these differentiated personalities, given the adoption of different cultural values, may interpret the growing interdependence or division of labour in ways that might lead to either self-regulation or self-deregulation.[8]

In brief, the interesting problem generated by Elias's substantive work is not whether a universal linkage can or cannot be established between interdependence and self-regulation; the really interesting problem is to explore the complex conditions where social differentiation and interdependence are linked to civilizing processes, and the conditions where they are not. To examine this matter seriously requires refining and supplementing Elias's terms, and then building on that improved base more restricted, context-bound theories. Such a shift of emphasis is perfectly feasible in the figurational tradition, given that Elias's emphasis on actors' games and strategies in his methodological/theoretical writings is itself averse to the blanket, contextless generalizations found in positivistic sociologies (correlations of 'variables' leading to universal laws), or in neo-evolutionist modernization theories (of the Rostow or McLleland genre). As already mentioned, the empirical work by Dunning and his colleagues on sports already follows this much more fruitful direction.[9]

This brings me to the theoretical issues that are raised by figurational sociology.

3 THEORETICAL AND METHODOLOGICAL ISSUES

Elias's well-known reluctance to take into serious account developments in sociology that were not strictly and directly congruent with his own approach had, of course, a negative effect on his overall *oeuvre*,[10] though it did produce some positive side effects. It made it very easy for him to resist the fads and fashions to which sociologists particularly are vulnerable, and which often disorient and retard the development of sociology as a relatively autonomous discipline quite distinct from philosophy or psychology, for instance.

I greatly admire and appreciate his refusal to indulge in purely philosophical discussions, and his insistence that sociological theory should chiefly concern itself with the construction of sensitizing concepts that lead directly to historically-oriented empirical research. Norbert Elias, therefore, was against the fashionable postmodern tendency to blur the boundary between sociology, philosophy and neighbouring fields. Although deeply knowledgeable in philosophy and other disciplines, he was not ashamed of calling himself a sociologist (in frequent contrast to theoretically-oriented colleagues nowadays), or of considering an excessive preoccupation with (for instance) the ontology of the social a 'flight into philosophy' and a refusal to put theory at the service of the more empirical exploration of human networks and their long-term transformations.

His cautiously sparse approach to concept-building is equally admirable. Unlike Parsons and other prominent theorists today, he based his theoretical writings on his socio-historical investigations, so that his approach to theory-construction resembled Merton's rather than Parsons': it avoided the construction of overelaborate grandiose, all-inclusive conceptual frameworks. Instead, he chose to concentrate on a small number of interrelated concepts, aiming to sensitize students to the risks of reification, and to help them ask interesting empirical questions about the constitution and transformation of human groups.[11]

Finally, despite his radical political views and his overall anti-establishment orientation,[12] Elias categorically refused to give in to the tendency (rife among Marxists in the 1960s and 1970s) of discarding all idea of detachment and objectivity in the social sciences. Contrary to a certain pseudo-radical fashion that identifies any discussion of scientific objectivity with the crude, positivistic 'value-free' position, Elias in his enquiry into involvement versus detachment basically reiterates the clear Weberian distinctions between value reference, objectivity and ethical neutrality. Weber made it clear that the quite inevitable intrusion of the sociologist's own values into his social science research does not necessarily lead to relativism and so does not eliminate the possibility of more or less objective analysis. Elias went a step further than Weber:[13] (i) seeing involvement and detachment as a continuum, and (ii) locating the notion of scientific objectivity within the broader phenomenon of the growing capacity for detachment that the civilizing process entails.

Let me now move on to some more problematic aspects of Elias's approach to sociology. Figurational sociology claims to have overcome the conventional distinction between agency and structure, since the concept of figuration entails both: it refers to agents (individual or collective) and their conflictual or co-operative interdependencies (structure). For Elias,[14] actors are not 'closed atoms' and cannot be conceived of separately from their interrelationships, so the distinction between actors and structures is nonsensical. It must inevitably result in reification, in the transformation of structures into mysterious entities regulating everything on the social scene.

It is perhaps useful to note here that the figurational approach is at the opposite pole from Parsonian functionalism. In so far as Parsons, in his late work, has underemphasized interaction and shifted his focus from the unit-act to social wholes as systems divided up into subsystems (his AGIL scheme), these subsystems do not refer to groups or actors; they consist of institutionalized norms that are analytically grouped together because they contribute to one of the social system's four functional requirements. In other words, the famous four societal subsystems refer to institutions rather than to actors (to the economy, polity, law, kinship/religion). Moreover, since each of the subsystems is further subdivided into four sub-subsystems and so on, there is no theoretically worked out place for collective actors or groups in Parsons' oversystemic scheme. In consequence, when reference is made to classes and other groups in Parsonian analysis, they do not really fit into the AGIL scheme.[15]

When Parsonian functionalists study the social structure of societies, therefore, they are concerned either with stratificational features (the way in which social traits, such as income or educational chances, are distributed among statistical categories), or with institutional structures (the way in which norms or rules cluster in institutionalized complexes in terms of their contribution to society's four functional requirements – economic, political, legal, religious/kinship). In the latter sense, then, social structure entails not conflictual/co-operative relationships between agents or groups as in figurational sociology, but linkages of compatibility/incompatibility between institutionalized norms.

Another way of seeing the difference between institutional and figurational structures (and using a vocabulary derived from linguistics) is to argue that the latter relate to the syntagmatic and the former to the paradigmatic level.[16] Indeed, figurational structures refer to actual relationships between particular actors or groups as they unfold in time and space (a good example, and one Elias is very fond of, is two football teams playing an actual match); institutional structures, on the other hand, refer to a set of interrelated rules that constitute, on the paradigmatic level, a virtual order outside time and space. As Giddens has aptly put it, such rules only exist as memory traces in the heads of actors, and are instantiated when actors draw on them in order to communicate with each other.[17] With 'instantiation', therefore, we move – to use again the linguistic metaphor – from *langue* to *parole*, from the paradigmatic to the syntagmatic, from a virtual order of rules to an actual order of actions and interactions.

It is not difficult to see now in what sense Elias's figurational structures are the mirror image of Parsons' institutional structures. Elias constantly refers to actual relationships between groups as these develop in macro historical time; Parsons focuses primarily on virtual relationships between norms, roles, institutions. One stresses actual conflict/co-operation between actors, the other talks about incompatibilities/compatibilities between normative expectations. If Parsons' critics are correct when they say that in his sociology actors are endlessly rehearsing their roles without ever acting,[18] then it can also be said that in Elias's sociology actors are endlessly acting without ever rehearsing. The paradigmatic dimension in Elias is missing or underemphasized, in the sense that it is unproblematically or rather reductively derived from the syntagmatic.

Needless to say, both figurational and institutional structures are absolutely indispensable for understanding how social wholes are constituted and reproduced. Any attempt to derive the one from the other unavoidably leads to lopsided or impoverished accounts of the social world.

Last, in order to further clarify the distinction between institutional and figurational structures, I shall say a few words on how Marxism deals with it. If we look at the meaning of social structure in Marxist sociology, we find the term used in both the figurational and the institutional sense. So when Marxist-oriented sociologists talk about the social structure of a social formation, they mean the actual relationships and struggles among interest groups. They also, however, use 'social structure' when they are referring to contradictions between institutionalized complexes (between technology and property institutions, between economic and political or cultural institutions, etc.).[19]

As Lockwood has cogently and perceptively put it, Marxism allows one to view social formations both in terms of social integration/mal-integration (i.e. in terms of co-operative/conflictual relationships between actors), and in terms of system integration/mal-integration (i.e. in terms of compatibilities/incompatibilities between institutions).[20] Although some Marxist or Marxisand historians and social scientists put more emphasis on social integration (e.g. E. P. Thompson) and others on system integration (e.g. Althusser),[21] Marx's overall work helps one to view social development in terms of systemic incompatibilities between institutionalized complexes, as well as in terms of how actors do or do not perceive such incompatibilities. The distinction is purely analytical, of course, given that it is not possible in actual reality to separate the social- from the system-integration aspects of social arrangements. Nevertheless, it is a distinction that is absolutely essential, because these two dimensions of social life do not always change in the same manner; for instance, growing systemic contradictions might lead to social conflict or they might not.

Let me put the above schematically:

Paradigmatic level (virtual linkages of compatibility/incompatibility)	I Institution	I Institution
Syntagmatic level (actual relationships of co-operation/conflict)	A Actor	A Actor

For Elias, structure as figuration refers to actor-actor interdependencies (A–A).

For Parsons, social structure primarily entails an institution-institution linkage (I–I).

For Marxist sociology, social structure may mean both A–A and I–I.

Coming back now to Elias, any reference to I–I linkages (whether the term structure is used or not) is a reification. For him and his disciples, the only 'reality-adequate' concepts are those based on, or directly derived from, an A–A relationship – concepts like games, figurations, interdependence, the 'we–they' relationship, power differentials between groups, etc. It is at exactly this point that we come to the crux of the opposition of figurational sociology to other competing approaches: how justified are Elias and his followers in dismissing as reifications all concepts not based on A–A relationships?

I myself do not think this indiscriminate dismissal warranted. Leaving aside the epistemological and ontological problems entailed in the notion of 'reality-adequate' concepts, I think the qualification should not apply to single concepts at all, but to whole theories. The sin of reification is revealed by looking not at isolated concepts, but at how concepts relate to other concepts within a specific theoretical project.

To give an actual example: when Marx talks about contradictions between major institutions of the capitalist system (say between the forces and relations of production), this must lead to reification unless the system-integration (I–I) approach is linked to a social-integration (A–A) one, to an approach, that is, that focuses on the complex ways in which system contradictions are or are not associated with the development of class consciousness, class organization and class action. If the linkages between I–I and A–A are properly explored, then reification does not occur. If, on the other hand, I–I is overemphasized at the expense of A–A (as in Parsonian and Althusserian functionalism), then it is unavoidable for institutional complexes to become illegitimately transformed into anthropomorphic entities taking decisions, doing things, etc. – or, worse still, for the system's functional requirements to be teleologically transformed into causes.

To say it again, therefore: in order to assess whether or not a theorist reifies social phenomena one should look not at isolated concepts, but at the way in which specific concepts are located within an overall theory. Elias and his followers, despite much emphasis on the necessity of viewing individuals and groups in their complex relationships, do not extend this non-atomistic insight to the level of theory-construction. On that level, their insistence that each separate concept must be 'reality-adequate' leads straight into a theoretical/conceptual atomism that is as limiting as the atomistic treatment of actors.

What all of the above suggests is that Elias's concept of figuration (implying an actor–actor relationship) can not displace the concept of institutional structure. Figurational and institutional structure simply refer to different types of linkage – with figuration entailing an A–A, and institutional structure an I–I linkage. Both concepts are necessary for viewing social arrangements in a multi-dimensional manner, and (as noted before) any attempt to ignore one of the two linkages, or any reductive attempt to derive the one from the other, unavoidably leads to extremely one-sided views of social life.

If Parsons, therefore, by overemphasizing institutional structures at the expense of figurational ones, gives a teleological, reified account of how societies are reproduced and transformed, Elias, by overemphasizing the latter at the expense of the former, avoids reification but (as I pointed out when discussing the connections between interdependence and self-regulation) systematically ignores the relative autonomy of belief systems. By this I do not mean to resuscitate yet again the non-problem of whether it is material or cultural/ideal factors that are more important in social change.[22] I would rather point out that Elias, given the primacy he attaches to figurational concepts, does not seem to realize that similar structural conditions – such as the degree of division of labour, interdependence, competition, monopolization, pacification, etc. – can lead to radically dissimilar types of self-regulation/deregulation if the cultural context is different. In other words, figurational and institutional structures, although inconceivable in isolation from each other, can vary independently, and in consequence the latter cannot be derived from the former.

4 CONCLUSION

My argument in this chapter has been in favour of an approach to the agency–structure problematic that will neither abolish the distinction nor seek to derive institutional structure from agency or vice versa. Furthermore, I have argued that the term 'social structure' can refer to at least two major types of linkage, both crucial for understanding how social wholes are constituted, reproduced and transformed. In consequence I would propose that, instead of using social structure in an undifferentiated or vague manner, the concept of figuration (or figurational structure) should be used when referring to actor–actor relationships, and the concept of institutional structure for reference to institution–institution (or role–role) linkages.

Of course, the ways in which figurations and institutional structures are linked to each other constitutes one of the most interesting problems in sociological theory. I am not sure where its solution lies, but I am quite certain that no progress towards it will be made as long as we conflate, or refuse to distinguish between, the two types of linkage I have been discussing. Progress can be made only when it is accepted that these two dimensions of all social games must be seen both as distinct analytically and as intertwined with each other in practical reality. The question is not, therefore, whether figuration is a concept more 'reality-adequate' than institutional structure; the question is how these two concepts are systematically linked up with each other. This is the problem I shall try to deal with in the next chapter.

5

ON THE ARTICULATION
BETWEEN INSTITUTIONAL
AND FIGURATIONAL
STRUCTURES
Bringing Parsonian and Marxist sociologies closer together

In Chapter 4 I tried, via a critical discussion of Elias's work, to elaborate the fundamental distinction between figurational and institutional structures. In this chapter I shall look at recent attempts to revive Parsonian functionalism and evolutionism, and show how certain Marxist conceptual tools can help us establish more adequate linkages between institutional and figurational wholes.

1 THE NEO-FUNCTIONALIST ATTEMPT TO REVIVE PARSONIAN SOCIOLOGY

As mentioned already, Parsonian functionalism, after a rashly sweeping dismissal during the 1960s and 1970s, experienced a considerable revival in the 1980s and 1990s. This revival was, at least partly, related to the demise of Marxist and Marxisand sociologies during that period. The present feeling about Parsonian grand theory is that its critics, by dismissing in rather cavalier fashion the whole of Parsons' work, were throwing out the baby with the bathwater, and that, given the remarkable rigour and depth of Parsons' theoretical constructions, the present task of sociological theory should be not its overall rejection, but a thorough restructuring of its weaker, problematic dimensions.

Neo-Parsonians (as well as an older generation of Parsons' disciples, like Eisenstadt and Smelser) readily accept some of the conventional criticism concerning Parsons' underemphasis of the voluntaristic dimensions of social life and of group strategies and group conflicts, as fundamental mechanisms of social transformation.

Neo-Parsonians are eager to reassess especially the key concept of differentiation as redeveloped by Parsons during the evolutionist stage of his intellectual progress. As is well known, towards the end of his life Parsons tried to inject some dynamism into his rather static structural-functionalist paradigm by showing its connection with evolutionism.[1] His more critical disciples admit freely that Parsonian evolutionism – although avoiding the crude determinism of some classical evolutionist approaches – has failed to convey the extraordinary complexity and variety, as well as the contradictory character of differentiation processes leading to modernity.

In fact, Parsons' underemphasis of actors (particularly collective actors) as partly shaping the form that differentiation/dedifferentiation takes in particular social contexts, creates the impression that social development in general and modernization in particular is a smooth and harmonious process leading all societies towards greater complexity and adaptive capacity.[2] This impression of smoothness is, it seems to me, quite justified, if one takes into account that Parsons tries to explain the transition from less to more differentiated social systems via such disembodied processes as

(i)   the diffusion of values from more to less developed societies;
(ii) the 'strains' or incompatibilities between variously differentiated institutional subsystems within a particular societal system;
(iii) the 'functional requirements' or needs of societal systems – needs often operating teleologically as causes that push societies up the evolutionary ladder.

Neo-Parsonians want to save the key notion of differentiation, while at the same time refusing to view the whole process as a unilinear problem-solving operation, leading to higher levels of adaptive capacity via the satisfaction of systemic requirements. As Alexander and Colomy argue, neo-functionalists attempt to

> raise the explanatory framework of differentiation theory itself, replacing a problem solving and societal need approach with a more political model that emphasises group conflict, power and contingency.[3]

Perhaps the best way to illustrate this new turn in neo-Parsonian theory is to refer to Smelser's work. In the 1960s, Smelser's *Social Change during the Industrial Revolution*[4] was one of the major attempts to apply Parsonian conceptual tools to the explanation of long-term processes of functional-structural differentiation between work and family roles. In Smelser's seven-stage model of differentiation collective actors were absent, or at best playing a very peripheral role. The whole process was portrayed in an oversystemic manner: 'Dissatisfactions' with the *status quo* emerged and, after a state of 'handling and channelling', 'general ideas' appeared mysteriously to provide solutions to the initial dissatisfactions. At subsequent phases such ideas were 'specified', 'implemented' and 'commercialized', so correcting the initial dissatisfactions and allowing the whole societal system to reach a new social equilibrium at a higher level of differentiation.

During this entire process, 'who' questions are rarely asked. One hardly knows precisely which groups/actors were dissatisfied, whose ideas contributed to the solution of the problem, whose interests were promoted or undermined during the phases of 'handling' or of 'implementation', etc. It was as if a mysterious entity called Society or Societal System had set itself a problem-solving task and, by means of a complex set of impersonal processes, either achieved this task and so brought about a higher differentiation, or did not achieve it, in which case the system regressed to lower levels of differentiation.[5]

In his later work Smelser moved away from this oversystemic orientation without totally rejecting the Parsonian framework. He points out in a more recent re-examination of the differentiation between family and schooling during the industrialization process in England that, in order to understand the form taken by differentiation in specific cases, one should seriously consider the social forces (the collective actors and their interests) that contributed to the overall process in complex and often contradictory ways. He points out for instance that schooling in England was much more marked by class than it was in the United States. For one thing, there was a strong link in the United Kingdom between types of schooling and social class: public schools for the aristocracy and the upper classes, grammar schools for the middle classes, and primary education for the poor. Moreover, to explain (rather than simply describe) how the mass of the population was introduced into the educational system requires taking into account the multiplicity of social forces that promoted divergent and often conflicting interests.[6] On the parliamentary level, which is where the upper classes were mostly represented, there was marked concern with the growing crime rate and the generalized 'debauchery' among the lower orders. So for instance primary-schooling Bills were proposed as a means of controlling the poor and of instilling into their progeny the values of reverence for their betters and hard work. Another major force in bringing about educational reform was the Anglican Church, which competed with various dissenting movements in proselytizing lower-class children. The parents themselves were rather reluctant to send their children to school, given the need for child labour in agriculture. Moreover, the more enlightened ones, who appreciated the social value of education, wanted a different type of primary schooling.[7]

From the above it becomes obvious that there is a striking difference between the 'old' and the 'new' Smelser as far as the theory of differentiation is concerned. Whether his new emphasis on social forces and conflict is congruent with Parsons' overall framework is a matter I shall discuss after considering some further attempts at restructuring Parsonian evolutionism.

If we look at the work of Eisenstadt, for instance, another old disciple of Parsons', we find that from very early on he attempted to maintain the general Parsonian scheme, while at the same time injecting some more voluntaristic elements into the AGIL conceptualization. Eisenstadt argued that:

(i) incompatibilities within or between the four subsystems do not automatically bring about social change; whether differentiation or dedifferentiation occurs, and what form it takes, depends on various interest groups or 'institutional entrepreneurs' and their cultural orientations, their control of resources, their legitimizing ideologies, the complex coalitions they form, etc.:

> The clue to understanding such differences [between forms of differentiation] resides in the different elites, the visions they articulate, the coalitions they enter into, and the relation of such elites to other groups or strata in the society, especially their autonomy or embedment in broader ascriptive units.[8]

(ii) These carrier-groups provide a better basis for understanding the 'boundary exchanges' between the four subsystems (AGIL) than does Parsons' depiction of such exchanges in a disembodied, oversystemic fashion. As Alexander has aptly put it in describing Eisenstadt's seminal work:

> The introduction of economic classes into functionalist theory comes naturally from this emphasis on different concrete groups. *The boundary relations between functionally differentiated subsystems can now be seen as social relations between different groups*, and the groups that articulate the 'adaptive function' are, at least in early periods, economic classes.[9] (italics mine)

(iii) In view of the above, the enormous variability of institutional arrangements and solutions at similar stages of social differentiation requires much more emphasis:

> My previous work did not, however, fully and explicitly address

84

the problem of whether the different types of integrative solution create different degrees of differentiation, types of uneven
differentiation, types of uneven dedifferentiation or different
modes of differentiation with different institutional dynamics.
Similarly that work only touched upon the crucial importance
of institutional entrepreneurs or elites.[10]

As in the case of Smelser, the shift from the 'old' to the 'new' Eisenstadt is
very clear-cut. To what extent this new realization of the importance of
collective or macro actors and of figurational wholes is *ad hoc* is another
question. Does the emphasis on groups and their conflicts constitute a
theoretically coherent restructuring of Parsonian functionalism/evolution-
ism, or is it rather a cobbling together, which actually undermines the
internal coherence of the Parsonian scheme?

Before tackling that issue, I want to stress that the post-Parsonian shift
towards collective and/or macro actors is to be found not only in the work
of Parsons' older disciples. It is also a strongly pronounced feature in the
writings of a new generation of sociological theorists, who are intimidated
neither by Parsons' often labyrinthine constructions, nor by his radical or
postmodern critics.

Lechner, for instance, objects to Parsons' rather 'one dimensional,
unidirectional view of modernization', and suggests that the variety of
routes to modernization is due to the integration of the differentiated parts
operating in ways that undermine rather than enhance the autonomous
logic of various institutional spheres. When this happens, the logic of one
sphere dominates and even completely obliterates that of other spheres.
When, for instance, the political logic 'colonizes' the rest, this results in
totalitarianism of one form or another (fascism, communism); whereas
when the religious logic becomes dominant, this creates the kind of
fundamentalism that prevails in parts of the Islamic world today. For
Lechner, religious fundamentalism implies a type of dedifferentiation that
does not return the societal system to its traditional, non-differentiated past.
Instead, it results in a mixture of traditional and modern elements (e.g. the
coercion of women going hand-in-hand with growing reflexivity and
modern technologies).[11]

Colomy pursues a similar theme by stressing the unevenness of the
differentiation process, and the fact that to explain this unevenness requires
bringing strategic interest groups into the central focus. He points out, for
example, that political differentiation – in the form of passing from
oligarchic cliques of notables to post-oligarchic, centrally organized mass
parties – developed differently in the various states of *ante bellum* America.

The process advanced more in New York (where there was strong institutionalization of the post-oligarchic party form) and less so in South Carolina (where the gentry managed to sabotage the more differentiated and centralized political forms).[12]

2 A CRITIQUE OF NEO-FUNCTIONALISM AND NEO-EVOLUTIONISM

There is no doubt that the above attempts at restructuring Parsonian theory have pointed to dimensions of social change that are absolutely necessary if differentiation/modernization theory is to get out of the theoretical impasse into which Parsons' oversystemic approach has led it. However, the new additions to the Parsonian edifice (whether in the form of group conflict, disorder, dedifferentiation, coalitions of institutional entrepreneurs, etc.) fit badly into the original scheme. Despite the theoretical sophistication of some of the above reformulations, and although there have been some interesting attempts to restructure along more voluntaristic lines Parsons' unit-act,[13] on the level of the social system, there is no systematic attempt to work out the conceptual implications of the introduction of collective actors for the AGIL scheme – a scheme which is absolutely central to Parsons' theory of structural-functional differentiation. As far as the crucial links between the AGIL scheme and collective action are concerned, the old and the new stand side by side, without any serious attempt at effective theoretical integration.

To be more specific, most of the neo-functionalist theorists mentioned above systematically use Parsons' AGIL schema, while at the same time stressing the importance of groups as producers rather than products of social life, for explaining the way in which differentiation takes place within and between institutional spheres. But while they admit that Parsons has ignored or seriously underemphasized the role of collective actors in explaining modernization, they tend not to enquire whether and how groups can be theoretically reconciled with the AGIL scheme. What, for instance, are the precise linkages between Eisenstadt's institutional entrepreneurs controlling economic and political resources and Parsons' adaptation or goal-achievement subsystem? Just to state that Parsons' boundary exchanges between subsystems can be viewed as exchange relations between groups, does not solve the problem. It does not tell us how precisely economic groups are linked to economic institutions; or how, to use the terminology developed in the previous chapter, figurational structures are linked to institutional structures.

If Parsons has constructed his overall theory in such a way that agents or figurational structures are subordinated to systemically conceptualized institutional structures, then redressing the balance requires more than announcing that groups and their relations are important. It requires

(i) identifying the conceptual obstacles that prevented Parsons from achieving a better balance between system and social integration; and

(ii) removing these obstacles by restructuring some basic dimensions of Parsonian theory in such a way that the balance between institutional and figurational wholes is re-established.

3 AGIL: ITS RELATIONSHIP TO FIGURATIONAL AND INSTITUTIONAL WHOLES

It seems to me that one main reason is responsible for the AGIL scheme preventing the consideration of groups or collectivities as relatively autonomous agents of the reproduction/transformation of social systems. This is that Parsons' famous fourfold typology is supposed to apply to both concrete groups/collectivities (e.g. a formal organization and its departments and subdepartments), and to more abstract institutional wholes (e.g. the economy, polity, kinship, etc.).

I shall try to spell out this crucial point as clearly as possible. For Parsons, the notion of social system implies a whole that is the result of interacting units, and is characterized by an internal organization, as well as a clear separation between itself and the environment.[14] In that sense, institutional and figurational wholes are both social systems: they are both the result of interaction between human beings, they both have an internal organization (e.g. of norms in the case of institutional wholes, and of interactions in the case of figurational ones) and they both have clear boundaries *vis-à-vis* an environment (which consists of more encompassing institutional and figurational structures respectively).

Now Parsons does distinguish between social systems that are 'collectivities' and those that are not. He considers collectivities as a special type of social system, endowed with clear goals and decision-making processes. So for instance a large business organization has formally stated goals, and a number of specific decision-making bodies that try to elaborate and implement policies aimed at the achievement of those goals. From this point of view General Motors is a collectivity, whereas the economy is not, as Parsons and Smelser explicitly admit.[15]

Although the distinction is clearly made, however, the AGIL scheme does not actually take it into account. Not only is the AGIL typology supposed to apply to both social systems that are collectivities and others that are not (to both figurational and institutional wholes);[16] it is also supposed to apply to their subsystems, even if such subsystems are not subcollectivities.

This point needs further clarification. A business organization is a collectivity in Parsons' terms, and as such can be subdivided into four subsystem s: adaptation, goal achievement, integration, latency (AGIL). The organizations's adaptation subsystem does not necessarily refer to a specific department, i. e. to a subcollectivity with its own clearly defined goals and decision-making mechanisms. Given that the norms regulating the adaptation requirement (i.e. the resource acquisition problem) may be found in very different departments (the personnel department, the finance department, etc.), the organization's adaptation subsystem constitutes an analytic category,[17] which groups under its umbrella all norms and processes that contribute to the resource acquisition project, irrespective of the departments or groups within which they are located. It is precisely in that sense that Parsons conceptualizes norms (and processes partly regulated by such norms) in a disembodied manner. He sees norms mainly from a systemic, not an agency, perspective. So despite the fact that organizational subsystems are not groups or collectivities, each in turn is again given four functional requirements (a, g, i, l). Another way of putting this is to say that Parsons uses the AGIL scheme in order to subdivide and sub-subdivide both figurational (formal organizations, groups, departments) and institutional wholes (the economy, the adaptation subsystem of a business organization, etc.).

This strategy of subdividing both figurational and institutional wholes in terms of the AGIL logic has very serious disadvantages. When the fourfold typology is applied to institutional rather than figurational wholes or subwholes, it unavoidably reifies institutions and illegitimately transforms them into mysterious collectivities. To be more precise: it is perfectly legitimate to say that a car factory, as a relatively self-contained configuration of producers, has four basic reproduction requirements: AGIL. It is equally legitimate to conceptualize the factory's adaptation subsystem (A) as an analytic category, grouping under its heading all institutionalized norms dealing with the factory's resource-acquisition problem (norms about the recruitment of personnel, acquisition of raw materials, of financial capital, etc.). But when Parsons goes a step further and subdivides the factory's adaptation subsystem into four sub-subsystems (A → a, g, i, l), then this is not acceptable. For the adaptation subsystem, in so far as it does not refer to a concrete subcollectivity, is simply an analytic category, and as such has no functional requirements that have to be met for it to survive.

To be blunt about it, it is right to argue that in order to survive an actual factory needs to solve its resource-acquisition problem; and it is wrong to argue that the factory's adaptation subsystem (in so far as it refers to all norms contributing to the adaptation requirement) has a resource-acquisition problem. Similarly it is one thing to argue that a car factory has a goal-achievement requirement (to produce cars and make profits) and another to say that the factory's adaptation system (A) has a goal-achievement subsystem (g).

To reiterate this once more: it is perfectly legitimate to attribute goals and resource-acquisition desiderata to collectivities/figurational wholes, but doing the same to institutional wholes unavoidably leads to reification: it illegitimately transforms institutional wholes into decision-making, goal-achieving entities.

This means that the Achilles' heel of Parsonian functionalism is the application of the AGIL logic to social wholes or subwholes that are not collectivities.

The above argument can be represented schematically by distinguishing legitimate from illegitimate modes of subdividing wholes into parts:

LEGITIMATE OPERATION
Figurational whole → A, G, I, L
(e.g. formal organization)
ILLEGITIMATE OPERATION
Figurational whole → A, G, I, L

a, g, i, l   a, g, i, l   a, g, i, l   a, g, i, l

If the above is given due consideration, it becomes obvious that when Parsons subdivides the societal system along institutional lines, and when he goes on to subdivide each institutional subsystem into institutional sub-subsystems (A → agil) and so on, he not only reifies institutional wholes, but also leaves no conceptual room for collective actors as partial producers of the social system. Institutions are wrongly presented as collectivities and, given the onion-like, system-within-system type of conceptualization, collective actors are banned from his conceptual framework.

This means that collective agencies (such as class organizations or interest groups) either disappear altogether, or they appear as passive products of institutional/systemic determinations. Of course, in some empirical analyses both Parsons and his disciples (old and new) do deal with collective actors as relatively autonomous agents contributing to stability or change.

But this is done in an entirely *ad hoc* manner. Where groups and group conflict appear, it is despite, not because of, the Parsonian framework.

Is it possible to remedy this situation without entirely rejecting the AGIL scheme? I think it is, if the link between AGIL and agil is broken, i.e. if institutional subsystems are not further subdivided into institutional sub-subsystems. To repeat, to see society as divided into four institutional orders (economic, political, legal, religious/kinship) is legitimate. It is equally legitimate to subdivide a less encompassing collectivity (a formal organization) or subcollectivity (a department within an organization) according to the AGIL logic. But the additional move from AGIL to agil must be rejected.

If we do not subdivide the major institutional spheres (economy, politics, law, kinship/religion) according to the agil logic, how else can we conceptualize them so that the actors (who are, in the last analysis, their creators) are not peripheralized; so that the linkages between institutional and figurational wholes are re-established in a theoretically coherent manner? This for me constitutes the central problem in any attempt at restructuring (rather than totally rejecting or simply further embellishing) Parsonian theory.

4 AGIL: THE TECHNOLOGICAL, APPROPRIATIVE AND IDEOLOGICAL DIMENSIONS OF MAJOR INSTITUTIONAL ORDERS

I believe that the Marxist subdivision of institutional spheres, particularly the economy, may show us a more appropriate way of linking institutional wholes to actors and their co-operative/conflictual relationships – a better way, that is, of linking institutions to figurations and vice versa.

What are the major subdivisions of the economy in the Marxist discourse? To answer this question we have to look at the mode of production concept. A dominant mode of production, as a set of institutionalized norms/processes that contribute to the fulfilment of a social formation's 'adaptation' requirement, is basically subdivided into forces and relations of production: i. e. into economic technologies (broadly speaking) and the manner of their appropriation.

To focus first on technologies or forces of production, these entail material tools, the knowledge leading to their creation and rules concerning the work arrangements related to the technical rather than the political division of labour.[18] Since for Marx human beings transform their natural and social environment primarily through the use of tools, this means that from a more historical perspective the way in which men and women create and control economic technologies is crucial for understanding how complex social wholes are constructed, reproduced and transformed. In other words, the emphasis on the technological aspects of economic institutions is fundamental for Marxism if one is to take a constructivist approach to institutional orders – if, that is, one wants to avoid reification and views society not as a mystical entity, but as the intended and/or unintended result of actors trying to achieve their ends through the use of resource-producing technologies.

Moreover, although Marxists emphasize the technological aspects of institutional orders, they avoid purely technicist views of the social by putting equal if not greater emphasis on the appropriative aspects of institutional complexes: on institutionalized rules that regulate the way in which technologies, and the resources they entail, are controlled.[19]

Finally, a third major aspect of the Marxist treatment of institutions is the stress on their ideological dimension. Not only are there institutional-ized rules on how technologies are controlled/appropriated, there are also normatively regulated processes which legitimate or distort (via conceal-ment or other means) the way this is done. Marxism therefore, via the concepts of mode of production and ideology, emphasizes the technologi-cal, appropriative and ideological dimensions of, if not all institutions, at least economic ones.

However, given its inherent economism (which cannot be overcome by merely paying lip service to the relative autonomy of so-called super-structural spheres), Marxism's understanding of the crucial importance of the technological and appropriative dimensions is limited to the economic sphere only. Even worse, via the economic base–superstructure dichot-omy, it leads to a view of ideologies or 'ideas' generally as a residual category located exclusively in the superstructure.[20] But if one rejects the base–su-perstructure dichotomy as well as economic reductionism in all its forms, then it becomes quite obvious that the technological, appropriative and ideological (t, a', i')[21] are three basic dimensions of all major institutional spheres. Whether one looks at economic, political, religious or educational institutional spheres, it is always possible to identify social arrangements or rules that are predominantly technological in nature, others that are appropriative, and others ideological.

To take religion as an obvious example, it is easy to identify within any particular religious sphere of a complex society technologies through which Parsons' latency requirement is partly achieved (e.g. administrative appa-ratuses, techniques of indoctrination, of religious socialization, modes of praying or fasting, technical exercises enhancing spiritual development, etc.). Moreover, these religious technologies are controlled/appropriated in particular ways (e.g. by rules on whether the means of indoctrination are controlled from the top, the middle or the bottom of the religious hierarchy). Finally, one can always find specifically religious ideologies that either conceal the relatively unequal character of appropriative arrangements, or justify them by reference to holy scripture, divine revelation and suchlike.[22]

What I am trying to say here is that technologies, their mode of appropriation/control and the way in which such controls are depicted and legitimized on the ideological level should not be conceptualized in terms of the economic base–superstructure straitjacket. Instead, the technological, the appropriative and the ideological should be considered as constitutive elements or dimensions of all major institutional spheres. So in highly differentiated societies, and whether one looks at their economic, religious or political spheres, one can usefully identify:

(i) technological means (means of social construction) through which human beings more or less deliberately construct, reproduce and transform their social existence;
(ii) patterned ways in which technologies are appropriated/controlled;
(iii) a set of dominant ideological themes which, via distortion and/or other means, justify the appropriation arrangements.

Going back to Parsons' social system now, its four basic subsystems (AGIL) consist of institutionalized norms that cluster into roles, and those in turn form broader institutional complexes. At this point, instead of further subdividing each of the four subsystems along agil lines, we should differentiate norms/roles in terms of the technological, appropriative and ideological (t, a', i') dimensions. Within each subsystem (adaptation, goal achievement, integration, latency) we can then try to identify which norms/roles have a predominantly technological, appropriative or ideological character. For instance, if the system reference is a capitalist enterprise, there are certain norms/roles the character of which is predominantly technical (e.g. the role of the engineer), appropriative (the capitalist owner) and ideological (public relations manager).

Why does it matter to differentiate norms/roles along the t, a', i' rather than the agil logic?

In a negative sense it is important because it avoids reification. As I have argued already, an institutional order, being a virtual system of norms/roles, has no goals or functional requirements. To ascribe goals or requirements to it illegitimately turns it into a concrete collectivity. On the other hand, it is perfectly legitimate to try to identify the technological, appropriative and ideological aspects of a set of institutionalized rules. In other words, whereas the AGIL → agil subdivision leads to reification, the AGIL → t, a', i' one does not.

In a positive sense now, the differentiation of institutional orders along their technological, appropriative and ideological dimensions helps us to consider societies in constructivist terms. It allows us to see norms/roles not simply as a means for the societal regulation of actors, but also as a means through which actors constitute, reproduce and transform social orders. Whether in the sphere of the economy, polity, religion or elsewhere, social construction always implies normatively regulated technological, appropriative and ideological arrangements.

This means that the t, a', i' differentiation of institutional complexes permits us to build bridges between institutions and agents, between institutional and figurational wholes, between Giddens' institutional analysis and analysis in terms of strategic conduct. By contrast, Parsons' AGIL → agil conceptualization prevents the construction of such bridges.

Since this is a very important point in the overall argument of this book, I shall, at the risk of repetition, develop it further. Viewing institutions in their technological, appropriative, and ideological dimension not only makes us see society as a human construct, but also obliges us constantly to ask 'who' questions. Given that technologies produce resources, the concept of appropriation unavoidably raises the question of who controls these technologies and the resources they generate. As to the concept of ideology, this brings up the equally crucial question of how the inequalities that are brought about by the differential appropriation/control of technologies are legitimized. These are the kind of critical questions that Parsonian functionalism ignores, and that Marxism – although often in crude and reductive manner – brings to the fore.

In brief: as long as its economic reductionism is avoided, the Marxist paradigm furnishes the most theoretically congruent linkages between institutional analysis and analysis in terms of strategic conduct.

A focus on appropriative norms (e.g. on the institution of private ownership of the means of production in a capitalist economy) provides a theoretically coherent basis for the conceptualization of structural cleavages between those who have and those who do not have access to the control of technologies. This means that we can ask interesting questions about the chances for the development of group consciousness and group conflict. This is a type of conflict that does not simply entail competition over the distribution of various types of reward (as in social-stratification approaches), but which draws attention to the fact that the rewards that are being contested are an intrinsic feature of the relationship between the antagonistic groups and the resource-producing technologies. In other words, the emphasis on the technological and appropriative aspects of institutions (economic, political, religious, etc.) necessitates a look at actors *relationally* rather than in aggregate, social-stratificational terms.

It is here that there is a major difference between the Parsonian social-stratification approach and Marxist class analysis. Marxist class exploitation is not primarily the result of market competition over the distribution of rewards; it entails a particular type of conflict, where the resources/rewards over which the antagonists are fighting derive directly from their relations within the system of production. As I have already said, this Marxist emphasis on the relational rather than stratificational[23] becomes even more fruitful when, going beyond economism, it is employed not only in class analysis but in the analysis of other types of interest groups contesting the control of non-economic technologies (political, cultural, etc.).

To come back to the central point, the technology/appropriation/ideology (t, a', i') conceptualization is Janus-faced: it leads us to view social practices from both an institutional-systemic and an actor-agency point of view. The more we focus on norms/roles referring to the technological, appropriative and ideological (t, a', i') dimensions of institutional orders, the more we ask systemic questions about the logical compatibilities and incompatibilities between these three institutional complexes. The more, on the other hand, we shift our analysis to actors' strategies, that is, the more we ask 'who' questions, the more we bracket institutional analysis and ask how actors (as producers of the social world) react to their roles or use their roles and institutionalized norms (t, a', i') in order to achieve their often antagonistic projects.[24] I would agree with Lockwood, therefore, when he argues that despite its serious deficiencies

> Marxist theory remains unique in seeking to establish a coherent relationship between system and social integration. In this respect at least its model of society still presents a formidable challenge to 'Bourgeois social science'.[25]

Concluding this argument, the link between institutional and figurational structures can be summarized by the AGIL → t, a', i' formula. Looking at institutional orders in terms of their technological, appropriative and ideological dimensions reveals their logical compatibilities and incompatibilities. This then leads quite naturally (without the need to resort to *ad hoc* operations) to the study of figurations, to the conflicting and co-operative interdependencies between groups.

Given for instance growing incompatibilities between technologies and appropriation arrangements (systemic, institutional analysis), what happens on the level of actors? In what ways, if at all, are actors experiencing such incompatibilities, and what do they do about them? These are the kind of questions that Parsonian sociologists are not conceptually equipped to raise. In Parsonian theory, incompatibilities between institutionalized parts cannot be articulated with actors' strategies and struggles. Therefore, whenever institutional incompatibilities lead to social transformation (e.g. to further differentiation), this transformation is either not explained at all, or it is explained in teleological terms (by social requirements being transformed into causes). Let me finally put the main points made so far into more schematic form.

Parsonian theory	*Proposed restructuring*
1 The AGIL subdivision applies to *all* social systems (those that constitute collectivities and those that do not);	The AGIL subdivision makes sense only when applied to collectivities;
2 Each institutional subsystem (A, G, I, L) can be further subdivided into four sub-subsystems: A → agil, G → agil, etc.;	Each institutional subsystem must be conceptualized in terms of its technological, appropriative and ideological dimension: A → t, a', i', G → t, a', i', etc.;
3 Incompatibilities between a, g, i, l do not lead to analysis in terms of 'strategic conduct'.	Incompatibilities between t, a', i' lead to 'strategic-conduct' analysis.

5 APPLICATION

By way of follow-through I shall try to show the utility of the above conceptualization by looking more closely at Colomy's analysis of strategic groups and political differentiation in the *ante bellum* United States (see section 1).

Colomy rightly points out that an effective method for moving from description to explanation of processes of uneven differentiation is to focus on strategic agents. The only way, for instance, of explaining why political differentiation (in terms of the transition from oligarchic political clubs to mass parties) was more advanced in New York than in other states is by paying attention to the projects, value orientations and complex alliances of the groups both for and against the political innovation that is entailed by mass parties. Moreover, it is necessary to look not only at elites, but also at their followers and at the complex coalitions among innovators, conservatives (opposed to political differentiation) and 'accommodationists'. Finally, for Colomy, the above voluntaristic perspective should be linked with a structural approach, which would point to the formation of institutional cleavages (class, ethnic, racial), to the opportunities/possibilities created by the constitution in each state, as well as to the cultural system (in some states egalitarian values were more pronounced than in others).

Now it seems to me that the linkage between the 'voluntaristic' and 'structural' dimensions is rather problematic in Colomy's analysis – particularly since he claims to work 'within the neo-functionalist tradition'.[26] If we focus for example on his use of the structural-cleavage concept, how is this key notion linked to the Parsonian conceptual framework?

For reasons I have already explained, Parsonian functionalism focuses on the type of institutional incompatibilities which take the form of 'tensions' between the social system's four subsystems or between the four further subdivisions of any subsystem (ending up with 'role strains' at the level of the individual). To use Colomy's example, let us hypothesize that with the help of Parsons' scheme we can (before the emergence of mass parties) identify an institutional incongruity or strain between norms that are located within the political system G (which is characterized by ascriptive, particularistic values and orientations) and more universalistic, achievement-oriented norms that are located within the educational subsystem L. The clash between particularistic and universalistic norms creates strains on the level of both the social system as a whole (a cluster of norms/roles in the G subsystem clash with a cluster of norms/roles in the L subsystem), and on the level of the role player (any single role player has to cope with conflicting normative expectations as s/he moves from G to L and vice versa).

There is another type of institutional incompatibility, however, which cannot be accounted for in the above manner, and which Colomy, as well as many other political scientists, calls structural cleavages. In what sense do structural cleavages differ from strains on the level of the role player or the social system as a whole?

To answer this question necessitates looking at institutional spheres in terms of the AGIL → t, a', i' rather than the AGIL → agil schema. To return to Colomy's analysis, one can conceptualize the phase of the oligarchic, pre-mass party as a situation where the government's administrative technologies were controlled by oligarchic relations of domination – i.e. by a set of appropriative norms that granted the rights of access to and rights of control over political technologies to a restricted number of notables, the majority of the population being virtually excluded from active political participation. Here again we are looking at norms, but we see them not from the agil but from the t, a', i' perspective. We are particularly concerned with norms of a predominantly appropriative character; norms which regulate the way in which rights of access to and control over the state machinery are distributed between rulers and ruled. Given the highly unequal distribution of rights during the 'club-of-notables' period; and given that this inequality is not merely statistical/stratificational, we are led to identify a chasm, a cleavage created by how political rights are entrenched in a complex of interrelated and potentially antagonistic roles and positions.

Moreover, structural cleavages can be identified in other institutional spheres if, for instance, we enquire how rights of appropriation/control are embedded in interrelated roles in the economic, religious or educational spheres. Once class, political, racial or ethnic cleavages are made apparent, we can investigate how much they overlap. To what extent, for instance, do those who control economic technologies monopolize also administrative/political technologies?

The above shows why the structural-cleavage rather than the strains approach to norms/roles/institutional complexes conduces to a theoretically coherent way of linking institutional with strategic-conduct analysis, or system with social integration. Once the focus is on structural cleavages (based on the differential access of actors to economic, political and cultural technologies), the researcher is more or less compelled to ask 'who' questions. In the case, for example, of the considerable overlap between socio-economic and political cleavages, how are those actors who are legally or otherwise excluded from the political arena going to react? Why did the reaction of the politically underprivileged in New York differ from that in South Carolina? How and why have the anti-oligarchic forces in the former case managed to radically change the relations of domination (by broadening political participation), and why have they failed in the latter?

Colomy does raise some 'who' questions, and does provide some satisfactory answers – but he does so *despite*, not because of, the Parsonian framework. Moreover, given that his concept of structural cleavage is introduced in rather *ad hoc* fashion, the complex ways in which such cleavages are linked to the control and legitimation of economic, political and cultural technologies are not explored systematically. This means that in Colomy's analysis the structural-cleavage concept comes out of the blue, it is not theoretically related to Parsons' AGIL scheme.

6 CONCLUSION

Because Parsons does not seriously theorize the notions of technology (t), appropriation (a') and ideology (i'), he can deal only with institutional incompatibilities that take the form of strains or incongruities between his four subsystems (AGIL) or his four sub-subsystems (agil). This theoretical strategy does not permit him to accommodate in his theory the kind of institutional incompatibility that results from the unequal access of actors to economic, political, legal and cultural technologies.

A basic weakness of Parsonian theory is, therefore, its incapacity to coherently integrate into its AGIL scheme cleavages resulting from the unequal distribution of appropriation rights related to resource-producing technologies. This means that such structural cleavages are either brought into the analysis in an *ad hoc* manner or are ignored altogether. The end result is that the dynamism of the functionalist paradigm is restricted to the concept of role strain or to the notion of incompatibilities between the AGIL subsystems. This leads to an overemphasis of the stratificational approach, at the expense of a figurational, relational analysis of how the mode of appropriating resource-producing technologies renders various groups interdependent.

Given all this it is not surprising that the neo-functionalists' emphasis on the importance of strategic groups for explaining social differentiation has led them to deal with actors in an arbitrary, non-systematic fashion. Whether one takes the late work of Smelser or Eisenstadt, or the analyses of a younger generation of functionalists and evolutionists, there always seems to be a conceptual chasm between their acceptance of the basic pillars of Parsons' functionalism/evolutionism (AGIL, pattern variables, differentiation, etc.) and their growing awareness of the importance of strategic-conduct analysis. Collective actors are either brought into the analysis in *deus ex machina* manner (like Eisenstadt's institutional entrepreneurs), or structural cleavages leading to figurational/group analysis are not systematically linked to those dimensions of institutional orders (technological, appropriative, ideological) on which they are based.

To close this discussion, in this chapter a way was proposed of bringing closer together Parsonian and Marxist sociologies by linking the AGIL scheme with the Marxist notions of the technological, appropriative and ideological dimensions of social life. In doing so I have tried to keep clear of two extremes:

(i)   the *ad hoc* introduction of 'conflict' elements into Parsons' scheme
(ii) the 'purist' position which argues that, given the radically different

domain assumptions of Marxism and Parsonian functionalism, a theoretical rapprochement between the two paradigms is impossible.

I think that the proposed tentative synthesis manages to safeguard the theoretical sophistication, wide applicability and non-economistic orientation of Parsons' AGIL scheme with the capacity of the Marxist paradigm to articulate in a non-reificatory manner institutional structures and their incompatibilities with agents and their struggles.

A final word about the limitations of the above analysis. I have not tried to restructure Parsonian theory along conflict/voluntaristic lines in a comprehensive manner (for instance, I have not dealt with the problem of how my reformulation of the AGIL scheme affects Parsons' unit-act theorization); neither have I tried to develop further the AGIL – t, a', i' scheme by showing how intra-institutional incompatibilities between the t, a', i' are linked with interinstitutional incompatibilities and struggles. Nor, finally, have I attempted to develop in any systematic manner a theory of collective action. My aim was much more modest. It was to show, in a tentative and limited way, the type of transformation that the AGIL scheme should undergo if one wants to link it in a theoretically coherent way with groups as both producers and products of their social world.

6

THE 'PARTICIPANT–SOCIAL WHOLE' ISSUE
Parsons, Bourdieu, Giddens

1 INTRODUCTION

The previous two chapters dealt mainly with social wholes. In Chapter 4, a comparison between Parsons and Elias tried to establish the fundamental distinction between institutional and figurational structures; in Chapter 5, via a Parsons–Marx comparison, I worked out a way of conceptualizing the linkages between these two types of structure.

In the present chapter the focus shifts from an 'externalist' to an 'internalist' perspective,[1] in order to examine the relationships between participants and social wholes (figurational and/or institutional). I hasten to say that this is not the classical and much criticized individual-versus-society problem. As I see it, the participant–whole problematic differs from the individual–society one in two fundamental ways:

(i) 'Participant' does not necessarily refer to the individual. A participant of a social whole may be a formal organization, a powerful elite, or a nation-state.[2]

(ii) A social whole does not completely overlap with the notion of society. In its figurational form, social whole may refer to a set of interrelated players on the level of a small group, a formal organization, or the world economy/polity. In as far as institutional wholes refer to sets of interrelated institutionalized rules, such a set may be limited to a small village community, or it may stretch widely in time and space and embrace a whole country or a cultural area encompassing several countries.

I think that in the above sense the participant–social-whole conceptualization is capable of dealing with the crucial problem of how agents orient themselves to an interrelated set of institutionalized rules on the paradigmatic level, or to a figuration of interacting actors on the syntagmatic level, while avoiding the numerous pitfalls created by the individual–society dichotomy.[3]

As in the two previous chapters, I shall again adopt a comparative approach. Section 1 will focus principally on Bourdieu's work, showing how his key concept of *habitus* could provide interesting linkages between Parsonian role theory on the one hand, and the various interpretative micro sociologies on the other. Section 2 will examine briefly Giddens' structuration theory, since it resembles Bourdieu's approach in various ways. I shall argue that, as in the case of Bourdieu's *habitus*, Giddens' key notion of the duality of structure fails to synthesize or 'transcend' structural and interpretative sociologies but, if properly restructured, can help us understand better the way in which participants relate to social wholes.

2 BOURDIEU'S NOTION OF *HABITUS*

2.1 The seminar game

I do not intend here to give a systematic account of Bourdieu's complex and ever-changing *oeuvre*, and shall focus only on his key concept of *habitus* as directly relevant to the concerns of this chapter. Let me begin with a short definition:

> The habitus, a product of history, produces individual and collective practices – more history – in accordance with the schemes generated by history. It ensures the active presence of past experiences, which, deposited in each organism in the form of schemes of perception, thought and action, tend to guarantee the 'correctness' of practices and their constancy over time, more reliably than all formal rules and explicit norms.[4]

Since Bourdieu's style, to put it mildly, is not always easy, the best way of showing what he means by the concept of *habitus* is to take a practical, mundane example and to show how his key concept differs from two related notions: role/social position, and interactive situation. The example chosen here is a social game very familiar to me as well as to many readers of this book – the game of a graduate seminar. Let us suppose that three researchers, influenced respectively by Parsons, Mead and Bourdieu, attempt to investigate the game of a specific seminar. What are the aspects or dimensions each would emphasize most?

2.1.1 Parsonian role theory

The Parsonian researcher will attempt to understand the seminar by emphasizing its role/social-position dimension, and thus explore the roles of the teacher, the students and that of the person giving the paper. S/He will attempt to find the formal and informal norms or normative expectations inherent in each of these roles, as well as the complex relationships between them. Our researcher will also try to link the social system of roles with the cultural system (which entails 'core values') and the personality system (which refers to needs/dispositions).

More concretely, let us assume that a normative expectation of the seminar teacher's role is to assess the students' performance universalistically rather than particularistically. According to Parsons, on the social system level, this norm can and should be linked with both the cultural and the personality systems. On the level of the cultural system, universalism may constitute one of the major societal or educational values; and this abstract, disembodied value is institutionalized in terms of normative expectations inherent in the teacher's role on the level of the social system, and internalized in the form of needs/dispositions on the level of the personality system.

2.1.2 Bourdieu's approach

The Bourdieu-influenced researcher will argue that the Parsonian triad of cultural system → social system → personality system covers only one dimension of the seminar game. What it ignores or neglects is the *habitus*: the system of generative schemata that each seminar participant (via a variety of past socializations) brings to the game. These schemata or predispositions are not directly related to and cannot be derived from the actual roles played in the seminar by the teacher, the students, the paper giver.

More specifically, in order for the researcher to comprehend my actual conduct as the seminar teacher, s/he should not only have some knowledge of what is entailed by a teacher's role, but must also take into account my class background, the schools I went to, my religious or non-religious upbringing, etc. Internalized, all my past socializations (which reflect the various social structures in which I was raised) constitute the system of predispositions Bourdieu calls *habitus*.[5] So the fact that I grew up in Greece rather than England might explain why, in my teaching, I activate gesticulatory schemata of action, whereas my educational training might explain the use of schemata or perception or comprehension that are too rationalistic, or schemata of evaluation that are manicheïstic.

While Parsons does not ignore processes of socialization/internalization, the core values → roles/norms → needs/disposition triad tends to lead the researcher to look at socialization processes directly linked to the specific role under investigation. For example, concerning my role as a seminar teacher, the Parsonian researcher will ask how I was socialized into my teaching role (via reading formal regulations, consulting older colleagues, being briefed by the departmental convener, etc.). S/He will be rather less concerned with schemata of action, perception and evaluation acquired in extra-educational contexts. And this precisely is the reason why Parsonian theory does not take seriously into account the strong possibility of a systematic or permanent incongruence between normative expectations on the social-system level and need dispositions on the personality level.

In other words, when trying to explain any specific game Bourdieu, much more so than Parsons, stresses the *habitus*/dispositional rather than the role/positional dimension. As he himself has pointed out, the schemata of the *habitus* tend

> to guarantee the correctness of practices and their constancy over time, more reliably than *all formal* rules and explicit norms.
>
> (my italics)[6]

These generative schemata of action, perception and evaluation refer to two 'historicities': the historicity of each player's personal biography, which is based on a hierarchized set of socializations; and the historicity of the various 'objective/external' social structures that the players internalize.

2.1.3 The interpretative, interactionist approach

The Meadian researcher, finally, will tend to put the main emphasis on a third fundamental dimension of the seminar game – the interactive-situational dimension. Interpretatively-oriented sociologists (whether influenced by Mead, Garfinkel or Goffman) maintain that neither the study of social roles or positions, nor that of dispositions can in itself give us an adequate account of the complex practices of the seminar game. One has to see how precisely the players use, or rather manipulate, their normative expectations, as well as the schemata of their *habitus* when they are playing the actual game – a game which has its own *interactive logic*.

To be more specific again, any adequate explanation of my seminar performance must take into account not only how I handle normative expectations, or how I activate those schemata of my *habitus* that are relevant to my seminar teaching, but it must also consider that the seminar might have a dynamic that derives from neither roles nor dispositions. So for example my adopting an aggressive or defensive teaching strategy might have to do with *emergent situational meanings*, which can only be grasped by shifting the focus from positions and dispositions to the way the interactive situation unfolds syntagmatically in time and space. For instance, via complex processes of intra- and interaction, of reflexive accounting, of interpretations and counter-interpretations, the seminar participants might come to the joint opinion that my teaching is inadequate; realizing this will make me adopt a more aggressive teaching style. Or, to use Boltanski and Thévenot's very suggestive terminology, a certain assessment of participants' reactions may make me change radically my mode or regime of justification: instead of justifying what I teach in terms of 'what the Founding Fathers said', I might adopt a style that legitimizes my teaching on the basis of divine inspiration, professional values or civic virtues.[7]

It should be noted that this outcome is not purely conjunctural or idiosyncratic. It is a practice that is based on a certain articulation of the role, dispositional, and interactive-situational elements of the seminar game. As such it is perfectly amenable to sociological analysis.

2.2 Six remarks on Bourdieu's *habitus*

2.2.1 The positional, dispositional and interactive-situational dimensions of social games

As I have tried to show with the seminar example, the emphasis by Parsons, Bourdieu and Mead is on three different dimensions of social games – respectively on social roles, on dispositions and on the interactive situation. Each of these dimensions portrays a specific logic which, as far as I am concerned, is irreducible to the other two.[8] The role dimension entails predominantly a normative logic, the interactive-situational dimension a voluntaristic logic, and the dispositional dimension a practical logic – i.e. a logic which, as I shall explain more fully later, entails neither a theoretical knowledge of norms and formal rules nor a conscious elaboration of strategies.[9]

This is not to imply that each of the three approaches completely ignores the other two, it is rather a question of where they put the greatest emphasis. So Parsons does indeed talk about interactive situations (his ego–alter interaction) as well as about dispositions (where norms have been internalized into need-dispositions). His work as a whole, however (particularly the middle social-system and the final neo-evolutionist phases), and (most importantly) the way his disciples use Parsonian tools, make it quite obvious that so much emphasis is laid on social roles and normative expectations that the interactive and the dispositional dimensions of games are systematically undervalued.[10] This precisely is the reason why Parsonian functionalism has been repeatedly criticized for portraying human beings as mere puppets driven by society's core values.[11]

Another way of putting this is to argue that Parsonian sociology implicitly assumes that there is no friction between social positions, dispositions and interactive situations, so that knowledge of the role/positional dimension is more or less sufficient for understanding the actual game played. This becomes clear if one looks at how Parsons deals with the issue of social order and disorder. Whereas he for his part tries to account for social disorder by such notions as failure of social controls, ineffective socialization or tensions and strains between roles, conflict theorists from Rex to Coser and Dahrendorf dismiss that position as trivial, and try to account for social disorder in terms of power inequalities and the ensuing interest differences between groups.

The positional, dispositional, interactive-situational distinction suggests a source of order or disorder that is fully covered neither by Parsonian functionalism nor by conflict theory. This source is the frequent, almost unavoidable clashes/incompatibilities between social positions, dispositions and interactive situations. Looking at extreme or ideal-typical cases, total harmony between social positions, dispositions and situations would entail circumstances where actors are socialized in such a way that their dispositions are perfectly congruent with the normative expectations of their roles. In such a case actors tend to wish and to expect what their roles prescribe. Moreover, not only is there perfect position–*habitus* congruence, but also the logic of interactive situations is such that players are invariably acting in accordance with their dispositions and the normative expectations entailed in their roles.

A good example of this 'seamless web' type of harmony is John Campbell's classical analysis of a transhumant Greek community – that of the Sarakatsani, whose lack of geographical fixity was compensated for by a strongly institutionalized system of values and roles that was a perfect fit with both the dispositions of its members and the situations they had to cope with in everyday existence.[12] Whether this really was the actual situation among the Sarakatsani or not, it is a fact that such total concord between social positions, dispositions and situations is extremely rare if not impossible, given the fragile, discontinuous, often chaotic nature of social arrangements. This means that constant tensions and incongruities between the logic of social positions, dispositions and situations is the rule rather than the exception.

To illustrate this, I shall draw again on the rich ethnography of modern Greek society. In contrast to Campbell's analysis, Jane Cowan's more recent anthropological study of a small-town community in Northern Greece shows that the 'seamless web' character of social arrangements disappears as traditional female roles are being contested.[13] Her young women, whose dispositions were partly formed via the mass media and the 'global culture', have come to resent the androcentric, patriarchal normative expectations that stress subservience to the husband, suppression of sexuality, 'shame', avoidance of all public spaces (except that of the church), etc. Now what reinforces their quasi-feminist, anti-traditional dispositions is the emergence of new institutional contexts (like the Western-type cafeteria) which – in contrast to the traditional *kafeneio* (from which women are excluded) – allows young people of both sexes to meet much more freely. Here the situational logic of the cafeteria reinforces the young women's anti-patriarchal dispositions and contributes to undermining the hold that traditional role expectations have on their conduct.

Comparing the two studies one can hypothesize that in Campbell's case the relative harmony between positions, dispositions and interactive situations was partly the result of the Sarakatsani's relative isolation from the outside world. This meant that all members of that community were socialized in a uniform manner – or, to put it differently: in so far as the *habitus* (as Bourdieu argues) is the result of an individual's past socializations, the varied socializations of each Sarakatsani (in the family, the church, the market place, etc.) were so congruent with each other that in any specific situation the individual's disposition was a perfect match of the role/normative expectations.

In Cowan's case, on the other hand, given the massive intrusion of extra-community socializing processes (the mass media, tourism, travel, etc.), the members' various socializations tended to be contradictory. This meant that in specific situations young women's dispositions (the result of earlier conflicting socializations) might clash with the normative expectations of significant others.

Now a Parsonian sociologist would simply talk in such a case of tensions or frictions within or between roles. This is not wrong, but neither is it informative. It does not help us to ask questions about the source of role friction. Whereas if one looks at the problem in terms of the congruence/incongruence of roles, dispositions and interactive situations, one obtains a much clearer idea of how frictions come about and how they relate to specific situations. In other words, the notion of the three-dimensional aspect of social games introduces into role analysis the idea of time (dispositions as 'embodied' history) and social space (the logic of specific interactive situations).

Needless to say, the degree of compatibility/incompatibility between positions, dispositions and interactive situations, as well as the players' reactions to such incompatibilities, are empirical questions that cannot be tackled in an aprioristic fashion. What can be said with certainty, however, is that the two ideal-typical extremes (of total congruence and total incongruence) are extremely rare if not altogether impossible. Most societies, and particularly complex, differentiated ones, portray neither a seamless-web type of harmony, nor do they entail circumstances where positions, dispositions and interactive situations are constantly at war with one another.

The distinction between the positional, dispositional and interactive-situational dimensions of social games can be extremely useful in dispelling some persistent confusions in micro–macro debates in sociology. Consider, for instance, Goffman's contention that the interaction order has a *sui generis* character. In his famous 1983 address to the American Sociological Association, Goffman argued that the interaction order, an order based on face-to-face social encounters, has a logic quite distinct from society's broader 'institutional order'. For him the interaction and the institutional orders are only 'loosely coupled' – this looseness implying that it is impossible to reduce the one to the other. It is impossible, for instance, to derive the rules that regulate face-to-face micro encounters from broader macro institutional features such as a national language or various forms of cultural knowledge. For Goffman, although actors bring into social encounters forms of broadly spread knowledge acquired via socialization, such knowledge does not determine what happens during the interaction process. In order to fully explain what happens, one has to see these forms of knowledge in conjunction with rules which are specific to the interactive situation.[14]

Although I fully agree with the notion of the interactive situation having a logic of its own, I disagree with the way in which Goffman links 'interaction order' with micro and 'institutional order' with macro. As already pointed out in Chapter 1, interactive as well as institutional structures can be both micro and macro. If one accepts this, then there is a much better way of conceptualizing the *sui generis* character of the interaction order: by stressing that micro as well as macro games entail the three fundamental dimensions of positions, dispositions and interactive situations. All three dimensions have a logic of their own – in the sense that one cannot automatically derive the one from the other.

Consider, for instance, a macro game like a meeting of the top managers of a multinational corporation in which important decisions are taken affecting a large number of people. In this specific macro encounter/game participants play certain roles, they bring into the game their dispositions acquired during various and differing socializations and they face a specific interactive situation which, as Goffman argued, has a logic of its own. In this case all three dimensions – positional, dispositional, interactive – have a macro character; in that sense they contrast sharply with the dimensions of a micro game like a face-to-face encounter of low-rank officials within a local branch of the same corporation. Such a game as well entails positions/roles, dispositions and a *sui generis* interactive logic. But in this case the three dimensions constitute a game whose consequences stretch very little in time/space.

2.2.2 Types of social games

While the role/positional, dispositional and interactive-situational dimensions are all indispensable for a full understanding of any social game, there can be no doubt that (depending on the nature of the game) one of these dimensions may be more important than the other two.

For example, in a highly ritualistic game – a traditional Greek Orthodox Mass, say – it is the role/positional dimension that is dominant, in the sense that one can understand the whole game from beginning to end by a thorough knowledge of the roles of the priest, the churchgoer, the thurifer and so on. On the other hand, a full explanation of a game of poker – a game the uncertainty of which requires intuition, the ability to predict the other players' next moves, etc. – gives pride of place to the interactive-situational aspect. Finally, in a game of tennis, where unconscious, virtually automatic schemata of perception, evaluation and action play a prominent role, it is the dispositional dimension that becomes all-important (without, of course, completely displacing the other two).

For all that we must never lose sight of the fact that each of the three basic dimensions of games to some extent involves the other two. So it is quite impossible to think of an interactive situation where the dispositional dimension is totally absent; to a lesser extent the same is true about the role dimension.

This does not mean, of course, that on an analytical/theoretical level it is possible to conflate the three aspects, or to reductively derive one from the other.[15] Each dimension has its own logic, and any attempt to reduce the one to either (or both) of the others must result in a distorted view of social life.

2.2.3 Habitus *and intentionality*

Bourdieu insists that the notion of *habitus* does not entail intent or strong voluntaristic elements. His *habitus* has an impersonal and quasi-automatic character: quasi-automatic in the sense that the actors are not necessarily aware of the generative schemes that result in their varied practices; and impersonal in the sense that these schemata cannot be explained exclusively by reference to the actors' idiosyncrasies. As internalizations of 'objective' social structures, the elements of *habitus* are shared by all human beings who have experienced similar socialization processes.[16]

In the above perspective, Bourdieu's notion shows certain similarities with Levi-Strauss' hidden codes – which is hardly surprising, since the latter's structuralism was a major influence on Bourdieu's early work. There are also important differences, of course. First of all, the *habitus* is not as 'hidden' as the unconscious codes of Levi-Strauss.[17] A more important difference is that Bourdieu, after an initial structuralist phase, came to think that social phenomena do not portray the order, symmetry and logical consistency implied by the codes of Levi-Strauss. He was persuaded that the structuralist methodology employs a theoretical logic that belongs more in the theorist's imagination than in the actual social practices of everyday life. In this sense Bourdieu's post-structuralist *habitus* is based on practical rather than theoretical logic – on a logic which recognizes that dispositions are extremely flexible, polysemic and polythetic, in that they take a great variety of forms according to the situation that activates them. *Habitus* can therefore be seen as the missing link between structuralism and pheno-menological/ethnomethodological approaches.

Another way of seeing how *habitus* articulates with structuralism and ethnomethodology is to use again Saussure's famous distinction between *langue* and *parole*. The hidden codes of Levi-Strauss operate on the level of *langue*, because they focus on rules that are discovered when social institutions are viewed on the paradigmatic level (as wholes made up of elemental parts, whose linkages are brought to the surface by the structu-ralist methodology).[18] On the other hand, Garfinkel's ethnomethods tend to operate on the level of *parole*, since they mainly consist of practical techniques that laypersons use in their attempt to facilitate interpersonal communication. So for instance the famous 'etcetera' principle cannot be derived from the study of grammar and syntax. It can only be understood empirically by looking at how laypersons manage the transition from the paradigmatic to the syntagmatic level, from language as a self-contained set of abstract rules, to talking as a social and practical accomplishment.[19]

With regard now to the notion of habitus, this pertains to both the paradigmatic (*langue*) and the syntagmatic (*parole*) levels. In the first case, *habitus* points to the unconscious, quasi-automatic dispositions that (like the hidden codes of Levi-Strauss) throw considerable light on the way social games are played. On the other hand, Bourdieu insists that the *habitus* is based far more on practical than theoretical logic, since the schemata of action, thought and evaluation do not have the elegance and rigour of Levi-Strauss' codes. As already mentioned, they rather portray the flexibility, malleability and practicality of the techniques of communication – the ethnomethods explored by Garfinkel and his disciples.

The notion of *habitus*, therefore, is located between the codes and the ethnomethods. From the former it takes the idea of non-intent or of non-theoretical knowledge/awareness, and from the latter it takes the practical techniques that link the paradigmatic with the syntagmatic.

2.2.4 Bourdieu's 'transcendence' of objectivist and subjectivist sociologies

The above makes it understandable why Bourdieu uses the *habitus* concept as a major means for transcending the perennial social sciences debate of objectivism versus subjectivism. He maintains that the various subjectivist micro sociologies centre their analysis on relatively autonomous subjects who act and interact in a highly voluntaristic, conscious manner. The objectivist sociologies, on the other hand (from Parsons to Levi-Strauss) portray human beings as the passive products of roles, institutions or hidden codes.

For Bourdieu the *habitus* refers to generative schemata that are quite different from the normative expectations of Parsonian roles, the hidden linkages of the Levi-Strauss' codes or the reflexive accounting of ethnomethodology. If Parsons considers the major source of social order to be common values and norms, Levi-Strauss the effectiveness of hidden codes and Garfinkel the situational meanings and interactive techniques that laypersons use, Bourdieu, in contrast to all of them, considers the foundation of social order to be the *habitus*.

I do not, however, think that Bourdieu has managed to transcend the subjectivism–objectivism distinction in the social sciences. Neither do I think that his *habitus*, when combined with other key notions of his conceptual repertoire (such as fields, capital, practices) replaces sociology's structural, structuralist and phenomenological approaches. His rather megalomaniacal attempts at 'transcending' existing approaches, distinctions or concepts may have more to do with the *habitus* of a certain type of French intellectual (who, by caricaturing or completely ignoring what already exists,[20] is obsessively concerned with the 'new', even where this merely means putting new labels onto old bottles) than with any serious elaboration of a genuinely new theoretical synthesis. In view of this it is not surprising that the supposedly 'transcended' distinction between subjectivism and objectivism is reintroduced by the back door in the form of the distinction between objective and internalized structures, or between social position and stance.[21]

Let me develop this critical point further. It has been objected that Bourdieu's linkages between his notions field (a set of interrelated 'objective' social positions), *habitus* and practices are mechanistic/deterministic – in that the field → *habitus* → practice nexus portrays human beings just as passively as does Parsons' functionalist sociology.[22] Bourdieu rejects the above critique by asserting that neither the passage from field to *habitus*, nor that from *habitus* to practices, is mechanistically determined. (I have already pointed out that Bourdieu stresses the flexible, polysemic and polythetic character of *habitus*.)

However, Bourdieu's defence is little more than rhetoric. The only way to convincingly demonstrate the non-mechanistic character of his linkages would be to create conceptual tools for analysing the supposedly non-deterministic character of the field → *habitus* → practice linkages. Surely the only way to create such non-deterministic concepts would be to take much more seriously than Bourdieu does the voluntaristic, interactive-situational dimension of social games.

Let us consider his claim that the generative schemata of *habitus* are not automatic internalizations of objective social structures. If this is true (which I think it is), it is due to the fact that social beings, even when submitted to similar external pressures or influences, and even if they belong to the same social class, are able to accept, reject or selectively internalize external social structures. To explain why some accept, others reject and still others selectively adopt institutionalized norms one must seriously take into account the relatively autonomous logic of the interactive situation: one has to remember that laypersons are capable of reacting in a highly conscious, deliberate manner to external influences, and that the way in which they internalize (if at all)[23] 'objective' social structures has to do with the way they interact with each other.

In other words if, as Bourdieu argues, individuals do not automatically follow formal rules or normative expectations, this is due not only to the flexibility of the *habitus*, but also to the logic of specific interactive situations.[24] The adaptable and polythetic character of the *habitus* presupposes that its generative schemes enable players of social games to act (in varying degrees and in the logic of any specific interactive situation) voluntaristically – that is to say, on the basis of a rational calculation of the consequences of alternatives, and by consciously adopting specific strategies and counter-strategies.

When Bourdieu insists that consciously worked out strategies are rare and less effective than strategies that are not deliberately calculated,[25] his argument is untenable on two counts. First, it is simply not true that voluntarism, in the form of rational decision-making, planning, the 'calculated' elaboration of strategies and counter-strategies, refers to extreme or rare situations. In all types of society there are games where *conscious* strategies (not strategies in the peculiar meaning in which Bourdieu uses the term)[26] play a crucial role. This is particularly so in modern and postmodern situations, where deliberately set up formal organizations proliferate and become dominant in all institutional spheres.

Second, even if consciously generated strategies were rare or ineffective, this would be no reason for refusing to theorize them. However rare they may be, Bourdieu cannot deny that they often play a crucial role in shaping the world we live in (think for example of the perfectly or imperfectly rational games played by multinationals competing for the control of world markets). In whatever way we look at the problem, therefore, conscious strategies and rational decision-making cannot be neglected as fundamental dimensions of certain games.

This being so, Bourdieu will have to tell us how they fit into the field → *habitus* → practice model. How are calculated strategies related to the generative schemes of the *habitus*? Given that dispositions have a non-volitional, quasi-automatic character, how is one to account for practices that are predominantly the result of conscious, reflexive monitoring of others' and one's own actions and interactions? If the *habitus* is stretched to cover both volitional and non-volitional strategies, then it loses its analytical edge. If it is limited to its present form, then quite obviously there is a 'black box' in Bourdieu's sociology of action. If one is going to reject deterministic linkages, the *habitus*–practice articulation requires the introduction of conceptual tools to permit an investigation of the voluntaristic dimensions of social life; to the fact that laypersons are to varying degrees rational beings, consciously striving to increase their share of material and non-material 'profits' by planning ahead, by constantly reassessing their actions on the basis of their past mistakes, and so on. The fact that human rationality is never as perfect as some rational decision-making models assume is no reason for simply writing it off, for dismissing the possibility of the conscious construction of rational strategies altogether.

What has been said about the *habitus*–practice linkages also applies to the field–*habitus* articulations. Bourdieu argues that social position (as an objective dimension of the 'field') does not automatically determine stance (*prise de position*). Actors can adopt different stances or postures *vis-à-vis* the rights and obligations each position/role entails.[27] In view of this room for manoeuvre, how can the possibility be ruled out of actors standing back from their roles in order to consciously construct strategies of transformation or conservation? Such a conscious practice cannot be linked with *habitus*. Where does it come from then?

To put this differently: in so far as practices

> are the result of the encounter between the Habitus and its dispositions on the one hand and the constraints, demands, opportunities of the social field or market[28]

on the other, how are deliberate strategic orientations related to practices? Since neither a field's objective structure of positions, nor the disposition of the *habitus* entail calculated strategies, where do such orientations fit? Even if we accept Bourdieu's strange contention that calculated strategies are both rare and ineffective, in so far as they exist at all, their relations to practices must be theorized. The only way to do this is to admit that practices are the result of not only positions and dispositions, but also of interactive situations. To repeat myself: the only way to get out of the structure → *habitus* → practice cul-de-sac is to take more seriously the voluntaristic dimension of social games.[29]

It is precisely because of the lack of voluntarism in his work that Bourdieu is criticized (rightly, I think) for being a functionalist as little able as Parsons to provide adequate explanations of macro-historical transformations in terms of collective actors and the anticipated or unanticipated consequences of their more or less consciously constructed projects.[30]

In sum, the basic difficulty with Bourdieu's theory of action is that he sees his notion of *habitus* as antagonistic to the notion of interactive situation with its strong voluntaristic implications (a notion which has been developed by a series of micro-sociological approaches such as symbolic interactionism, ethnomethodology and phenomenological sociology). I myself see *habitus* and the interactive situation as rather complementary, in the sense that the games primarily based on conscious decision-making presuppose the quasi-automatic, non-conscious schemata of the *habitus* as much as do less 'voluntaristic' games. In as far as calculated decision-making does not take place in a socio-psychological vacuum, in as far as decision-makers operate on the basis of decisional premises they often take for granted,[31] the involuntary schemata of action, thought and evaluation that Bourdieu talks about may be viewed as key elements for enabling rational actors to intentionally elaborate strategies and arrive at more or less rational choices. In other words, not everything in decision-making is conscious, but the final result always derives from a mixture of conscious, less conscious and unconscious elements. The schemata of the *habitus* constitute the less conscious or unconscious premises that, together with more conscious ones, contribute to the construction of intentional strategies.

Finally (assuming that the *habitus* does not contradict but complements the notion of interactive situation), if all social games have a positional, dispositional and situational-interactive dimension, then, contrary to what Bourdieu thinks, his work has not displaced or transcended Garfinkel's ethnomethodology, Mead's symbolic interactionism, or Coleman's rational-choice theory: it simply complements all these approaches.

To say it once more: the present task for sociological theory is not one of 'transcendence', of looking *à tout prix* for the uncompromisingly and totally 'new'; neither is it to imperialistically impose the logic (subjectivist or objectivist) of one paradigm at the expense of all others. The task of sociological theory is, via the construction of appropriate conceptual tools, to build bridges between paradigms, and to enhance communications between theoretical approaches, so that compartmentalization is destroyed without at the same time destroying the autonomous logic of existing paradigms – without, that is, destroying the multi-paradigmatic character of sociology. This brings me to my fifth remark on Bourdieu's work.

2.2.5 The consequences of Bourdieu's underemphasis of the interactive-situational dimension

Bourdieu's overemphasis of the positional and dispositional aspects of social games at the expense of the interactive-situational one has, of course, direct consequences for his more empirically-oriented studies. Thus, much of Bourdieu's work on class, education and social reproduction is basically a very ingenious social-stratification exercise. For one thing, it is an attempt to measure or construct various sorts of indicators of both social positions (e.g. the social or cultural capital inherent in a specific position) and dispositions (patterns or schemata of action, perception, appreciation). Second, Bourdieu's work sets out to show how the above correlate with social background or 'class', which he ambiguously defines either in terms of occupational categories or in terms of the tripartite classification bourgeois/petit bourgeois/proletariate (corresponding to the Anglo-Saxon equivalent of upper, middle and working class). It is around these three pegs that, as Chris Wilkes to rightly puts it, Bourdieu

> weaves an elaborate thread of habitus, and it is through ceaseless
> examples of the habitus in its many elements – in its artistic compo-

nents, in eating habits, in the dispositions of the body, in theatre-visiting (or not visiting), in a concern for music or no music, in the political attitudes, the cars they drive, the men and women they marry, the sort of living rooms they construct – in all these ways the lives of classes are drawn.[32]

If one looks at his *Homo Academicus*, where Bourdieu's analysis avoids the static reproduction model of practice → *habitus* → position by partly focusing on the May 1968 events and their impact on the French university system – even there the analysis remains squarely within the social-stratification tradition. It is true, of course, that in *Homo Academicus* a certain dynamism is introduced into the simple reproduction model by showing how various crises break the usual correspondence between subjective expectations and the objective possibilities associated with social positions. But here as well the voluntaristic, interactive aspects of the crisis are peripheralized.

Specifically, Bourdieu shows how a dramatic increase in the number of social science students and a devaluation of their degrees undermines the fit between 'expectations' and objective possibilities. This disruption then brings about a similar disruption of the expectations of the social science teachers, whose chances of promotion are seriously undermined. On a broader plane, the arts and social science disciplines are doubly subordinated: by the traditional prestigious disciplines of law and medicine, and by the new dominance of science and technology.[33] But all the above descriptions of changes in the relations between different fields, or different positions within the same field, say nothing about how actors, particularly collective actors or groups, have reacted to these changes or crises. There is no systematic reference to the complex games the various groups were playing during this dramatic period, of their strategies and counter-strategies, their antagonisms, their attempts to maintain or transform the *status quo*. Bourdieu of course mentions numerous groups or social categories – but such mentions have a static social-stratificational rather than an interactive-situational character. He writes:

> Despite their popular image, the professors of the arts and social science faculties are no doubt overall more left-wing than the science professor ... despite the fact that, where public declarations are concerned (as in petitions, or declarations in favour of candidates for election) the left-wing minority is much more strongly represented ...
> As for the professors of law, who invest more strongly in politics than the professors of medicine, but who are no doubt less massively

concentrated on the right, they are more inclined to take up a public position on political problems, especially perhaps when they belong to the left-wing minority.[34]

Now all this is very fascinating, but it is based on a static analysis of the distribution of social traits (political orientations) among social categories (professors of social science, law, medicine). The way in which, say, actual social science professors interrelate antagonistically or co-operatively with professors of law or medicine and with other groups in connection with specific situations is not seriously explored. We are never shown how actors, more or less consciously, use the schemata of their *habitus* and the various 'capitals' entailed in the objective positions they occupy in order to actually play a specific game. In brief, there is a lot in Bourdieu's work about the rules of games, about the disposition of the players and the positions they occupy, but there is very little on how actual games are played, how actual games unfold syntagmatically in time and space.

Given this interactive-situational underemphasis, it is not surprising that Bourdieu's work totally lacks the kind of class analysis to be found in Marxist-influenced, historically-oriented social scientists (like R. Bendix, B. Moore, M. Mann), or in sociologically-oriented historians (like E. Hobsbawm, P. Anderson, F. Braudel). For them, classes are not static categories, useful for studying how social traits are distributed among a certain population; they consider that classes or fractions of classes can, given certain conditions, operate not only as the products but also as the partial producers of their social world. Bourdieu's caricaturing of Marxist class analysis cannot conceal the fact that, unlike non-dogmatic Marxism, his own approach may provide brilliant insights on how certain schemata (of action, perception and evaluation) or certain capacities and resources (inherent in social positions) are distributed among occupational categories, but it can not effectively explain how these distributions came about in the first place, and how they are being maintained or transformed.

2.2.6 Limited conceptual framework

Leaving the grandiose now for the modest (I find Bourdieu's work a strange mixture between the two), what is particularly useful in his theoretical work is that he adopts a Mertonian rather than Parsonian orientation to theory construction. He does not, *à la* Parsons or Giddens, aim at creating an all-inclusive, universal conceptual framework that will furnish an overall map of the social. In a much more limited and flexible manner he tries, like Merton did before him, to construct a restricted number of interrelated conceptual tools which, without offering ironclad philosophical foundations or universal methodological guidelines, are simply useful as sensitizing concepts facilitating empirical research.[35] As must be apparent by now, I am not against attempts at constructing a grand theory (after all, the second part of my book rests on the conviction that Parsons' work should neither be facilely dismissed nor 'transcended', and that instead one should build on it by reworking its oversystemic character, which is its major weakness.) All the same, I think that what we need most in the social sciences today is the more limited and modest theoretical approach of Merton and Bourdieu. I believe that more tactical rather than strategic theorizing is indicated if we are to get away from the absurdities of postmodern social theory, as well as from the sterile and unending battle of competing, imperialistically-oriented paradigms and subparadigms.

3 GIDDENS' DUALITY OF STRUCTURE

Moving from Bourdieu's tactical to Giddens' strategic theorizing, we see that there is much the works of the two men have in common, notwithstanding the obvious differences many commentators have pointed out. The most evident similarity is that Giddens, like Bourdieu, has set out to 'transcend' the object–subject dualism that is responsible for the never-ending antagonism between subjectivist and objectivist sociologies. Also, like Bourdieu (as I shall argue below), he has failed to transcend this divide, being obliged to reintroduce by the back door the very distinction he had set out to reject. Moreover, as in Bourdieu's case again, the 'transcendence' strategy led Giddens to the construction of concepts which, instead of bringing interpretative and structural/structuralist approaches closer together, have simply erected additional obstacles to their *rapprochement*.

Despite these shared negative features, Giddens' notion of the duality of structure and Bourdieu's *habitus* (when stripped of their 'transcendence' pretensions) are both extremely useful concepts for understanding how participants relate to social wholes (figurational and institutional). More specifically, if Bourdieu's *habitus* can help us see how social positions relate to real interactive situations, Giddens' duality-of-structure notion (when considered not as antagonistic but as complementary to subject–object dualism) can help us see how participants relate, via various social hierarchies, to social wholes on both the paradigmatic and the syntagmatic levels.

I shall begin with a very brief and rather elliptical exposition of Giddens' well-known structuration theory.

3.1 Brief exposé

The major purpose of Giddens' structuration theory[36] – an ambitious attempt to assume Parsons' mantle by providing an overall conceptual framework for the study of societies – is the integration of objectivist (structural, structuralist) and subjectivist or interpretative sociologies. Given its considerable impact on today's state of the discipline, it is pertinent to ask to what extent Giddens has been successful in transcending the objectivism–subjectivism dichotomy.

Structuration theory focuses on the central concepts of structure and social system. Structure consists of rules and resources that, like Saussure's *langue*, exist outside time and space.[37] It is conceptualized as a virtual system that is recursively instantiated as agents draw on it in order to act and interact on a routine basis. Structure, therefore, pertains to the paradigmatic. Social system, on the other hand, as a set of interactions or patterned relationships, refers to actors' concrete practices as these unfold syntagmatically in time and space. The term structuration, finally, signifies the process by which structures lead to the constitution of social systems.[38]

When Giddens claims that his concepts of structure, system and structuration operate in such a way that the subject–object dualism has become obsolete, it is because, for him, structure as a social object is not external to the subject, it is rather inseparable from the agent's conduct. In consequence, there is no dualism but duality. As a set of rules and resources, structure is both medium and outcome of the conduct it recursively organizes. In the capacity of medium it furnishes the rules and resources that make social conduct possible. *Qua* outcome, its reproduction and transformation result from the instantiation of rules in action and interaction. Just as language rules make it possible to formulate intelligible sentences while simultaneously, via these sentences, contributing to the reproduction of the language, so this same medium/outcome duality is to be found in all institutional spheres. Institutional orders, therefore, are reproduced by means of the duality of structure: through agents using, and thereby reproducing, rules and resources.

Lastly, given that Giddens' structures are not 'external' limitations but an element inherently shaping the actors' conduct, they are not only constraining but also enabling. Rules and resources as medium and outcome both limit and facilitate interaction, for they are the means through which social systems are constructed.

3.2 General critique

Although there is a lot more to structuration theory, the above sketchy summary is sufficient to show that its basic concepts lead to yet another dead end as far as the integration of subjectivist and objectivist sociologies is concerned.

To start with, the type of subject–object relationship that the duality-of-structure scheme implies does not exhaust the types of relationship subjects have *vis-à-vis* rules and resources, or towards social 'objects' in general. The duality of structure implies a practical, taken for granted, 'natural-performative'[39] orientation to rules and resources. To take language as an example again: all people routinely use language rules in order to interact with each other, and here the duality-of-structure notion is appropriate, rules being the means through which people communicate. But at other times actors view rules as topics rather than as means or resources. In that case they distance themselves from these rules in order to analyse or change them. When a linguist is studying the grammar of a language, for example, or a feminist is striving to change the prevailing rules regulating gender relationships, theoretical or strategic-monitoring orientations are stronger than natural-performative ones. Where the latter prevail, there is no distance between subject (the actor) and object (rules and resources), and it is legitimate to use the *duality*-of-structure concept. When theoretical and/or strategic orientations prevail, there is considerable distance between subject and object; hence the notion of *dualism* rather than duality is appropriate.

A similar point can be made when what is at issue is not a subject's relationship to a *virtual* order of rules on the paradigmatic level, but to *actual* social systems, to games or interacting agents situated in time and space. On this syntagmatic level too the subject may relate to actual social objects (the ongoing relationships between agents) in terms of both duality and dualism.

To take my earlier seminar example again: a participant may contribute so decisively to its major structural features that subject and social system are more or less inseparable; in that case it is inconceivable to see such a social system as 'external' to the subject-participant. Let us call this type of subject–object relationship syntagmatic duality. On the other hand, the same subject may be involved in much larger systems or games (a nation-state, say, or a multinational corporation), to the construction of which s/he contributes only minimally (in the sense that withdrawing from the game would not at all affect its major structural features). Here one can quite legitimately see this larger system as 'external' to the subject, in which case one should speak of the relationship as one of syntagmatic dualism.[40]

In the light of the above it becomes quite obvious why it is impossible to understand how hierarchically situated subjects relate to virtual rules, or actual social games or systems, via the duality schema. Subjects orient themselves to virtual rules and resources in both a practical and a theoretical-strategic manner, and moreover relate to a variety of actual social systems and games, some of which are more external to them than others; in consequence, the concepts of duality and dualism are both equally indispensable.

Let us take the authority structure of a modern industrial organization as an example. We shall assume that the workers at shop-floor level orient themselves to rules and resources primarily in a 'natural-performative' manner, which means that in a practical, taken-for-granted way they draw on rules and resources in order to do their job and earn a living. This is paradigmatic duality. The same rules and resources can, however, be a topic and focus of attention of foremen who, influenced by principles of so-called scientific management, want to analyse and change the work rules in order to increase shop-floor productivity. This is a case of paradigmatic dualism, since the foremen, as subjects situated in a hierarchically superior position, distance themselves from the rules or resources so as to study and change them.

On the syntagmatic level now, blue-collar workers relate in terms of subject–object duality to social systems or games for the construction and reproduction of which their participation is vital (such as small informal groups at shop-floor level). At the same time their relationship to more encompassing social systems (like the corporation as a whole), or to macro games taking place at higher levels (e.g. games among senior managers), is one of syntagmatic dualism, given that each individual worker can affect them only minimally. Moreover, what constitutes an 'external' social system or game for a micro actor (a blue- or white-collar worker) may be otherwise for a meso or macro actor (a manager), whose decisions stretch more widely and affect a great number of organizational members. From a hierarchical perspective, therefore, what is external for one actor may not be (or be less so) for another.

The above example will have illustrated how the notion of subject–object duality and dualism, on the paradigmatic as well as the syntagmatic levels, can be systematically related to the concept of social hierarchies. Occupants of subordinate positions tend to relate to games played at higher organizational levels in terms of syntagmatic dualism (since as single individuals they cannot affect them significantly); whereas they relate to rules initiated from above predominantly in terms of paradigmatic duality (since they are supposed to, and often do, follow them in a taken-for-granted manner). The opposite combination (syntagmatic duality and paradigmatic dualism) obtains if one looks at how occupants of superordinate positions relate to games and rules respectively on lower organizational levels.[41]

It may be useful to note, finally, that the fourfold duality/dualism typology as outlined above can help towards a better understanding of the relationships that Giddens wants to examine between conventional macro sociology, interpretative sociologies and various forms of structuralism. In so far as macro sociology in the Durkheimian tradition is based on the society–individual schema, it primarily focuses on orientations characterized by subject–object dualism on the syntagmatic level (society being 'external' to the individual); whereas the micro-sociological approaches influenced by Mead and Schutz are based on subject–object relationships characterized by syntagmatic duality (social systems emerge through interaction and are inseparable from the subjects' activities). In structuralist analyses, on the other hand, the subject relates to the codes underlying various institutional arrangements in terms of paradigmatic duality (i.e. by drawing on more or less 'hidden' rules in a natural-performative manner). Quite obviously, as mentioned already, it is on this partial case that Giddens bases his duality-of-structure notion.

3.3 Duality of structure and the distinction between institutional analysis and strategic conduct

Although Giddens, like Bourdieu, refuses to distinguish between agency and structure (as entailing a subject–object dualism), in certain parts of his work he is obliged to elaborate a distinction between institutional analysis and analysis in terms of 'strategic conduct'. For Giddens, institutional analysis

> places in suspension the skills and awareness of actors, treating institutions as chronically reproduced rules and resources.[42]

Whereas in the analysis of strategic conduct,

> the focus is placed upon modes in which actors draw upon structural properties in the constitution of social relations.[43]

This is, of course, exactly the distinction Lockwood made years ago with his concepts of system and social integration: social integration referring to relationships between actors, and system integration to linkages between institutions or 'institutionalized parts of a social system'.[44]

Now the utility of the agency–institution distinction is that it helps us realize that for a full explanation of social stability or change one must look at social phenomena from both an institutional and an agency perspective. Lockwood has argued quite convincingly that Parsons, by focusing exclusively on institutional incompatibilities (system integration or mal-integration), has ignored social conflict (social integration) as a major mechanism of social transformation. Marx, in his work as a whole, provides a more balanced framework for the study of social change, because he has combined a social- and system-integration approach. As already noted, he analyses capitalist societies both in terms of growing systemic or institutional incompatibilities (e.g. growing contradictions between technology and the institution of private property), and in terms of agents' struggles (for instance by enquiring into the development of class consciousness, organization and conflict).

The crucial point here is that although the system–social-integration distinction (or, to use Giddens' terminology, the strategic-conduct/institutional-analysis distinction) is an analytic one, it refers to aspects of social reality that can vary in relatively independent fashion – given that growing institutional incompatibilities do not automatically generate social conflict or a certain type of strategic conduct. Situations can be envisaged in which, for example, certain institutional incompatibilities, on the level of agency, lead to revolutionary, reformist or 'apathetic' conduct. (To revert to Marxism, it is only in the most crude and mechanistic forms of historic materialism that institutional incompatibilities are supposed to lead more or less automatically to revolutionary conflict and the collapse of a dominant mode of production.)

The above makes it clear that the distinction between institutions and actors (between system and social integration in Lockwood's formulation, or between institutional and strategic-conduct analysis in Giddens') becomes useful when one allows for agents to react in a non-fixed, not predetermined manner to institutionalized rules and their eventual incompatibilities. That is to say, it becomes useful for asking questions about how actors perceive institutional incompatibilities (if at all), and what they do about them. Who, for instance, is aware of such incompatibilities and how; who is trying to maintain, and who to resolve and transcend them? Such 'who' questions are absolutely indispensable for understanding how institutional analysis is related to an analysis in terms of strategic conduct, and they can be asked only if one introduces the concept of paradigmatic dualism – i.e. if one theorizes actors as capable, for theoretic and/or strategic purposes, of standing back from institutionalized rules (for example when they wish to attack or defend institutionalized rules or their variously perceived incompatibilities).

It is precisely at this point that Giddens' duality-of-structure notion runs into difficulties. For if one opts exclusively for a subject/object duality approach, the only way of conceiving the relationships between subject and structure is to see the latter as medium/outcome – which means conflating agency and structure, and eliminating the possibility of actors distancing themselves from rules and resources in order to view them strategically.

What all this amounts to is that Giddens' duality-of-structure notion contradicts and therefore jeopardizes his useful but not original distinction between institutional and strategic-conduct analysis. It is precisely because of this that his ambition to transcend the agency-versus-structure controversy and to integrate structural and interpretative sociologies, has not been achieved. Instead of providing bridges, the duality-of-structure notion erects insurmountable barriers to an effective integration of approaches emphasizing strategic conduct, and those emphasizing institutions. A fundamental precondition for an effective integration is the conceptualization of the subject/object or the agency/institutionalized-rules relationship in terms of duality and dualism – which means the agents must be seen as related to institutionalized rules both in a taken-for-granted and in a strategic-monitoring manner.

Finally it is worth mentioning that Giddens, in post-structuralist fashion, rejects not only the agency–structure distinction but also the micro–macro one. For him the two distinctions are linked in the sense that social scientists tend to associate micro with agency and macro with structure. But given that this association is neither logically necessary nor endorsed by everybody, it is difficult to understand why Giddens should prefer outright rejection to clarification and restructuring. This puzzle becomes still greater when Giddens attempts to replace the micro–macro distinction by that of social/system-integration. For the author of *The Constitution of Society*, social integration refers to

> reciprocity of practices between actors in circumstances of co-presence, understood as continuities in and disjunctions of encounters,

whereas system integration refers to

> reciprocity between actors or collectivities across extended time-space, outside conditions of co-presence.[45]

Therefore it is co-presence or lack of it that becomes the criterion for distinguishing micro from macro. It follows that for Giddens, encounters entailing face-to-face interaction are micro phenomena. This makes him fall into a trap not dissimilar to that of micro sociologists, who consider any face-to-face interaction as a micro event – irrespective of the power of the interactants.

Giddens' attempt to 'transcend' the micro–macro distinction not only ends up by replacing two perfectly useful distinctions (i.e. micro–macro, and Lockwood's version of system- and social-integration) with a useless one; it also leads him to link micro with face-to-face interactions – a linkage that is as absurd as the association of agency with micro and of structure with macro.

4 CONCLUSION

The above analysis of Bourdieu's and Giddens' attempts at transcending objectivist and subjectivist sociologies allows us to make a closer identification of a defect common to the conceptual framework of both theorists. This flaw is that neither of them provides adequate concepts for showing the obvious fact that actors are capable of standing back from game rules or actual games so as to, quite consciously, construct strategies of transformation or conservation.

To recapitulate: given that Bourdieu's *habitus* refers to quasi-automatic schemata that preclude conscious strategies of action, and given his dismissal of rational-choice models as well as the voluntaristic orientations of interpretative sociologies, he has no conceptual means for dealing with interactive situations where actors, in perfectly conscious and deliberate fashion, distance themselves from their social positions (on the paradigmatic level) or from actual games or practices (on the syntagmatic level), in order to rationally assess the situation (both paradigmatically and syntagmatically) and, on the basis of this assessment, construct more or less intentional, calculated strategies of transformation or conservation. To put this into Giddens' duality/dualism vocabulary, Bourdieu's *habitus* does not allow researchers to view actors in terms of subject–object dualism: it does not allow them to see actors as able to stand back from rules or from any specific interactive situation for purposes of strategy or monitoring.

The same is true the other way round. Giddens' duality of structure does not sensitize one to the fact that Bourdieu's position–disposition–practice triad misses the voluntaristic aspects of all human games. Therefore, *habitus* and duality of structure complement and reinforce each other negatively. They both divert the student of social games from viewing participants as capable and willing to take a discriminatory stance *vis-à-vis* institutional and figurational wholes, in order consciously to generate transformational or conservational projects. The upshot is that both Bourdieu's and Giddens' key concepts hinder the explanation of situations where actors try, in quite deliberate and conscious manner, to use rules and resources (in Giddens' case) or their positions and dispositions (in Bourdieu's) not as means but as topics.

It would be quite possible, of course, to argue that the above critique is contradicted by the fact that both authors, in their more empirically-oriented analyses, are constantly talking about conscious strategies. Giddens' notion of strategic conduct, of knowledgeable subjects, of reflexive monitoring; and Bourdieu's references to social fields as spaces of 'struggles', to the stances or postures that actors adopt *vis-à-vis* their social positions, to the notions of reflexivity and 'socionalysis'[46] – all these concepts lead directly to a view of actors as strategists often, and quite deliberately and consciously, distancing themselves from rules or interacting players.

But what must be stressed is that such references and concepts flatly contradict what the two theorists say about their key notions of *habitus* and duality of structure. These are incompatible with their authors' constant references to actors as strategists and partial producers of their social world.

What – to reiterate it for a last time – creates this schizophrenic situation is not the concepts themselves. The difficulties and contradictions are due to the exclusionary, 'transcending' manner in which they are presented: Bourdieu is not prepared to see that his *habitus* complements rather than displaces the voluntarism of interpretative sociologies; Giddens dismisses the concept of subject–object dualism as *passé*.

I think it is time to reassert as clearly and as forcefully as possible that the agency/institutional structure or the subjectivist/objectivist distinction, in so far as it is not replaced by a more adequate conceptualization, cannot be dismissed as easily as Giddens and Bourdieu (as well as Elias for that matter) try to do: i.e. by simply caricaturing theories which use the distinction and by rhetorically declaring its transcendence while reintroducing into their conceptualizations logically equivalent distinctions.[47]

To end on a more positive note, I would like to affirm once more that outside the 'transcendence' problematic both *habitus* and duality of structure are extremely useful tools for understanding how social players orient themselves to figurational and institutional wholes. Bourdieu's *habitus* can show that neither the role/position (stressed in Parsonian sociology) nor the interactive situation (stressed by interpretative micro sociologists) is sufficient for a full understanding of how players relate to each other in specific games. The unconscious, quasi-automatic, polythetic schemata we all carry inside us are absolutely fundamental for making sense of how we react to the normative expectations of the roles we play, and to the emergent meanings that every interactive situation generates. If it is essential to see *habitus* as complementary to the notions of role/position and interactive situation, it is equally essential to see Giddens' duality of structure as complementary to the notion of subject–object dualism. When this is properly realized, the duality–dualism concepts will be able to generate interesting questions about another fundamental dimension of the participant–social-whole problematic, questions about the distance or non-distance subjects take up *vis-à-vis* virtual objects (institutionalized rules) and *vis-à-vis* actual objects (other interactive subjects). Such questions would illuminate the hierarchical aspects of the participant–social-whole issue. As I have argued earlier, to talk about micro–macro, or about participant–social-whole linkages without taking into account social hierarchies is like trying to swim in an empty pool.

7

SYNTHESIS AND APPLICATION
A sociological reconsideration of functionalism

As I have been arguing throughout this book, the way to assess new concepts or conceptual frameworks is to demonstrate their utility by either tackling successfully persistent theoretical puzzles and misconceptions that sociologists have been unable to solve so far; or by applying them directly to empirically-oriented research. Since in a previous book[1] I have mainly followed the latter criterion, here I will put greater emphasis on the 'puzzle-resolving' one. More precisely, I think that the various conceptual tools I have developed in the foregoing chapters can throw some light on the ongoing debates on the status of functionalism. These debates seem to drag on endlessly because social theorists do not bother to give a clear definition of their basic terms (such as social structure, social whole, functional requirements, etc.). As a result they keep talking at cross-purposes, or take refuge in ontological/epistemological arguments that often get in the way of the sociological dimension of the problem, displacing or occluding it.

1 FUNCTIONALISM: LEGITIMATE AND ILLEGITIMATE FORMS

I shall start with the assumption that the minimum requirements for calling an approach or explanation functionalist are (a) the notion of a whole consisting of interrelated parts, and (b) the notion of 'externality'.

As regards (a), in the light of what I have argued in Chapter 4, a social whole can refer both to a system of interrelated actors (i.e. to a figurational whole) and to a system of interrelated rules, roles or social positions (institutional whole).

When R. K. Merton set about purging functionalist analysis of a series of widespread misconceptions, he pointed out that the degree of the interrelatedness of 'parts' is an empirical question:[2] that functionalism *per*

127

se implies neither high social harmony in figurational terms nor high compatibility of norms/values in institutional terms. Moreover, he left open the question of what constitute parts of the social whole. Parsons on the other hand, as mentioned already, sees parts primarily in terms of institutions rather than actors, and opts for an institutional rather than figurational analysis of part–whole linkages.[3] I shall argue that a great deal of confusion about functionalism derives from the fact that theorists talk about social structures without making clear whether they view wholes in institutional or figurational terms.

Concerning now the second basic requirement (b), this pertains to the idea that for an analysis to be called functionalist it is not sufficient to view social phenomena in holistic terms; another fundamental precondition is the adoption of an 'externalist' rather than 'internalist' perspective.[4] What exactly does an externalist perspective imply? It is more than a question of observer's versus participant's perspective, because the observer may be a participant observer in the tradition of interpretatively-oriented research. It is rather that externality implies the major focus of analysis being on the social whole (institutional and figurational), and this in two respects:

> *first*, that one pays greater attention to how the social whole affects participants, than to the way participants shape or do not shape the social whole;
> *second*, that in so far as one raises questions about how social wholes are maintained or changed, the focus is again on system- rather than actor- or participant-oriented issues.

Let me spell out in greater detail these two ways in which functionalists emphasize social wholes at the expense of social participants.

1.1 The social-whole → participant emphasis: acceptable functionalism

One of the major forms of functionalist emphasis on the whole (i.e. one major dimension of externality) lays greater stress on how (in terms of either constraint or enablement) a system of interrelated actors or of interrelated roles affects the participants, rather than on how these participants construct, reproduce and transform such systems.

For example, Durkheim arguing that the collective conscience is both constraining and external to individual consciences – without explaining how the *conscience collective* is formed and whose interest it serves – is a clear case of institutional whole → participant functionalism.

I would like to stress here that, whatever Durkheim's critics may say, this type of analysis does not necessarily reify social reality.[5] Although in many respects not very satisfactory, such an analysis is an acceptable form of functionalism. It is acceptable in the sense that the assumptions about externality (the shared norms having existed before any particular participant was born) and constraints (such shared norms setting certain limits to any specific participant's room for manoeuvre) are, if properly interpreted, quite realistic. It is acceptable also because it is perfectly legitimate to ask what impact those pre-existing (from the point of view of a specific participant), strongly institutionalized norms and values may have on the conduct of the participant.

On the other hand, although the analysis is quite legitimate, it is not very satisfactory because it discourages the researcher from asking the equally legitimate question of how individual or collective participants shape or fail to shape the collective consciousness. Another way of making the same point is to argue (as in the preceding chapter) that functionalists tend to overemphasize the role/positional dimension of social games and to underemphasize the interactive-situational one. Due to this one-sidedness, functionalists tend to merely describe or give only very partial explanations of stability or change.

This form of functionalist explanation may be schematically presented as follows:

$$\text{Social whole} \rightleftarrows \text{participant(s)}$$

Here the weak arrow indicates that although the model emphasizes the whole → participant(s) rather than the participant(s) → whole relationship, there are no conceptual obstacles to investigating the reverse linkage. It is precisely this that makes this type of functionalism legitimate.

1.2 Unacceptable functionalism I: Parsons

If we now move to Parsons, the situation becomes more problematical. Like Durkheim, Parsons starts with core values and shows how they are institutionalized into normative expectations and internalized into need dispositions. Quite faithfully following in the Durkheimian tradition, he never asks questions systematically as to how these core values appeared in the first place or how they are being maintained or transformed. That means that he too accentuates the institutional-whole → participant(s) relationship. But Parsons' one-sidedness is not simply unsatisfactory, it is also unacceptable in methodological terms, given that, as argued extensively in Chapter 5, his AGIL → a, g, i, l scheme does not merely discourage but actually excludes the investigation of how participants affect the whole.

To repeat briefly a point already made, inasmuch as Parsons subdivides each major institutional order into four institutional sub-subsystems, he creates conceptual obstacles that prevent the effective articulation of institutional and figurational structures, as well as the examination of how agents are not only products but also producers of institutional wholes. Moreover, when turning from his early analysis of social action to his analysis of social systems, Parsons systematically underemphasized the interactive-situational aspects of social games.[6] In consequence, his critics are not unjustified when they accuse him of presenting actors as social or cultural dupes, or when they object that when relatively autonomous agents appear in Parsonian analysis it is in spite and not because of its core conceptual framework.

In view of the above, the temptation to resort to teleological explanations is great indeed. Once relatively autonomous agents disappear, there is no explanation for the stability or transformation of social wholes other than by reference to social needs as 'causes', or to 'hidden codes' in the Levi-Strauss tradition.

Schematically the Parsonian model of functionalist explanation can be given as:

$$\text{Social whole} \rightleftharpoons \text{participant(s),}$$

the broken arrow indicating that Parsonian functionalism not only does not encourage, but actually prevents questions about how participants shape or fail to shape social wholes.

1.3 Unacceptable functionalism II: Althusser

If we now look at Althusserian functionalism, we find the teleological bias still more pronounced. Althusser's agents, unlike Parsons', are *deliberately* presented as puppets. Whether one looks at his theory of ideology (where the agent's sense of autonomy is viewed as false consciousness), or his theory of classes (conceptualized as 'carriers of structures'), in terms of theoretical intent and conceptual tools offered, practices for Althusser are always – by definition, so to speak – the 'effects' of structural determinants.[7] So while he did manage to overcome some of the most objectionable aspects of Marx's economism, he introduced into Marxism a form of extreme structuralism which, in actual fact, obviates questions about the participant(s) → structure relationship. Here teleology is not, as in Parsons, the unintended consequence of inappropriate conceptual tools, but an explicit and strongly held theoretical position.

In other words, in Parsons' case the passive portrayal of actors was due to inadequate conceptualization rather than to a belief in the total lack of a voluntaristic dimension of social life. In Althusser's case the lack of voluntaristic concepts is fully intentional, and based on a view of social development, where

> The real subject of all partial history is the combination on which the elements and their relationships depend – that is to say, something which is not a subject. So it could be said that the chief problem of a scientific history, a theoretical history, is identifying the combination on which depend the elements that are to be analyzed.[8]

In the light of the above one can schematically represent Althusser's functionalism as:

$$\text{Social whole} \longrightarrow \text{participant(s)},$$

the $\longleftarrow$ sign signifying that the obstacles to analysing participant(s) $\rightarrow$ whole relationships are both conceptual/practical and theoretical.

2 FUNCTIONAL REQUIREMENTS AND CONDITIONS OF EXISTENCE

Moving now to the second way in which functionalists emphasize social wholes at the expense of participants, here (in contrast to the previous case) questions concerning the maintenance or survival of the social whole are asked indeed, but these questions are system- rather than action-oriented. They are not 'who' questions (implying a participant $\rightarrow$ whole relationship, such as who created the whole? who tries to maintain or change it?), but questions about the necessary but not sufficient conditions of existence of the whole, and whether specific institutionalized processes, viewed from a system- rather than social-integration point of view, strengthen or weaken these conditions of existence. In other words, the typical issues raised by functionalists in this context concern the minimum conditions in which the whole (institutional or figurational) can go on in its present form, as well as how certain conditions can strengthen or weaken its present state.

2.1 The logic of Parsons' functional requirements

The famous functional requirements or 'needs' of the social system (as used by Parsons, for example) can be translated without any loss of meaning into a conditions-of-existence vocabulary. In that sense to criticize functionalism for its 'biologistic' bias, for its tendency to reify social wholes by its constant reference to mysterious systemic needs is quite simply to draw attention away from what matters. When theoretically sophisticated functionalists talk about social needs or functional requirements, they simply mean conditions of existence. Given that the debate concerning the legitimacy of talking about needs is still going on, it is important to spell out the argument as plainly as possible.

For example, when Parsons maintains that a formal organization like a factory has an adaptation requirement or 'need', he is merely saying that in order to survive in its present form it has to have a certain amount of human and non-human resources (like workers, machines, raw materials) for its basic operations. Since the acquisition of such resources is not random, Parsons then asks systemic questions about the norms (and the processes these norms regulate) that deal with the acquisition-of-resources problem.

To repeat: the assumptions behind this type of functionalist reasoning are (a) that a minimum of resources is necessary if this particular formal organization is to continue functioning in its present form, and (b) that coping with this minimum requirement entails a set of institutionalized rules/processes. These assumptions are good plain common sense, but they do not create into any methodological difficulties. Questions raised on the basis of such assumptions – such as: which rules are primarily oriented towards solving an organization's adaptation requirements? – entail neither reification nor teleology.

The same is true of questions about the 'functional' or 'dysfunctional' consequences that certain norms and practices have for the social whole. Does the adoption of a new scheme for recruiting managers facilitate or hinder the acquisition-of-resources problem? It is true that, such questions being systemic, they do not usually tell us who loses and who gains by the introduction of the new scheme. But while 'who' questions are important, there is nothing wrong with asking systemic questions, i.e. questions about whether or not a new rule or institutionalized practice enhances or weakens the functioning of the whole (to repeat, regardless of which group of participants gains or loses). As Merton pointed out long ago, once it is made clear that the functional or dysfunctional consequences exerted by a social item on the social whole must not be used as a cause explaining how this item came about, then it is perfectly legitimate to ask questions about whether or not this item strengthens or weakens the social whole. Despite all the subsequent debates, I think that Merton's distinction between teleological and non-teleological (i.e. legitimate) functionalist analysis continues to be both valid and useful.

The above arguments are made a great deal clearer and more acceptable by translating 'social needs' or 'functional requirements' into 'conditions of existence'. I will say it again: there is nothing wrong with asking questions about the conditions of existence of a social whole (viewed in either institutional or figurational terms). Sociologists like Giddens, who reject functionalism altogether, are only avoiding the conventional terminology (of needs, functions, systemic requirements) while retaining the functionalist logic: they continue to ask externalist questions about the conditions of existence of institutional or figurational wholes.[9]

2.2 Passing from necessary to sufficient conditions

It is one thing to ask methodologically legitimate questions about the necessary conditions of existence of a social whole, and quite another to explain how it came about. Conflating necessary with sufficient conditions is illegitimate, because it entails the transformation of necessary conditions into sufficient causes. To put this differently: there is a fundamental distinction to be made between possible and actual conditions of existence.

Let me give a specific example. It is one thing to argue that a necessary condition of existence of the capitalist mode of production (at any rate in its developed form) is the existence of a state that provides a minimum of welfare, but it is quite another to enquire into how the actual welfare state developed in specific capitalist societies.[10] It is with respect to this crucial passing from 'necessary' to 'sufficient' that functionalist analysis differs from an analysis emphasizing the participant → whole relationship.

To start with the latter, one way of moving from the necessary to the sufficient level, from the counterfactual to the actual, is to adopt an internalist perspective and to ask 'who' questions. Who performed what roles? What types of strategies and group struggles led, intentionally or unintentionally, to the formation of a welfare state in Great Britain, say, or Sweden? As already mentioned, functionalists tend not to put this kind of question – or, if they do, they cease, strictly speaking, to be functionalists.[11] So instead of asking 'who' questions they adopt an externalist perspective and ask 'how' questions – how certain disembodied processes (i.e. processes regarded from a system-integration point of view) reproduce, or fail to reproduce, a social whole.

To go back to our previous example, given that one of the necessary conditions of existence of a factory is the acquisition of a minimum of resources, how is this condition actually met in a specific factory (say a General Motors factory)? How are these norms (and the social processes regulated by them) used for dealing with the 'adaptation' problem in this particular factory? How do these norms and processes relate to other norms and processes that cope mainly with the factory's other necessary conditions of existence (e.g. the norms and processes referring to goal achievement, integration or latency)? [12]

Functionalists too, therefore, pass from the counterfactual to the actual, but they do so by asking systemic 'how', rather than 'who' questions. This means that whereas from the internalist, participant perspective, norms and social processes are directly viewed in terms of actors (intentionally or not) shaping social wholes, from a functionalist perspective subjects are 'decentred', and therefore social norms and processes are seen from the point of view of the requirements or conditions of existence of the whole. As I said before, in functionalism the organizing principle underlying the study of norms and processes is not the relatively autonomous social actor related interactively and situationally with other actors, but the social whole and its conditions of existence.

Now while it is perfectly legitimate to ask systemic questions, to do so is not enough. As many critics have pointed out, systemic enquiries only describe or can at best provide very partial explanations of how social arrangements persist or change. Inasmuch as they decentre or peripheralize actors, inasmuch as they view social processes or practices exclusively from a systemic perspective, they can never result in a satisfactory causal account of how social wholes are constituted, reproduced or transformed. Given that social causality entails the conception of participants as partial producers of their social world,[13] any decentring or peripheralizing of agency can only lead to descriptions, partial explanations, or illegitimate, teleological accounts of social stability or change.

This brings us to the connections between functional and action analysis.

3 FUNCTIONAL ANALYSIS AND ACTION ANALYSIS

As I have already pointed out more than once, non-teleological functionalism is methodologically legitimate in the sense that there is nothing intrinsically wrong with the whole → participant kinds of questions, or with questions about the conditions of existence of social wholes. However, for a more comprehensive and more cognitively adequate analysis of social phenomena, functional analysis must be combined with an analysis focusing on the participant → whole relationship. Schematically this more comprehensive approach can be represented as:

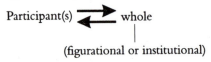

Participant(s) ⇄ whole

(figurational or institutional)

There is, of course, nothing new or original in the above position. It is so obvious that, apart from methodological fanatics, few social scientists would object to it nowadays; or, at least, those who object usually reject the terminology but accept the substantive logic of the position. It is generally accepted today that the total neglect of either the participant → whole or the whole → participant relationship leads to extremely lopsided views of the social world. It either (as in the various interpretative micro sociologies) presents the social world as an aggregate of interactions occurring in an institutional or figurational vacuum; or, at the other extreme, social actors and their interactions are portrayed as the passive product of structural determinations or of 'society' conceptualized as a reified entity.

Arguing that we need both the social whole → participant, and the participant → social whole relationship does not, however, spell out the conceptual tools or rules that can make this *rapprochement* theoretically possible.

As in the case of the relationship between the institutional and figurational structures (see Chapters 4 and 5), here too the problem for sociological theory can be solved neither by some foundationalist search for epistemological or ontological first principles nor by a psychoanalytic attempt at constructing yet another theory of the subject. It needs a more mundane and straightforward approach: it requires devising sociological concepts that refrain from the radical disjunction of social structures (or social wholes) and social participants, or the reduction of the one to the other, or the conflation ('transcendence') of structures and participants/agents. In brief, the problem is to avoid, via the creation of adequate conceptual tools, both reification and reductionism.

If the AGIL → t, a', i' schema provided constructive bridges between institutional and figurational wholes, I think that the concepts I have worked out (on the basis of my discussion of Bourdieu's *habitus* and Giddens' duality of structure) can help when dealing with participant → whole relationships. These concepts refer to:

(i) the three-dimensional nature of all social games or interactions (positional, dispositional, interactive-situational);
(ii) the duality/dualism distinction on both the paradigmatic and the syntagmatic level; and
(ii) the notion of hierarchies as this was tentatively deployed in both Parts I and II of this work.

I do believe that the above conceptualizations, once their linkages are clearly spelled out, can help us see how participants relate to a variety of hierarchical structures or hierarchized wholes (both institutional and figurational). It is these hierarchized structures or social wholes that constitute the chief means for understanding how players, whose actions and interactions stretch only little or moderately in time and space (i.e. micro and meso actors) link up with macro actors, with the individual or collective players whose actions stretch more widely in time and space.

3.1 The positional, dispositional and interactive dimensions of games

Human beings are capable, via symbolic language, of detaching themselves from the here and now; they are capable, in Mead's terminology, of imaginary rehearsal and role-taking; as a result they operate or orient themselves constantly on two interrelated but analytically distinct levels. These are the virtual, paradigmatic level of institutionalized rules or norms (these being the constituent elements of roles or social positions) and the actual level of concrete actions and interactions. To put it differently, people constantly orient and reorient themselves to both the 'rules of the game' (as a virtual set of norms instantiated only when games are being played), and to actual games of interacting players as these unfold syntagmatically in time and space.[14] In so far as the rules of the game constitute what sociologists call role or social position, it is useful to refer to the virtual or paradigmatic dimension of games as the positional dimension, and to contrast it with the interactive-situational one. The first pertains to norms or rules as a set of potentialities or possibilities of rule-governed conduct; the second refers to the instantiation and realization of such rules in actual, situationally specific actions and interactions.[15] Finally, as Bourdieu points out, human beings are able to play games because they carry within them a set of dispositions, a set of generative schemata of action, perception and evaluation.

Contra Bourdieu I have argued in the preceding chapter that a full understanding of actual games cannot be obtained by referring exclusively to social positions and dispositions; it is equally necessary to take into account the relative autonomy and the situational logic of the interactive dimension. This being so, the *habitus*, the set of dispositions that actors acquire through various forms of socialization, helps them to bring together the positional and the interactive-situational dimension. It is, partly at least, because of our dispositions that we are able to learn the rules of a game *in abstracto* (i.e. paradigmatically), as well as to apply them when we wish in actual situations on the syntagmatic level.

Bourdieu underemphasizes the voluntaristic, interactive-situational dimension of games, and so rejects the distinction between learning the rules and actually applying them while playing concrete games. He considers rules as often unconscious, so that our only knowledge of them is practical, and such knowledge cannot be separated, analytically or otherwise, from the actual playing of a game. From the point of view of the present analysis, the distinction between *langue* and *parole*, between the paradigmatic and the syntagmatic, between the virtual and the actual, is fundamental. Although the two levels are closely interrelated, they must never be conflated. Given that the two dimensions can have different logics, they may vary in diametrically opposed fashion.

For example, the dispositions of certain players may enable them to deal more effectively with the paradigmatic than the syntagmatic. They may be great experts in the detailed theoretical knowledge of game rules, but totally inept when it comes to applying them to actual situations. To use Chomsky's distinction, they may score high on competence and low on performance.[16] Think of a highly inefficient manager with Ph.D. degrees in Business Administration, and efficient ones who never even went to high school; or take players whose dispositions encourage them to adopt a contemplative or 'theoretical' rather than performative, action-oriented attitude to games (in the sphere of politics, sports, sex, etc.) and vice versa. I think that it is perfectly justified to distinguish between contemplative and active/performative dispositions, and an actor or categories of actors may well be stronger in one than in the other.

It will be clear from the above that the *habitus*, as already argued, is a concept compatible (rather than incompatible) with the notion of the interactive-situational dimension of social games. To say it again: the three dimensions (positional, dispositional and interactive-situational) are mutually complementary, but each has its own relatively autonomous logic and dynamic.

3.2 Duality and dualism

The distinction between competence (contemplative) and performance dispositions leads to my second major conceptualization, derived from restructuring Giddens' structuration theory: the distinction between subject/object duality and subject/object dualism. The competence/contemplative disposition indicates a subject–object dualism *vis-à-vis* rules on the paradigmatic level; the performance disposition often implies a taken-for-granted attitude to rules, which is to say a paradigmatic subject–object duality.[17]

I shall start with paradigmatic duality/dualism. If this distinction is seen not in terms of either/or, but rather indicating 'more or less', if it is seen as the two poles of a continuum, it can then be used in order to spell out the various ways in which participants orient themselves to institutional structures – that is, to a virtual order of rules seen from a systemic point of view.

The first point to make here is that the relationship between participant and institutional structure does not, as I have repeatedly pointed out in Part I, correspond to a micro–macro relation, where 'participant' entails micro and 'institutional structure' macro. Both participants and institutions can be micro as well as macro. 'Participant' can refer to a rank-and-file member of a company (micro), to a branch manager (meso) or to the company president whose decisions directly affect thousands or even millions of people (macro). In similar fashion the term institutional structures can refer to institutionalized rules limited to a single company, to a group of companies or to all companies within a national economy. As already mentioned, the failure of micro sociology to break away from the errone-ous notion which decrees that individual actors or face-to-face interaction implies micro, and institutional structures macro, has (more than any other distinction in sociology) prevented the establishment of effective linkages between micro and macro analysis.[18] Given this, it becomes obvious that a proper study of the linkages between a micro and a macro approach should *not* take the form

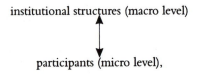

but the more complex configuration

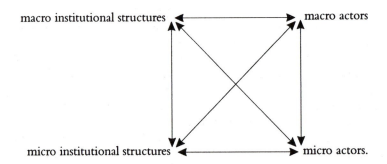

Having established the above, we can now proceed to explore the conditions in which participants (micro, meso, macro) orient themselves to a virtual order of rules more in terms of duality, and in which conditions orient themselves more in terms of dualism.

First of all, when rules are completely hidden (like those of Freud's unconscious), it is obvious that participants can in no way distance themselves from them, given that they have no idea of their nature, or perhaps even of their existence (unless, of course, they are psychoanalysed or are familiar with psychoanalytic techniques). This, therefore, is a clear-cut case of paradigmatic duality: rules (or structures, in Giddens' terminology) are 100 per cent the medium and outcome of action.

To a lesser extent this is also true when participants have only a practical (rather than a theoretical) knowledge of rules (as in Bourdieu's *habitus*).[19] Although in this case they are aware of the existence of rules, the lack of theoretical knowledge would encourage participants to use them in a taken-for-granted manner – i.e. in terms of subject–object duality.

When, however, participants are both aware of rules and have a clear theoretical knowledge of them, then these rules may easily become a topic rather than a resource/means of interactive communication. In that case we move from paradigmatic duality to paradigmatic dualism.

Speaking more generally, when rules (for whatever reason) become problematic for the participants, then the chances of being looked at and challenged (paradigmatic dualism) become stronger. To take an example already mentioned, when there are, as Parsons argues, 'strains' or incompatibilities between roles or institutionalized norms located within or between different subsystems (e.g. universalistic norms prevailing within the economy, and particularistic roles within the polity)[20] – then the chances are greater for individual or collective actors to ask questions about these rules, to challenge or defend their validity, to attempt to transform or maintain them, and so on. A similar shift from taken-for-granted to theoretical/strategic orientations to rules may happen when there is no or very little concordance between the positional, dispositional and situational-interactive dimensions of social games.

To use the example again given in the previous chapter: in the pastoral Sarakatsani community that John Campbell has described so admirably, the almost total fit between social positions, dispositions and situations meant that actors were orienting themselves to the community's highly institutionalized rules in a taken-for-granted manner (i.e. in terms of paradigmatic duality). In contrast, Jane Cowan's anthropological study of a Greek small-town community in Macedonia stresses the variety of 'voices', the multiplicity of interpretations of gender roles and the systematic incongruence between traditional female roles, young women's dispositions and emerging situational contexts.[21] These circumstances quite understandably make the norms problematical, and imply a strategic/monitoring rather than taken-for-granted attitude towards them (paradigmatic dualism).

Another interesting case where game rules are rendered problematical is when institutional and figurational structures do not completely overlap. When, for instance, conflicting figurations cut across institutional cleavages (between capitalists and workers, say, or blacks and whites, men and women) and lead to coalitions where capitalists and workers, blacks and whites, feminists and anti-feminists all join forces against another figurational whole that contains similar social forces, then the disjunction between the 'institutional' and the 'figurational' means that participants cannot unambiguously follow the normative expectations that their roles entail – or, at least, they cannot take them for granted. It means, in other words, that the interactive and dispositional dimensions of the game have become more important than the role/positional ones.

Last, as already mentioned in the previous chapter, if we take into account the perspectival character of the duality/dualism problem and the fact that participants often operate within hierarchized wholes we can establish some systematic linkages between paradigmatic duality/dualism and the hierarchical dimensions of formal organizations. Work rules, for example, which are, or are supposed to be, taken for granted by rank-and-file members of an industrial organization (a case of paradigmatic duality), are not supposed to be taken for granted by participants higher up in the formal hierarchy (e.g. foremen, managers). In their case, operating rules become topics of analysis. In a more general way, decisions about rules taken at a certain hierarchical level (paradigmatic dualism) tend to become taken-for-granted decision premises at lower hierarchical levels (paradigmatic duality). These decision premises then become the basis on which lower-placed organizational participants take decisions of a more limited or circumscribed nature.[22] The same rules can therefore be means/resources at one hierarchical level (paradigmatic duality), and topics at another, higher level (paradigmatic dualism).

The above points about hierarchies bring us to the notion of syntagmatic duality-dualism. At this level as well, the duality-dualism notion has a marked perspectival character: as already mentioned, what is a transformable, malleable figuration for a highly-placed participant (syntagmatic duality) is 'external', intractable, immutable for participants lower down in the bureaucratic hierarchy (syntagmatic dualism). Therefore, the perennial problem of whether figurational wholes are internal or external to the individual is a non-problem. Once the highly misleading and confusing individual–society schema is radically rejected, as well as attempts to solve the problem at the level of ontology or psychoanalysis; once the problem is being tackled in terms of *sociological* theory proper, it simply disappears. In so far as 'external' signifies relatively non-transformable, it is quite obvious that from the point of view of any specific hierarchically-situated participant certain games are clearly external, in the sense that his/her contribution to their constitution, reproduction and transformation is minimal or non-existent, whereas other games are less so. Moreover, what is an external and non-malleable game from the perspective of a micro or meso actor, may be less external and more malleable from the point of view of a macro actor.

In consequence of the above, it seems to me that a shift of emphasis from philosophy to sociological theory, and a determination to dismantle misleading conceptualizations, can enable us to see that the famous internality/externality problem is non-existent. It has been unnecessarily and artificially created by theorists who, instead of trying to improve our considerable knowledge of the social world, seem determined to replace common sense with vacuous philosophizing or craftily disguised nonsense.

3.3 Social hierarchies

It should now be clear that the notions of paradigmatic and syntagmatic duality/dualism can help us conceptualize the orientations and interactions of participants within a dimension of social life that is rather under-theorized: the hierarchical one.

To repeat myself: in the context of bureaucratically organized hierar-chies, for participants occupying hierarchically low authority positions, games played at the top are relatively external, i.e. non-malleable (syntag-matic dualism); whereas games played at their own or lower levels of authority are less external, more malleable (syntagmatic duality). The situation is reversed on the paradigmatic level in respect of participants' orientations to a virtual order of bureaucratic rules. Here, rules, which are taken for granted and are seen as means/resources by hierarchically low-placed participants, tend to become topics for analysis and strategic manipulation for more highly placed participants. This is to say that, other things being equal, rank-and-file positions entail paradigmatic duality *vis-à-vis* rules imposed by management,[23] and syntagmatic dualism *vis-à-vis* games played at the top of the bureaucratic hierarchy.

Hierarchies do not, of course, take the form only of bureaucratically constituted organizational authority structures, but vary considerably ac-cording to the type of linkages they establish between lower and more highly placed participants. In order to deal more systematically with such linkages I shall use Bourdieu's notion of different types of capital, and modify it in such a way as to make it congruent with Parsons' AGIL typology.

One can argue that in all hierarchically organized games the participants, at whatever level they may find themselves, are struggling to increase their capital – capital here meaning power, the overall capacity to mobilize not only economic and political resources but also social and cultural ones. One can, therefore – following Bourdieu's fruitful distinction between different types of capital (economic, social, cultural, symbolic) and Parsons' AGIL scheme – talk about economic capital (A), political capital (G), cultural capital (L) and social capital in the form of social prestige (I).[24]

If players succeed in considerably increasing one of their four types of capital, they may then not only become able to contribute more decisively to the game they are playing, but they may also move up and become participants in hierarchically superior games entailing much higher stakes. If winners move up, losers will have to move down and become participants in hierarchically lower-grade games that entail rather more petty rewards or profits.

Another important point to be taken into account is that whenever games are hierarchized, players higher up influence games and players at the lower levels by creating both limits and opportunities. This is why in a bureaucratically organized state apparatus (Parsons' G-subsystem) decisions taken by high bureaucrats (decisions resulting from the complex games they play among themselves) both restrict the room for manoeuvre of those below, and at the same time provide them with some of the means for playing games and taking decisions of a more circumscribed nature.

Something similar happens in hierarchies based on market linkages between 'high' and 'low' participants. In market hierarchies (A-subsystem) the limits and opportunities that high participants create for low participants do not have the formal, legalistic character of bureaucratically organized hierarchies, but they may be equally if not more effective in decisively shaping lower-level games. To take an everyday example: small local merchants in a village community are influenced (both in terms of limits and enablements) by the activities or games played by economically more powerful merchants at regional or national level. So setting the price of a commodity at one level (whether via oligopolistic, monopolistic or competitive games) more or less automatically, without the imposition of legal-bureaucratic rules, creates specific limits and opportunities for profits lower down in the hierarchy of trading games.[25]

The situation will, of course, change qualitatively in the case of hierarchies entailing neither bureaucratic nor market linkages between superordinate and subordinate levels. If one considers hierarchical games that rank players in terms of social prestige in the community (I-subsystem), here, via mechanisms of influence and imitation, participants enjoying high social prestige exert an influence (in terms of limits and opportunities) on social games played below. Here, therefore, the linkages between hierarchical levels are more diffuse and fragmented. If ranking rules are not contested, low-level players attempting to augment their social capital take into account or are influenced by games of social prestige played higher up. These latter games may take the form of (a) conspicuous consumption, of following as strictly as possible the social etiquette entailed in ascriptively inherited status positions; or (b) they may by contrast take the form of competition for the acquisition of civic merit as a result of offering or performing a variety of public-spirited, more or less altruistic activities. Whether or not the social games have (in Parsonian terminology) an ego or community orientation, both (a) and (b) have to do with the accumulation of social capital or prestige derived from ascriptive or achieved social positions.

The important thing to stress here is that, as with games over economic capital, games focusing on the acquisition of social capital tend to be hierarchized in the sense that superordinate players set limits and create opportunities for subordinate ones. In the present case the limits/opportunities are not prescribed by bureaucratic or market mechanisms, but by the constitution of reference groups that set standards, models and lifestyles to be emulated.

Whether one considers macro activities or games played by 'high-society' individuals, by the very rich, or by those who have achieved fame and glory by offering public services – in all these cases subordinate but aspiring players, in their attempts to increase their own social capital (in one or several of the above dimensions), will be watching carefully what is happening higher up.

It may be useful to distinguish between struggles over social (I) and over cultural capital (L). Roughly speaking, in the first case the power acquired is based on one's position or conduct (altruistic or not) as member of a social community. In the second case the power is related to the possession of socially legitimate knowledge, or a capacity for mobilizing, manipulating or creating symbols that contribute to the reproduction or transformation of the cultural heritage of a society or a social whole. Although the two notions overlap considerably, on a practical level it is quite easy to distinguish the 'social' from the 'cultural'. For instance, in the U.K. an upper-class or aristocratic family background, or a good reputation in the community achieved through commendable conduct (honesty, bravery, generosity, etc.), enhances one's social capital. Cultural capital is gained via the acquisition of socially valued knowledge, artistic taste, literary skills and suchlike. In that sense, experts of all kinds (for example in the natural sciences, the humanities, arts or religion) struggle mainly over the acquisition of cultural rather than social capital.

The social and the cultural may go together, but they may also be diametrically opposed. One need only think of the heroic or 'saintly' person (high in social capital) who is totally deficient in cultural matters or, on the other hand, the Jean Genet type of literary genius whose considerable cultural capital is accompanied by a very low or negative social capital.

In the same way that struggles or games over the acquisition of social capital tend to be hierarchized, so do games for cultural capital. We can speak about cultural hierarchies, which operate more or less like social hierarchies: the cultural games played at high levels set standards and therefore provide limits and opportunities for cultural games further down. They create limits in the sense that they orient the energies and attention of subordinate players towards one problem and one form of analysis rather than another; and they create opportunities in the sense that they provide conceptual means for constructing a space for debate – a space where more limited cultural capital can be increased, decreased or lost altogether.

To give an example related to this book: cultural games played at the top of the social sciences' cultural hierarchies (between such internationally known social theorists as Habermas and Lyotard, say, over the nature of modernity) have an important impact on academic and cultural circles whose respective 'influence stretch' varies in time and space.

In conclusion, following Bourdieu's notion of different types of capital and Parsons' AGIL scheme, it is possible (in complex, differentiated societies) to distinguish between economic (A), legal-bureaucratic (G), social (I) and cultural (L) hierarchies. Each of them is related to struggles over the acquisition of one type of capital. All of these games are hierarchized, in the sense that (via market-, bureaucratic-, social- and cultural-influence mechanisms) those taking place at the top of the pyramid both set limits and create opportunities for more subordinate players.

It must by now be beyond question that hierarchies should not be conceptualized simply as rankings of social positions. Given that social positions or roles constitute only one of the three basic dimensions of games (the other two being the dispositional and the situational-interactive dimensions), a more useful and comprehensive view of hierarchies is in terms of hierarchically organized games or of hierarchically organized spaces within which games are played.

3.4 Relations between hierarchies

Looking at hierarchies from the point of view of any single participant (micro, meso or macro), we see that s/he is involved, to a greater or lesser degree, with all four types of game.[26] S/He is unavoidably involved in struggles over the acquisition or control of economic, political, social and cultural capital, and a serious success in any one of these hierarchized fields may allow the player to move up and start participating in a superordinate game and/or to augment his/her capital in the other three fields. Let us take the classical instance of a village merchant whose successful venture in trade allows him to shift his operations from the local to regional, national and eventually international level. This process means a move from micro to meso to macro games via the acquisition/control of economic capital.[27] Furthermore, his upgrading may allow him to increase his political weight as well as his social and his cultural capital.

An increase of one type of capital does not, of course, bring about an automatic increase in the other three. To take again the merchant example, if his gains in economic capital are based on quasi-illegal dealings, the increase in wealth will be obtained at the expense of his social capital; or rather, the increase in social prestige that wealth brings about will be counteracted by the social stigma of fraudulent, unscrupulous conduct. An opposite example is the children of wealthy but uncultured parents, whose attempts at establishing their independence from parental control or domination may increase their cultural capital to the extent that, through neglecting financial matters, their economic capital suffers dramatic diminution.

Looking at the linkages between economic, political, social and cultural capital from a long-term developmental or evolutionary perspective, one can argue that, given the state's weak societal penetration in pre-industrial formations, hierarchies tended to be decentralized, diffuse and segmental. This means that at each level the economic, political, social and cultural hierarchies greatly overlapped. Players tended to be consistently high- or low-ranking in all four dimensions. So for instance the position of the *ancien régime* court aristocracy in France more or less automatically entailed the possession of wealth (a necessity for maintaining the required lifestyle at court), of political power, social prestige and 'culture'. At the other end of the social scale, those directly involved in agricultural production tended to be very underendowed with all four types of capital. The emergence and dominance of the nation-state in the nineteenth century, and the decline of economic, political, social and cultural localism, brought both greater centralization and greater differentiation of all four types of hierarchy, this differentiation implying a lesser overlap between the four types of capital. In other words, as far as modernity is concerned, Weber was more accurate than Marx when he argued that one should look at class, status and party as three systems of stratification that can vary independently of each other.

The post-industrial era has brought the fragmentation of hierarchies through global capitalism, and created a situation where micro, meso and macro games are hierarchized not by strict reference to the nation-state, but also by reference to a multiplicity of interregional and transnational networks. In terms of fusion or overlapping, this postmodern situation leads to further disruption between economic, political, social and cultural capital. For example, a local branch manager of a transnational firm may possess considerable economic capital but, given his transnational horizontal mobility, his social and political capital may be insignificant by comparison with that of an indigenous entrepreneur.

3.5 Hierarchies as technologies

Having clarified the concept of hierarchy, it is now time to close the circle by establishing some theoretical linkages between technologies and hierarchies.

Let me start with macro games. Macro players, by struggling to maintain or increase their various types of capital, contribute decisively to the construction of the macro space where hierarchized games of a certain type are played. This occurs as a result of their macro interactions, strategies and decisions providing the general parameters for subordinate games. In other words, macro players, whether deliberately or not, operate as catalysts for those below them. They mobilize subordinate players by both setting limits and by delineating and providing opportunities for increases in capital at the meso and micro levels.

The vertical chain of games below macro players can, therefore, be seen as the means or technology (economic, political, social, cultural) for symbolic and material construction: the meso and micro games together with the material or symbolic resources they generate being, from a macro perspective (as well as from the point of view of outside observers) the means through which social realities or orders are constructed.

Let me illustrate this further by reverting to the earlier merchant example. In the economic sphere (A), oligopolistic or more open forms of competition between wholesale merchants (macro actors) of a commodity sets the general parameters (in the form of setting the basic price framework) for merchants at the meso and micro levels. In so far as a macro actor, or a group of them, manages to control the price game at the national level via market mechanisms, this exerts an influence on the vertical chains of the game at the regional and local levels. In other words, the dominant players at the national level have privileged access to the symbolic and material means by which the overall economic market space is constructed. 'Access' here means the capacity for a decisive shaping of the terrain where meso and micro trading-games and strategies are to be deployed. The similarities between vertical chains of games, and technologies in the Marxian sense,[28] become clear when one considers that such chains portray

(i) *instrumentality*: as already mentioned, they constitute the intended or unintended means through which are produced capital/profits for the players, and 'services' or 'goods' for the consumers;

(ii) *differential access*: dominant macro actors have privileged access to such chains, and contribute much more to their reproduction or transformation than do micro players.

It is not difficult to give similar examples for the non-economic spheres; for national political leaders (G) whose agreements or disagreements influence regional and local politics; for society celebrities or civic leaders (I) who respectively set the dominant social fashions or the moral standards for the national community; for famous artists or cultural gurus (L) who shape a nation's artistic or intellectual patterns. All these macro actors, in their attempts to maintain and augment their capital, contribute decisively, via the mobilization of vertical chains of games, to the construction, reproduction and transformation of political, social and cultural macro spaces.

Macro actors are not, of course, the sole producers of the social world. But their contribution, as already argued, is much more decisive than that of micro actors.[29] To put this differently: inasmuch as all actors are both products and producers of the social world, macro actors (economic, political, social, cultural) are much more producers than products.

147

CONCLUSION

In the preceding pages I have argued that the emergence, with Parsons, of sociological theory as a specialized subdiscipline of sociology is not as disastrous as early critics of Parsonian functionalism would have had us believe. In so far as sociological theory as a subdiscipline aims at constructing not substantive, universal/foundationalist generalizations but conceptual tools for facilitating empirical research, this type of specialized and often highly abstract endeavour has a legitimate place within the growing division of labour among social science disciplines and subdisciplines. Moreover, it can also play a leading role in combating the tight compartmentalization that characterizes the unavoidable proliferation of theoretical paradigms and empirical specializations in sociology today.

If this is accepted, and even if one disagrees with Parsonian theory, the type of division of labour that was initiated primarily by Parsons is here to stay. This means that the real problem today is not to turn our backs on sociological theory as a subdiscipline specializing in the construction of conceptual tools (Generalities II), but to make sure that the conceptual tools offered become increasingly more useful, and that the type of linkages Parsons and his disciples have established between theory and empirical research (between Gen. II and Gen. III) will be both strengthened and improved.

More specifically I have argued that Parsonian theory, in its endeavour to provide an overall conceptual framework for the study of cultural, social and personality systems, has overemphasized 'systemness' at the expense of agency, on the micro as well as the macro level of analysis. This fundamental flaw was partly overcome on the micro level by the spectacular development of the various interpretative sociologies. These, however, by tending to identify action/interaction with micro, and institutional structures with macro, were unable to link micro and macro approaches effectively, and to deal satisfactorily with the Parsonian underemphasis of

148

macro actors. This lopsidedness – which led to a systematic neglect of social hierarchies and to an ever-widening rift between micro and macro sociology – was not corrected by relevant theoretical developments outside interpretative micro sociology, such as rational-choice analysis. Neither was it corrected by writers who, although in some of their works follow the specialized construction of conceptual tools that Parsons has institutionalized, are determined at all costs to transcend functionalism in general, and Parsonian functionalism in particular. By focusing on aspects of the work of Elias, Giddens and Bourdieu, I have shown that their attempts at 'transcendence' have failed, and that the functionalist logic, if not its vocabulary, clandestinely creeps back into their analyses.

The persistent failure to link micro with macro, and action with institutional structure, in post-Parsonian sociological theory has made it lose momentum. The main energies of theoretically minded sociologists are now turned towards epistemological issues and/or to debates in disciplines such as linguistics, semiotics or psychoanalysis. This shift in focus, from sociological-theoretical to philosophical, linguistic and psychoanalytical issues has weakened the ties between theory and empirical research. The underdevelopment or stagnation of sociological theory proper means that it has not been possible to effectively translate insights drawn from philosophy or from theoretical developments in neighbouring disciplines, into conceptual tools that would facilitate rather than hinder empirical research on the constitution, reproduction and transformation of social systems, particularly societal ones.

This, finally, has resulted in a situation where the inherent paradigmatic pluralism of sociology has degenerated into anarchy and cacophony, a total lack of communication between warring theoretical schools; it has also led to a postmodernist abolition of such fundamental distinctions as micro–macro, agency–system, representing–represented, etc. In combination with the abolition of boundaries between disciplines and subdisciplines, this has led to a free-for-all where anything goes, and where the analysis of societies by means of various reductive explanations (in terms of 'texts', the unconscious, chains of signifiers, desire, etc.) has regressed to pre-Durkheimian standards. We are faced, in other words, with a situation of theoretical dedifferentiation or theoretical primitivism which, instead of building on what has already been achieved by the classical sociologists and their followers, takes us back to extremely crude, facile and even grotesque forms of sociological analysis.

Believing that it is not enough to criticize, and that it is important to progress from diagnosis to tentative remedies, I have tried in Part II of the book to show as concretely as I could how sociological theory – as a practice portraying a logic distinct from that of philosophy and other neighbouring disciplines – can help sociologists clear and prepare the ground for the empirical investigation of how social wholes are constituted, reproduced and transformed. I have tried to show that this can be done by sociological theory solving puzzles, eliminating persistent confusion and replacing less by more useful conceptual tools.

More particularly, in Chapter 4, via a critical analysis of Elias's figurational sociology, I submitted that it is absolutely vital to maintain the agency/institutional-structure distinction, and that any attempt to conflate institutional and figurational structures, or to reduce the former to the latter (as Elias does), leads to one-sided, distorted accounts of the social world. I pointed out that Elias's underemphasis of institutional structures (as wholes having a logic of their own, and therefore varying independently from figurational structures) led him to establish quasi-universal generalizations between growing social interdependence and self-discipline. Such generalizations, in so far as they neglect institutional/cultural contexts, tend to be either wrong or trivial.

In Chapter 5 I tried to further consolidate the institutional/figurational-structure distinction by suggesting specific ways of moving from disconnection or reduction to an effective articulation of the two notions. To this end I presented a critique of the Parsonian AGIL scheme, and argued that Parsons' further subdivision of each of his four subsystems along the same 'institutional/systemic' logic disconnects, that is to say, creates obstacles to an effective articulation of institutional and figurational wholes, and indirectly leads to the reification of societal subsystems. I also pointed out that recent neo-functionalist attempts to inject a figurational, 'group-struggle' component into Parsons' theory are more decorative than substantive – in the sense that the introjected elements do not fit well with existing ones, such as the AGIL scheme.

I then suggested that, instead of applying such *ad hoc* embellishments to the Parsonian edifice, a theoretically congruent way of providing linkages between institutional and figurational wholes (i.e. wholes of institutionalized roles, and wholes of interrelated actors) would be to take seriously into account that within each institutional order (A, G, I, L) it might be useful to view institutionalized norms/roles not in terms of the agil logic (i.e. not in terms of the further subdivision of each of the four subsystems into four sub-subsystems), but in terms of the technological, appropriative and ideological dimensions of institutional wholes.

Such dimensions, which are at the centre of all Marxist thought, should be radically disconnected from all forms of economic reductionism and from the highly misleading base–superstructure dichotomy. We should view technologies, their mode of appropriation/control, and the way in which such controls are legitimized, not in base–superstructure terms, but as inherent elements of all institutional spheres (economic, political, legal, educational/familial/religious). This will provide us with appropriate tools for showing in non *ad hoc* manner how institutional incompatibilities lead, or fail to lead, to group conflicts on the economic (A), political (G), legal (I) and cultural (L) level. It will also allow 'who' questions about the constitution, reproduction and transformation of societal wholes. The key idea that men and women use various material and non-material technologies in the construction of their everyday existence, and that these technologies (economic, political, legal, cultural) are differentially appropriated/controlled, leads 'naturally' to the notion of hierarchically organized or situated actors; to the fact that different agents (individual or collective, micro, meso or macro) have different degrees of control over these technologies, and to the fact that differential control of technologies may lead to social conflict.

In Chapter 6 my focus shifted from linkages between institutional and figurational structures to a concern with 'participants–social-whole' relationships. Here, by a critical reconceptualization of Giddens' structuration theory, I tried to demonstrate the utility of the notions of both subject–object duality and dualism for understanding how participants relate to institutional wholes on the paradigmatic level, as well as to figurational wholes on the syntagmatic level. I then showed how the notions of paradigmatic and syntagmatic duality/dualism can be systematically linked to social hierarchies, i.e. to the complex ways in which social positions/roles are hierarchically arranged on the paradigmatic level, and how specific actors are hierarchically related in time/space on the syntagmatic level.

With the help of the above conceptualizations I have submitted that the micro–macro and externality–internality issue can be adequately tackled once the interaction=micro and institution=macro connection is rejected, and once the perspectival character of both role linkages and actors' relationships is emphasized.

Chapter 6 also dealt with Bourdieu's notion of *habitus*, with the help of which I developed the idea of the role/positional, dispositional, and interactive/situational dimensions of social games – maintaining that these three dimensions are not reducible to each other.

As I believe that conceptual tools (Gen. II) can be assessed properly only if it is shown how they can be useful in empirical research (negatively, by eliminating confusion; positively, by raising interesting, empirically-oriented issues), in Chapter 7 I attempted to show two things: (a) how the conceptual tools I am offering (i.e. figurational/institutional wholes, para-digmatic and syntagmatic duality/dualism, social hierarchies, the positional/dispositional/inter-actional dimensions of games) relate to each other; and (b) how these conceptual tools can eliminate some fundamental misconceptions about functionalist explanations in sociology.

The conceptual tools and distinctions I have elaborated by restructuring other theorists' work do not, of course, constitute final or foundationalist solutions to the micro–macro, agency–structure issues, or to the problems inherent in functionalist analysis. They are tentative suggestions or guide-lines in a field of study which, due to its very nature, is constantly changing. As I kept pointing out repeatedly, I see the major task of sociological theory as not only providing fully worked-out, conceptual edifices (à la Parsons or Giddens), but also as providing tentative, flexible, open-ended, transi-tional frameworks useful for the empirical, comparative investigation of specific sociological problems. In other words, I think that, in addition to the strategic, grand theorizing of Parsons and Giddens, we are urgently in need today of more tactical, modest theorizing such as developed by Merton, Gouldner or Lockwood. By 'modest' I do not mean middle range. I mean more the elaboration of a small number of interrelated concepts which, rather than offering a global map, are useful for reducing 'distorted communication' and asking interesting empirical questions on specific problem areas.

What I would like to stress once more in closing this analysis is that our primary concern as theoretically-oriented sociologists should be neither the hopeless modernist quest for philosophical foundations and/or univer-sal generalizations nor the vacuous postmodernist efforts at theoretical dedifferentiation that lead to such extremely crude, reductive accounts of the social world. If, *contra* modernism, we accept that the only interesting substantive generalizations (Gen. III) in the social sciences are those that take into full account context in terms of time and space; and if, *contra* postmodernism, we respect the autonomous logic of sociological theory, then we should put at the centre of our preoccupations the modest and ever provisional production of a set of interrelated tools that can prepare the ground for the empirical investigation of the social world.

I would like to make two qualifications to the above:

(i) To say it one more time: I am not arguing that sociological theory should ignore philosophy or other relevant disciplines, but that its relationship with them should be such as to maintain and enhance its relative autonomy, its specific logic. This means that it should translate the insights of other disciplines into conceptual tools for broadening and enriching the empirically and comparatively oriented sociological analysis of social arrangements.

(ii) I am not saying that the construction of Gen. II should be the only concern of sociological theory. There is obviously ample room within the subdiscipline for a variety of other theoretical activities, such as the constant reassessment, interpretation and analysis of classical texts, the history of social thought, social and moral philosophy, philosophical anthropology, etc.

For all that, the construction of Generalities II should be at the centre of our preoccupations. I believe this should be so for the simple reason that, given the inherently multiparadigmatic character of sociology, the main task of sociological theory is to maintain and enhance its pluralism by trying to transform 'compartmentalized' into 'open' differentiation, and by opposing both the senseless and destructive quarrels generated by paradigmatic dogmatism/exclusionism and the postmodern attempt at theoretical levelling, at destroying the various logics of sociological analysis by means of the crude strategy of theoretical dedifferentiation.

In other words, and speaking metaphorically, what we need today is the establishment of a highly decentralized, 'democratic' or 'dialogic' federation that will respect the internal logic and dynamic of each theoretical orientation or tradition, while at the same time removing all obstacles to the free communication of ideas and insights between them. Sociological theory can and must play this key strategic role. In order to do this effectively, its postmodern wing should stop subjecting itself to the tyranny of intellectual fashions, to the obsessive need to 'transcend' at all costs whatever exists already, to its predilection for ignoring the old and to automatically opt for the new, irrespective of its truth value. Its more 'modernist' wing, on the other hand, should discard its fundamentalist luggage and shift its attention from universalist schemes and philosophical groundings to flexible, tentative conceptualizations, sensitive to the problems and dilemmas of empirical research, and ever willing to modify the conceptual tools on offer in the light of new theoretical insights or new empirical findings.

APPENDIX TO THE CONCLUSION: TENTATIVE GUIDELINES

In this Appendix to the concluding chapter I would like to put forward eight major points, which can be seen both as a summary of the arguments developed in the book, and as guidelines or rules useful for theoretically-oriented sociological analysis.

I Foundationalism, essentialism, holism

I.1 Sociology should resolutely abandon foundationalist projects, but it should never abandon the effort to explain social phenomena in a holistic manner.

I.2 Sociology should also abandon projects based on essentialist assumptions, but this should not lead it to reduce society to language or to non-hierarchized chains of texts/discourses/signifiers.

II Generalities II and III

II.1 It is important, when assessing a theory, to examine whether it is predominantly a conceptual framework (Gen. II) or a set of substantive propositions (Gen. III). The criteria of assessment are different in each case.

II.2 Greater attention should be paid to what theorists actually do with their conceptual tools (i.e. how they use them) rather than to what they say they will do. This means that more attention should be paid to theorists' first- rather than second-order theoretical discourses – to the actual application of Gen. II in empirical research, rather than to rhetorical pronouncements and methodological blueprints.

II.3 Gen. III, which are universal (in the sense of neglecting historical and cultural contexts altogether), tend to be either trivial or wrong. This does not apply to Gen. II, given that their main purpose is to prepare the ground for analysis leading to context-sensitive Gen. III (negatively, by dispelling confusion and communication blockages, and positively, by raising interesting questions and providing tools for the comparative analysis of social wholes).

II.4 Sociological theory as a subdiscipline of sociology, primarily concerned with the construction of conceptual tools (as developed by Parsons and others), is here to stay. Despite the obvious weaknesses of Parsonian theory, the specialized preoccupation with the construction of tools that may facilitate the empirical investigation of the social world is absolutely essential if sociology is to avoid empiricism and/or the compartmentalization of conflicting paradigms.

II.5 Sociological theory is not and should not become an underling or adjunct of philosophy, linguistics or psychoanalysis. Neither should it turn its back on the above disciplines. Instead, it should relate with them from a position of relative autonomy: a position that stresses the distinctive logic of sociological theory and which, on that basis, strives (a) to increase interparadigmatic communication, and (b) to translate and integrate the insights of other disciplines into the sociological corpus.

III Institutional and figurational wholes

III.1 It is essential to view social wholes from both a figurational and an institutional point of view: in terms of conflictual or co-operative relations between actors/groups on the syntagmatic level, as well as in terms of incompatible or compatible relations between sets of institutionalized rules on the paradigmatic level.

III.2 The neglect of figurational structures or wholes leads to reification, and the neglect of institutional structures or wholes leads to various forms of reductionism.

III.3 Institutional wholes should be conceptualized in such a way that their linkages with figurational wholes can be established in a theoretically congruent manner.

III.4 An effective way of doing this is to focus on the technological, appropriative, and ideological dimension of all institutional orders (economic, political, educational, religious, etc.). When sets of institutionalized rules are viewed from such a perspective, the articulation of institutions with figurations, the linkages between institutional incompatibilities and social conflict, can be effected in a non *ad hoc* manner.

IV Micro–macro

IV.1 In so far as micro is not linked to agency nor macro to structure, the micro–macro distinction is a very useful one. Whether we are dealing with actors/interactions or institutional structures, macro refers to cases where the impact of institutionalized rules (when instantiated) or actors' practices stretch widely in time and space; micro applies where this impact is very limited.

IV.2 The micro–macro distinction has the character of 'more or less' rather than of 'either/or'.

IV.3 The micro–macro distinction, when not hypostasized, sensitizes the student to different levels of analysis as one moves from less to more encompassing social systems or social games. When the distinction is ignored, the door is open to all forms of crude, facile, reductionist explanations as one is tempted to jump from an analysis of less encompassing to an analysis of more encompassing social systems or games without taking into account the emerging complexities.

IV.4 If the above points are taken seriously into account then there *are* micro and macro sociologies. The point is not to ignore their obvious differences (as post-structuralists and other social theorists do), but to construct concepts that break down the barriers and strengthen the bridges between them.

IV.5 Whether the focus is primarily on micro or macro levels of analysis, social wholes can be viewed from both an 'internalist' and an 'externalist' perspective, both from an agency (social-integration) and an institutional (system-integration) point of view.

IV.6 Not only is Lockwood's distinction between social and system integration relevant at both micro and macro levels, but the two perspectives must also be dealt with in a balanced fashion. To paraphrase Durkheim's dictum, macro 'facts' must be explained by other macro facts before one moves 'downwards' to meso and micro levels of analysis.

V Duality/dualism

V.1 The subject–object distinction is another one that it is impossible to eliminate without paying too high a price. Subject–object dualism refers to situations (from the point of view of the participant or observer) where there is distance between subject and object, and duality to situations where such a distance tends to diminish or disappear.

V.2 On the syntagmatic level, subject–object dualism refers to situations where a subject's participation in a game does not seriously affect its outcome, whereas duality refers to situations where the opposite is true.

V.3 On the paradigmatic level, actors can, for strategic/monitoring reasons, distance themselves from rules (paradigmatic dualism); or they can use rules in a taken-for-granted manner (paradigmatic duality).

V.4 As with the micro–macro distinction, the divide between objectivist and subjectivist sociologies should neither be ignored (as in post-structuralism), nor transcended in a decorative, rhetorical manner (à la Bourdieu, Giddens or Elias). The point is not to go beyond the divide; it is rather, via the construction of appropriate conceptual tools, to bring subjectivist (internalist) and objectivist (externalist) approaches to social phenomena closer together.

VI Social hierarchies

VI.1 The gap between micro and macro sociologies cannot be bridged unless the hierarchical dimensions of complex societal wholes are seriously taken into account.

VI.2 Both those who link micro with face-to-face interactions and those who reject the micro/macro distinction altogether, tend to neglect social hierarchies. The former do so because they do not take seriously into account that those involved in face-to-face interactions have varying degrees of power; the latter because they do not have the conceptual means to show how less and more encompassing social wholes relate to each other. Whatever the reason, the neglect of social hierarchies leads to a highly distorted, 'flat' view of the social world as well as to reductionist explanations of how social wholes are constituted, reproduced and transformed.

VI.3 Actors at the top of hierarchically organized wholes play games the consequences of which tend to be macro (i.e. they stretch widely in time and space). The opposite is true for games played by those at the bottom of social hierarchies.

VI.4 The duality–dualism conceptualization can help us show in theoretically congruent manner how actors/participants relate to hierarchically-linked games. Actors relate to hierarchically superior games (i.e. games the outcome of which they cannot seriously affect) in terms of syntagmatic dualism; they relate to hierarchically subaltern games in terms of syntagmatic duality.

VI.5 With respect to taking up distance from institutionalized rules, low-rank bureaucrats in bureaucratically organized situations are supposed to adhere to rules and orders in a taken-for-granted manner (paradigmatic duality); whereas high-rank organizational members are supposed to distance themselves from the same rules for strategic/monitoring purposes (paradigmatic dualism).

VI.6 There is a logical link between the notion of social hierarchies and the technological/appropriative/ideological dimensions of institutional spheres. The idea that men and women use a variety of material and non-material technologies in the construction of their everyday existence, and that these technologies (economic, political, social, cultural) are differentially appropriated and controlled, leads 'naturally' to the notion of social hierarchies – to the fact that different participants (individual/collective, micro/macro) have different degrees and types of control over such technologies.

VII The three-dimensional character of games

VII.1 A full understanding of any social game requires focusing on its role/positional, its dispositional and its interactive/situational dimension. Each of these three dimensions has its own logic and dynamic, which can vary independently, and can therefore never be automatically, aprioristically, derived from the other two.

VII.2 It is wrong to view what Goffman calls the 'interaction order' as micro and the 'institutional order' as macro. Both orders can be micro and macro. When face-to-face interactions have consequences which stretch widely in time/space, they are macro. On the other hand, when institutions are embodied into role-positions which entail low levels of power (or games whose outcomes do not stretch widely), then they are micro.

VII.3 The importance of each dimension varies from one type of game to another, of course.

VII.4 One of the reasons why modern societies portray such a fragmented, discontinuous, fragile social organization is the growing discrepancy between the positional, dispositional and interactional dimensions of social games. The greater the discrepancies between the three dimensions, the greater the chances that participants distance themselves from the rules that each of the three dimensions entails.

VIII Functionalism

VIII.1 Functionalism implies both a holistic orientation to social phenomena, as well as the adoption of an externalist/systemic perspective.

VIII.2 A systemic/externalist perspective leads researchers to ask questions about the necessary but not by themselves sufficient conditions of existence of a social whole (functional requirements), as well as about actual or counterfactual conditions that enhance or weaken its internal cohesion. When putting forward such systemic, externalist questions, the emphasis is on the social-whole→participant, rather than on the participant→social-whole relationship.

VIII.3 Functionalist explanations/analyses become illegitimate when necessary conditions of existence or functional/dysfunctional consequences are turned into causes (teleology); or when the social-whole →participant relationship is conceptualized in such a way that it is not possible to ask questions about how participants are not only influenced by, but also themselves influence social wholes (this impossibility leads to the reification of social wholes).

VIII.4 When functionalists avoid both teleology and reification, their analyses are perfectly legitimate but invariably incomplete, since a complete analysis requires both the social-whole→participant and the participant →social-whole perspective .

VIII.5 The only way of eliminating non-teleological functionalism from sociological analysis is to categorically refuse the adoption of an externalist perspective altogether. This is precisely what many interpretatively oriented micro-sociologists do; but the price they have to pay is that they provide us with extremely one-sided and shortsighted views of the social world. One can easily eliminate functionalist terminology. But one cannot eliminate functionalist logic without paying an unacceptably high price.

APPENDIX
Hierarchical aspects of life trajectories

In Chapter 7 I have explained how we can apply the concepts of hierarchy, duality/dualism and the three-dimensional aspects of games to the solution of puzzles generated by the debate on functionalism. In this Appendix I shall show how the same concepts can also be useful in areas more directly related to empirical problem areas. Following Bourdieu's practice and his advice that sociologists should be reflexive of their own social milieu or background, I shall use some of the concepts developed above for an analysis of my father's and my own life trajectory along the four hierarchies, and the struggles over capital they entailed. I shall not, unless absolutely necessary, involve other family members, since it is not the purpose of this exercise to provide a family biography, but simply to show the practical utility of the concepts developed in the preceding chapters.

1 HIERARCHIES AND THE PURSUIT OF CAPITAL

My father, Panayiotis Mouzelis, was born at the turn of the century in the small Greek village of Amphiklia (or Dadi) in the province of Phiotis. His parents were poor peasants. When he and his two older brothers were all in their teens they moved to Lamia (the capital of Phiotis), where they began their careers with small manual jobs in the minor trading firm of a distant relative. Through hard work and some luck they managed, first, to become the principal partners in the firm, and then to expand their entrepreneurial activities both vertically (from trading cotton to the construction of cotton mills) and horizontally (from the export of cotton to that of tobacco).

Having become well off, Panayiotis Mouzelis married the daughter of a local landlord, whose declining economic fortunes made my parents' arranged marriage a quite typical alliance between newly acquired wealth and established social prestige. When his two brothers (who never married) moved their residence and economic headquarters to Athens, my father became the dominant economic player in Lamia. In that capacity his firm's trading, industrial and banking activities[1] set clear limits and created opportunities for a number of other (cotton) merchants operating in Lamia and in the various villages of the province. With respect to the economic games played at the local level, my father's position was one of syntagmatic duality, whereas his position *vis-à-vis* games played at the national and international level was one of syntagmatic dualism (in the sense that these games were 'external', beyond his control). If, for the purposes of exposition, one considers as meso the level at which my father was operating in the middle of his life (he died in his eighties); and if one adopts an A to E grading scale, I would say that his *economic* capital at the meso level was A.

In the Lamia of the pre-war and early post-war period even more so than today, economic power was closely associated with political power. My father, although never directly involved in politics, had considerable political influence (or capital) in the province, via such typical mechanisms as his financial support of local MPs, his close acquaintance with the nomarch, the mayor, the bishop and other dignitaries of the small town, his membership on various official or semi-official boards, his presidency of organizations such as the provincial Chamber of Commerce, etc. In view of the above I would assess his *political* capital, at the meso level where he was operating, as B.

As far as his *social* capital was concerned, a prestigious marriage was a definite plus, as well as the fact that his wife, my mother, was highly respected due to a variety of church and philanthropic activities. On the minus side was my father's reputation for being strict with his employees, and rather tight with his money. Although he always had a very good name in the market (Bourdieu's symbolic capital), his philanthropic activities and his contributions to the social welfare of the community were rather meagre. All in all, I would rate his social capital as C.

Finally, his *cultural* capital would be lower still, a mere D, since his interests in cultural matters were typical of a person who in his formative years had neither the family background nor the money to acquire a taste for good education or 'high' culture. Therefore, although with the financial help of his two brothers he did attend the University of Athens, academic and cultural preoccupations were very peripheral to his long life.

The early 1960s, when his brother George died, brought a dramatic change in my father's life. He had to leave Lamia and move to Athens, both in order to take care of his deceased brother's financial affairs, and because the Lamia industrial concerns were becoming technologically obsolete. In a way, this was a move up the ladder. For as far as the economic dimension is concerned, he was increasingly involved with macro rather than meso economic games, particularly so when, with the help of a younger partner, he began to import and later assemble Japanese cars. This business, in terms of both the number of people employed and capital invested, was much bigger than his Lamia operations.

The shift from meso to macro meant that from being a big fish in a small pond, my father became in his fifties and sixties a relatively smaller fish in a much bigger pond. His economic capital, although larger in absolute terms, in relative terms declined to B-C. With respect to his political capital, his move to Athens meant (for similar reasons) a drop from meso B to macro C-D. One can say that an analogous diminution occurred in his social capital, particularly since towards the end of their lives my parents' social activities were drastically reduced.

My father's trajectory as a whole shows a clear move along the four hierarchies, from micro games in his native village, to meso games in Lamia, and to macro games in Athens. Schematically this can be represented as follows:

Type of capital

Type of game	Economic (A)	Political (G)	Social (I)	Cultural (L)
MICRO early life Village	D	D	D	D
MESO middle life Lamia	A	B	B–C	D
MACRO late life Athens	B–C	C	C	D

2 POSITIONS, DISPOSITIONS, SITUATIONS: DEGREES OF CONGRUENCE

Another interesting point concerning my father's overall career is the extent to which the micro, meso and macro games in which he was involved showed a general tendency towards congruity between the positional, dispositional and situational dimensions. His childhood having been one of extreme poverty, the roles or social positions he occupied as a teenager and young man emphasized the ideal of material success. Normative expectations (particularly from his strong-willed and ambitious mother) required him to do well and get ahead in life. Given the financial impossibility for him to acquire a good education, and given the circumstances in Dadi at the beginning of the century, he had very few choices open to him. As a result, the normative expectations and my father's *habitus*/dispositions were quite congruent. In the context of strong family solidarity and the overall values and social organization of the Dadi community, my father's dreams and dispositions were consonant with what he was expected to do in order to succeed in life.

To put it differently, and in accordance with my discussion above, my father's early socializations within his village community (in respect of family, school, church, neighbourhood, playground) fully agreed with each other, so that dispositions and role expectations were a perfect match.

It should be added that the overall economic conditions during his early life were such that one could, much more easily than today, start from scratch and accumulate considerable capital. The ethic of hard work, frugality and accumulation was much more relevant and operative in turn-of-the-century Greece than it is today.[2]

Given this congruence between the positional (normative expectations), dispositional (capabilities and aspirations) and situational (favourable economic conditions) dimensions, it is not surprising that my father rarely distanced himself from the rules entailed in his business career. Rules were taken for granted as means and resources (paradigmatic duality), rather than considered as topics to be investigated or transformed.

With respect to my own career the picture was quite different. In my case, normative expectations and dispositions were in constant conflict. Concerning the former, I was brought up in a patrilocal and rather patriarchal family,[3] as the only male heir-to-be not only of my father's considerable business assets, but also of those of my two uncles who, as mentioned already, never married. Having moved quite early from my family home and from Lamia in order to attend Athens College (one of Greece's best private schools), my two uncles became my guardians. This meant I had three fathers, so to speak, all three of them expecting me to take over the family business eventually, so as to consolidate and increase an economic capital they had devoted their lives to building up. Their patriarchal and traditional values imbued them with a very strong sense of the need to carry on the family name and fortune. Therefore, although they were ready to offer me 'the best education money can buy', it was so that it might be used for the continuation, modernization and enlargement of the business. These expectations were not, of course, idiosyncratic. They were completely congruent with the kinship roles (and the father–son relationships they entailed) of a small-town Greek community in the 1950s.

Concerning now the dispositional dimension, all my inclinations were urging me away from a business career. Not only was I experiencing in acute form the typical father–son antagonism; but also, at Athens College the emphasis among the able students was on cultural rather than economic capital. This was partly due to the left-wing inclinations of some of the more inspiring teachers, and partly because some of my school mates came from *tzakia* families,[4] or from families that had been rich for several generations and were quite *blasé* about money. Furthermore, there was a certain spirit of idealism among young people of my generation that has completely disappeared from the Greek postmodern youth culture of today. All the above was reinforced in my case by a strong and rather punitive feeling of guilt for having been born into a well-to-do family, and a tendency to contemplation and meditation rather than practical action (paradigmatic dualism).

For all that, having no clear idea of what else to do, I decided to study business administration. I was trying to solve the role–dispositional conflict by doing what was dictated by my position rather than my disposition. My choice of university fell on Geneva, not because I thought it to be best in the subject, but because – following another typical pattern of Greek bourgeois upbringing – I had attended several Swiss summer schools to learn French and acquire 'civilized' manners. This brings me to an analysis of the situational dimension.

The BA degree course at the University of Geneva happened to be particularly uninspiring. All courses related to business were either purely technical (e.g. the mechanics of accounting, of statistical analysis), or they consisted of common-sense recipes on how to run a business, albeit dressed up in pseudo-scientific jargon. However, the structure of the degree course was such that one could choose a large number of non-business courses in philosophy, sociology, psychology, etc. Being particularly attracted to sociology and psychology (I had Piaget as a teacher), I decided, once I had finished my four-year course in business administration (*Licence ès sciences commerciales*) to get a second *licence* in sociology. This presented no difficulties because, via a system of *equivalences*, I was able to acquire my second degree in a relatively short time.

Wishing to postpone my return to Greece for as long as possible, I then persuaded my father to financially support my postgraduate studies at the London School of Economics (LSE), where I got my Ph.D. in sociology. This was during the 1960s, which were marked by the dramatic expansion of British university education in general, and of sociology in particular. It meant that even before I had finished my Ph.D. I was able to find a position as assistant lecturer in the Department of Sociology at Leicester.[5] These situational possibilities, in conjunction with my growing interest in sociology (which was particularly stimulated by the intellectually exciting environment of the Leicester Department)[6] finally made me opt for an academic career. This caused considerable disappointment to my father and uncles who, apart from anything else, had a very low opinion of sociology (as not 'marketable').

In sum, both my studies in Geneva, which had prompted me to shift from business administration to sociology, and the spectacular expansion of the academic market in the UK while I was doing my Ph.D. there, were two situational factors that led me to resolve the role expectations-dispositions dilemma in favour of the latter.

3 LINKAGES BETWEEN DIFFERENT TYPES OF CAPITAL

Concerning now the games I became involved in from the point of view of struggles for capital, my opting for an academic career in the UK brought with it a dramatic increase in cultural capital (as compared to my father's) but, as I shall explain below, at the expense of economic capital.[7]

It is, of course, my economically privileged background and my family's willingness to finance my rather long and expensive studies that partly explains such academic success as I have had, and the eventual accumulation of considerable cultural capital (via publishing several books and many articles, being given a Chair at the LSE, etc.).

On the other hand, it was my refusal to get seriously involved in the family business that led to a dramatic decline of the family's economic capital. After the death of his two brothers while he was in his late seventies and early eighties, my father, who had no intention of retiring, and a younger and very ambitious partner became involved in a highly risky industrial investment that failed, and soaked up most of his and my fortune.[8] Not only was I both unwilling and unable to prevent these fatal developments but, after my father's death, my academic commitments and my inexperience in business matters left me rather ill-fitted for unravelling the financial problems I had inherited.

Focusing now more closely on the internal structure of my academic career, after five years at the University of Leicester (1965–1969), and after absolving my military service in Greece, I was appointed Lecturer at the LSE (where I am still teaching part-time as a professor). In the middle period of my academic career it would have been possible for me – given that it was certain to take a long time before I could hope for a Chair at the LSE – to take up a position that would combine a reasonable academic status with a heavy dose of administrative responsibilities. This would have meant becoming a professor and/or head of department at some less well-established university, or at a London polytechnic, or directing a prestigious social sciences research institute in Athens. Such options entailed a different articulation of the 'four capitals': slightly higher economic capital (i.e. a higher salary); more political power (i.e. greater capacity for mobilizing human and non-human resources for the achievement of organizational goals); more social capital (i.e. more contact with influential people outside the department, and a greater capacity for mobilizing social networks); and less cultural capital (working in an intellectually less challenging environment and having less time for research). Given my well-to-do background (no need for a higher salary), my determination to follow a career diametrically opposed to my father's, and my contemplative rather than action/performance disposition, it is not surprising that I rejected, or refused to consider seriously, offers which would have shifted my career from academic-administrative to administrative-academic.

This did not mean that mine was an ivory-tower career with non-existent or minor hierarchical pressures. It simply meant that the pressures, or rather the controls/opportunities coming from above, were very different from those of an administrative-academic position. More specifically, the major limitations/enablements originated from other sociologists (whether personally known to me or not), who were involved in similar issues but stood higher up in the cultural hierarchy. Here the struggle for cultural recognition, although more subdued and 'civilized' than the economic struggles my father had been involved in, could be as intense and disruptive as those analysed by Bourdieu in his *Homo Academicus*. It is worth stressing once more that (in the cultural field) pressures and opportunities originating from above need not take the form of bureaucratic directives or market constraints, but can operate much more unobtrusively.

For example, to develop the key concepts in this work I had to resort to the work of theorists who have dealt with similar problems, and who have greater cultural capital and more intellectual influence than I do (e.g. Bourdieu, Giddens, Elias). Therefore, even though I do not know Bourdieu personally, his work is hierarchically related to mine: his writings both set limits and provide opportunities for the advancement of my research (and therefore of my cultural capital). In particular, my developing the positional/dispositional/situational notion of social games is due to a large extent to my persistent efforts to understand Bourdieu's key notion of the *habitus*.

This kind of influence does create limits, but it does not entail (as in more dogmatic disciplines) uncritical acceptance. The notion of limitations, in other words, simply implies the obligation to take seriously the work of someone else, who is better known and/or has done more work on the subject that one has oneself.[9] At the same time, this kind of influence also creates possibilities, in the sense that, within certain limits,[10] it encourages criticism that may lead to the elaboration of new or restructured concepts.

If it is possible to point to hierarchical linkages between my own and better-known works, one can also point to hierarchical linkages with social scientists whose work, in certain fields of common interest, is less well known than mine. For instance, my two books on the sociology of development (one on modern Greece and the other on the long-term socio-political developments of some Balkan and Latin American societies)[11] have influenced researchers who have equal, higher or lower cultural capital than myself. In the latter case the establishment of hierarchical linkages (if these are defined not in the narrow, formal–organizational sense) are perfectly clear – although such hierarchies are fuzzier and more transient than are bureaucratic or market ones.

4 FURTHER COMPARATIVE REMARKS

Looking more systematically at points of homology as well as heterology in my father's career and mine, the first striking difference can be analysed in terms of the paradigmatic duality/dualism distinction.

4.1 From duality to dualism on the paradigmatic level

If one considers a life trajectory as a prolonged overall game where, among other things, the player tries to increase his/her capital along economic (A), political (G), social (I) and cultural (L) dimensions, a marked divergence between my father's and my own 'overall' social game is that in his case there was relative congruence between his roles, dispositions and situations, whereas in my case there was relative discord. As already mentioned, my father, in terms of his trajectory as a whole, never experienced any profound conflict between role expectations, dispositions and situational opportunities. Despite the fact that he lived in a historical period marked by turbulent events and violent social and political upheavals (wars, military coups, civil conflicts, etc.), what was expected of him by 'significant others' (parents, relatives, friends, business partners, people considered important in his social world in Dadi, Lamia and Athens) was more or less what he himself wished or was disposed to do, and what favourable situational factors rendered objectively possible. In these circumstances, it is not surprising that his broad orientation *vis-à-vis* the rules of the overall game was a taken-for-granted, 'natural' attitude. In Giddens' terms, rules were simultaneously means and outcome (paradigmatic duality). They were used in a taken-for-granted, uncritical manner as the way of living one's life.[12]

In my own case the choice of a career, as I tried to make clear in the preceding section, brought a clash between role expectations and dispositions that marked profoundly both the nature of the overall game I have been playing ever since, and the manner or style of my playing it. With respect to the latter, my attitude *vis-à–vis* the rules of the game has almost unavoidably been much more reflexive than my father's (paradigmatic dualism). Such rules could not be taken for granted. There was agonized searching and questioning in regard of the validity of role expectations, the nature and strength of my dispositions, and the general legitimacy of rules stressing accumulation of any kind.[13] The varied and changing ways in which I have dealt with the ensuing dilemma need not be developed in this context. What is pertinent for the present discussion is that incompatibilities between the role, dispositional and situational dimensions of one's overall game tend to link up with an orientation to game rules that belongs to paradigmatic dualism; whereas congruity between the three dimensions leads to taken-for-granted attitudes *vis-à-vis* rules (paradigmatic duality).

4.2 Hierarchical fragmentation

Another interesting difference between my father's and my own trajectory is that in my case the hierarchies in which I was implicated have had a more fragmented, late-modern or 'postmodern' character. This marked fragmentation takes different forms.

Although geographically I have lived outside Greece for most of my life, I have kept up very strong links with friends, relatives and colleagues in my country of origin. The continued strength of these relationships is due to my academic job allowing me to spend long periods away from the university, to the relative strength and cohesion of Greek kinship structures,[14] and to my already mentioned research and economic interests in Greece.

As a result, ever since my student days I have been living abroad as much as at home, moving forwards and backwards at regular intervals. This today not so very unusual situation meant that I was involved in hierarchized games simultaneously in Athens and London (on the economic, political, social and cultural level). These two rather distinct hierarchized spaces overlapped to some extent, of course. In both Athens and London, the major organizing and balancing acts of my existence concerned my academic work (both teaching and research); the struggle for academic and intellectual recognition continued whether I happened to be in Athens or in London. So for instance the lectures I gave at the LSE were usually prepared in Greece during the long summer vacation. With respect to research, my moving between London and Athens did not prevent a continuity of focus and effort, especially since the social structure and historical development of modern Greek society has been one of my major research interests.

On the other hand, in many respects the Greek and British sets of hierarchized games have been quite different. Taking cultural capital, for instance, for Greek sociologists and even for the Greek intelligentsia my LSE position and my published work meant that the influence I exercised was considerable. The games I was playing (via informal contacts, lectures, participation in conferences, writing in Greek newspapers, etc.) to a large extent influenced games played further down in the cultural hierarchy. In London, on the other hand, given a much broader intellectual and cultural community, my cultural capital was lower.

Similar discrepancies have existed in the political dimension (G). In Greece, although I have always refused to become directly involved in politics (by joining a specific party, say), my political capital has been not completely insignificant. Some influential politicians have been my students or colleagues, and my writings, particularly my regular articles in *Vima* (the major quality Sunday paper in Greece) have had a certain impact on ongoing political debates. My political capital in the UK, on the other hand, has been quite insignificant.

In view of the above it should now be clear that my father's hierarchized space was much more unified and clear cut than mine. So for instance, in his mid-career his hierarchical subalterns who were directly affected by my father's business decisions (his employees, workers, other cotton traders, etc.) were all concentrated in a clearly delineated geographical region: that of Lamia and the surrounding villages and small towns of the Phiotis province. In my own case, those whose cultural capital is less than mine and who are directly influenced by my writings (students, young sociologists interested in the sociology of Greece, in development, sociological theory) are dispersed all over the world (particularly the Anglo-Saxon world, but also in Latin America, the Mediterranean area and Japan).[15] In other words, my two geographically, culturally and socially distinct but closely interrelated spaces portray the ambiguity, transience and fuzziness of postmodern/late-modern social situations. As such they are characterized by social syncretism and by various local/global combinations that displace the more rigid and clear-cut national hierarchies, which the emergence and dominance of the nation-state created in an earlier era.

4.3 Economic and cultural capital: homologies and heterologies

A great strength of Bourdieu's typology of capital is that it provides the conceptual means for seeing similarities, or rather homologies, in the kinds of logic of various institutional spheres, without reducing one to the other. Rejecting any idea of ultimate primacy, Bourdieu stresses that different 'fields' (i.e. institutional spaces) have their own logic and dynamic, while at the same time portraying fundamental similarities – hence the possibility and desirability of speaking of struggles over capital not only in the economic sphere, but also in the social and cultural ones, etc.

However, in his *Homo Academicus*, Bourdieu tends to stress homologies rather than heterologies. For instance, the ruthless competition among academics differs very little from cut-throat competition in the economic market place. However, comparing my father's situation with my own, I can identify (on the level of roles/normative expectations) some systematic differences which, as far as I can see, are not stressed in Bourdieu's analysis of the French academia. In my father's role as a businessman, success more or less automatically (within the limits imposed by the dominant business morality) equated with increasing his economic capital, expanding his investment and increasing his firm's profits. The instrumentalism underpinning the fundamental logic of the economic game was not hidden or qualified. One worked hard and took risks in order to make money. In my father's business community this straightforwardly instrumental orientation was neither something to conceal nor to feel ashamed of.

In academic circles, however, the struggle for fame and recognition (the equivalent of making money in the economic sphere) was less transparent. The dominant normative expectation (at least in the late 1960s English academic environment where I had my first university post) was that the major driving force in an academic's life should not be fame and glory, but a disinterested desire for the promotion of human knowledge, of the discipline's broad interests, of student welfare, and so on. Recognition was supposed to be a relatively unimportant and certainly unintended by-product rather than the main goal.

Given this non-instrumentalist normative focus, it is not surprising that the 'academic entrepreneur', who is so much concerned with the kudos of fame and/or managerial power that s/he gives low priority to scholarship, was decidedly not the dominant model. This meant that, however instrumental one's dispositions may actually have been, on the level of role expectations (on the level of social positions, that is) one had to take serious note of the emphasis placed by the academic community on collegiality, the disinterested pursuit of knowledge, etc. To use Parsonian terminology, on the level of academic values and norms, the stress was on the expressive rather than the instrumental, on community rather than ego orientations towards both students and colleagues. This normative emphasis did not, of course, transform all-too-human academics into disinterested saints. But it did have a serious impact on the level of the *habitus*. The disposition to 'accumulate' recognition *à tout prix* was weaker – if for no other reason than because it was always possible to opt for a 'relaxed' existence (which basically meant few publications, or refusing to give in to pressures for 'quick results' at the expense of quality), without being worried that at the end of the year one's 'productivity' was to be officially measured – and that, if the quantifiable (usually superficial) aspects of one's work were not very impressive, one would be criticized by the convener, or the head of the school, for contributing negatively to the national ranking of the department, school, university.

It is interesting that this 'gentlemanly' relaxed atmosphere did not lead to an overall deterioration of academic standards. There were always a few individuals, of course, who abused the system. But on the whole, my impression was that the abuses were peripheral, and their impact on the overall performance of a department insignificant. I think this was due mainly to the fact that, in sociology at least, most academics looked at their work as a vocation rather than a nine-to-five job. This made the really effective controls internal and/or professional, rather than bureaucratic in nature. It meant that, despite the 'relaxed' atmosphere, the quality of the work produced, in terms of both research and teaching, was very high. (This is quite obviously a rather impressionistic assessment, but it is based squarely on my comparative experiences of university education in Greece, French-speaking Switzerland and England.)

At an early stage in my academic career, therefore, and notwithstanding a fundamental homology between my father's struggle for economic and my own for cultural capital, there were some important qualitative differences between the two games. These differences were dramatically reduced in the 1980s and 1990s as, with the growing prevalence of neo-liberal, Thatcherite values, the managerial ethos started to penetrate and even to displace the scholarly attitude and so to undermine the relative autonomy of the academic sphere. As highly formalized audit exercises and routine productivity assessments began to replace the subtler, more informal (and more effective) controls the community of colleagues had been imposing on each others' work; as the ideal of the disinterested scholar was replaced by the ideal of the academic/cultural entrepreneur (who attracts massive research funds, is a media star, knows how to mobilize social networks, and achieves smooth co-operation between state bureaucrats, politicians, business people and academics); as academic standards of postgraduate research had to be lowered so that departments could achieve a higher productivity profile;[16] as there was reduced concern over students learning what their teachers considered the core elements of a discipline, and greater emphasis on enhancing 'consumer choice' – as, in brief, the university lost some of its autonomous logic and became more like a glorified supermarket or a business concern, the struggle between economic and cultural capital acquired an increasing similarity. Here, of course, one can detect a primacy: it is the economic market place that has imposed its logic and dynamic on academics. Significant differences remain, and the interpenetration between business and academia is not entirely unidirectional, but in Thatcherite Britain there can be no doubt that the major influence is from business to academia rather than vice versa. The end result, from the university point of view, is pretty negative.

NOTES

INTRODUCTION

1 See S. F. Nadel, *The Theory of Social Structure*, vol. 1, London: Routledge, 1962.
2 See L. Althusser, *For Marx*, London: Allen Lane, 1969, pp. 183–90 and 251.
3 T. Parsons, *The Social System*, London: Routledge, 1951.
4 In quite positivistic and foundationalist manner Parsons, in the middle and late phases of his work, claimed to be building a 'scientific' theory of society based on already existing 'empirical findings'. He also claimed that his underemphasis of social change during his middle phase had to do with the fact that empirical research was not yet sufficiently advanced to serve as the basis for a general theory of how social systems change. What in fact he did was to provide sociologists with a set of conceptual tools (Gen. II) that can be more or less useful in the empirical investigation of the social world. Taking Parsons' work as a whole, it mainly consists of Generalities II rather than Generalities III.
5 N. Smelser, *Social Change in the Industrial Revolution: An Application of Theory to the Lancashire Cotton Industry 1770–1840*, London: Routledge & Kegan Paul, 1962.
6 Note that the main difference between Parsons' and Smelser's books is not their degree of abstraction or grand sweep; some substantive theories (Gen. III) are just as abstract and all-inclusive as Parsons' *Social System*. As a matter of fact, in Smelser's *Social Change in the Industrial Revolution* there is a seven-stage model of social differentiation I consider a substantive, empirically verifiable theory, which is supposed to apply to all types of differentiating social systems, regardless of time or space. Like all contextless, transhistorical Gen. III statements, Smelser's theory tends to be either trivial or inconclusive.
7 See E. M. Rogers, *Modernization among Peasants: The Impact of Communication*, New York: Rinehart & Winston, 1969.
8 See D. C. McLleland, *The Achieving Society*, Princeton, N. J.: Van Nostrand, 1961.
9 See for instance C. W. Mills, *The Sociological Imagination*, New York: Oxford University Press, 1959.
10 In fact, if one looks at empirical work (whether of a positivistic nature or not) in political sociology, the sociology of religion, the family, small groups, organizations, and so on, Parsons' influence has been all-pervasive during the early post-war period in the United States and elsewhere. See among others

173

G. Almond and S. Verba, *The Civic Culture*, Princeton: Princeton University Press, 1963; B. Barber, *Science and the Social Order*, New York: Free Press, 1952; R. M. Bellah, *Beyond Belief*, New York: Harper & Row, 1970; K. Deutsch, *The Nerves of Government*, New York: Free Press, 1963; S. N. Eisenstadt, *The Political System of Empires*, New York: Free Press, 1963; M. Levy, *The Family Revolution in China*, Cambridge, Mass.: Harvard University Press, 1949; S. Lipset, *The First New Nation*, New York: Doubleday, 1963.

11 For a recent reformulation of such a critique, see J. H. Turner, *A Theory of Social Interaction*, Cambridge: Polity Press, 1990.

12 The passive portrayal of micro actors in Parsonian theory is not due to his alleged emphasis on actors' role conformity, on consensus rather than conflict, order rather than disorder, etc. (Parsons has, after all, repeatedly emphasized that the degree of role conformity, order or consensus in any specific social system is an empirical question.) The true reason for this passivity lies in his attempt to explain the conduct of actors exclusively or predominantly in terms of normative expectations, of the rights and duties entailed in their roles or social positions. The *role/positional* dimension, however, although relevant, cannot in itself explain the actual games actors play with each other (not even if we assume that they always adhere faithfully to the rules that belong to their role in each given game). A full explanation (as I shall argue below, see particularly Chapter 6) must also take into account the *dispositional* and *situational-interactive* dimensions.

13 For a typical work clearly reflecting the major weaknesses of Parsonian structural functionalism on the level of macro actors see N. Smelser, *Social Change in the Industrial Revolution*, op. cit. (As I shall discuss in Chapter 5, Smelser changed his position on collective actors in his late work.) For an approach to the same subject which, through its overemphasis of agency, goes to the other extreme, see E. P. Thompson, *The Making of the English Working Class*, London: Allen Lane, Penguin, 1963. Finally, P. Anderson's *Arguments within Marxism*, London: New Left Books, 1980, tries to strike a balance between an agency and a system approach. The systematic underemphasis of actors leads, on the level of macro sociology, either to the reification of institutional structures (a *system*–action imbalance), or to their reduction to an aggregate of micro interactions (an *action*–system imbalance). See N. Mouzelis, *Back to Sociological Theory: The Construction of Social Orders*, London: Macmillan, 1990.

14 See J. Elster, *Rational Choice*, Oxford: Basil Blackwell, 1986.

15 If one continues to use the evolutionist notion of differentiation, it can be said that, whereas with Parsonian functionalism the differentiation between the more theoretical and empirically-oriented branches of the discipline was accompanied by integrative mechanisms, in the case of post-structuralism, differentiation *not* being accompanied by integration has led to regressive dedifferentiation. See on this point Chapter 3, Sections 2 and 3.

16 J. Alexander's work tries to restructure Parsonian theory in a non *ad hoc* manner. See, for instance, his *Action and its Environments*, New York: Columbia University Press, 1988, Chapter 10.

Another major theorist who has attempted to restructure Parsonian theory by integrating systemic and life-world approaches is, of course, Habermas. But since his main orientation is philosophical rather than sociological-theoretical, and given that I have dealt critically with the 'system–agency' aspects of his work elsewhere (see N. Mouzelis, *Back to Sociological Theory*, op. cit. and Appendix I), I shall not discuss his work here in any depth.

17 See J. Habermas, *The Theory of Communicative Action, vol. II, Lifeworld and System*, Cambridge: Polity Press, 1987.

18 N. Mouzelis, *Post-Marxist Alternatives: The Construction of Social Orders*, London: Macmillan, 1990; and *Back to Sociological Theory*, op. cit.

19 See *The Collected Papers of Charles Saunders Pierce*, ed. by C. Hartshorne and P. Weiss, Cambridge, Mass.: Harvard University Press, 1932–5, vol. V, par. 9:

> In order to ascertain the meaning of an intellectual conception one should consider what practical consequences might conceivably result by necessity from the truth of that conception; and the sum of these consequences will constitute the entire meaning of the conception.

Although I am not persuaded by the latter part of the quotation, I do agree with the first: the best way to understand the meaning of sociological concepts (particularly any developed in convoluted and/or obscure theories like those of Parsons and Foucault) is to examine their practical consequences, i.e. to see how they are *used* by their creators and others in the empirical investigation of the social world.

Moreover, an effective way for some critic to question *my* interpretation of, say, Parsons' or Foucault's work would not be to point out that Parsons or Foucault said something different in such-and-such a text on such-and-such a date, but to show that the way in which they or their disciples *use* the concepts under discussion in empirical investigation is different from the way as described by me.

20 Concerning feminist theory, for example, there is no doubt that it has made serious contributions to our knowledge of gender as well as to substantive areas of sociology that were previously studied in a gender-blind manner. But as far as *sociological theory* proper is concerned (if one adopts the narrow definition I am proposing here), I do not think that the impact of feminist theory has been particularly marked. While feminist theory has drawn extensively from various theoretical traditions (phenomenological, ethnomethodological, post-structuralist, etc.) in order to study (among other things) the social construction of gender differences, the main influence has been from theory to feminism rather than the other way round. I am unable to think of any important theoretical paradigm the parameters of which have been significantly transformed via the development of feminist theory.

This is not surprising, since on the level of Generalities II, conceptual tools/frameworks tend to be quite neutral as far as gender or race is concerned. For example, in Part II of this book I examine Elias's concept of figuration and Giddens' duality-of-structure notion. Neither of these two concepts are 'male'- or 'female'-oriented, and I would argue that the same is true about the more inclusive conceptual frameworks (figurational analysis, structuration theory) in which they are embedded. Whatever the strengths or weaknesses of such concepts, they certainly do not stand or fall on the basis of their feminist credentials. Given their high level of abstraction/generality, they are supposed to help us ask questions about how human beings (whether men or women, black or white) relate to each other and form larger social wholes. As such, they can be more or less useful to both feminists and anti-feminists, to those who want to radically transform and those who want to maintain the patriarchal *status quo*.

This is not to deny that conceptual tools are indeed related in various ways to the substantive concerns whose empirical investigation they are supposed to prepare. But the connections are such, and the level of theory construction so abstract, that establishing direct linkages between feminist positions and, say, structuration theory or figurational sociology is not likely to be convincing. Of course, some radical feminists tend to think that no social theory, whatever its object or degree of generality, can ever be neutral *vis-à-vis* feminist issues and concerns. In the same way that dogmatic Marxists a few decades ago used to divide all social theorists into Marxist (i.e. 'scientific') and bourgeois (i.e. 'ideological'), so today there are feminists who, in equally Manichean fashion, divide all social science literature into feminist and anti-feminist.

As far as I am concerned, I do not accept this kind of procrustean dichotomizing. Therefore, in dealing with some fundamental problems of sociological theory (such as those of agency–structure and micro–macro) I do not feel that it is necessary to pay particular attention to the sociology of gender differences – just as I do not feel particularly obliged to deal with recent developments in other substantive areas of sociology (like the sociology of social movements, sociology of ageing, race, religion, etc.).

21 See on this point the difference between Parsons' rhetoric and actual practice in Note 4 above.

1 IMPASSES OF MICRO-SOCIOLOGICAL THEORIZING: OVERREACTION TO PARSONS

1 For an early discussion of the issue of whether or not the notion of organizational goals entails reification, see N. Mouzelis, 'Silverman on Organizations', *Sociology*, vol. 3, no. 1, Jan. 1969.

2 For a theoretical elaboration of the notions of political and cultural means of production see N. Mouzelis, *Post-Marxist Alternatives: The Construction of Social Orders*, London: Macmillan, 1990, Chapter 4.

3 For a development of this point see N. Mouzelis, *Back to Sociological Theory*, London: Macmillan, 1991.

4 See A. W. Rawls, 'The interaction order *sui generis*: Goffman's contribution to social theory', *Sociological Theory*, vol. 5, 1987; S. Fuchs, 'The constitution of emergent interaction order. A comment on Rawls', *Sociological Theory*, vol. 6, 1988; A. W. Rawls, 'Interaction vs interaction order. Reply to Fuchs', *Sociological Theory*, vol. 6, 1988; and S. Fuchs, 'Second thoughts on emergent interaction order', *Sociological Theory*, vol. 7, 1989. See also D. Levine, 'Parsons' structure (and Simmel) revisited', *Sociological Theory*, vol. 7, 1989; and J. Alexander, 'Against historicism/for theory: A reply to Levine', *Sociological Theory*, vol. 7, 1989. The two latter contributions are only indirectly related to the debate on the nature of the interaction order.

5 See A. W. Rawls, 'The interaction order *sui generis*', op. cit.

6 S. Fuchs, 'Second thoughts on emergent interaction order', op. cit., p. 121.

7 See on this N. Mouzelis, 'The interaction order and the micro–macro distinction', *Sociological Theory*, vol. 9, no. 2, Nov. 1991.

8 See P. Blau, 'Microprocesses and macrostructures' in K. S. Cook (ed.), *Social Exchange Theory*, London: Sage, 1987, p. 97.

9 To be more precise, there are two ways in which institutional structures can be micro. The one is when, as mentioned above, institutionalized rules/norms are embodied into the role structure of a micro-social system. In this case, despite the fact that such rules may also be found in different and/or broader social systems, they are micro in so far as they are constituent elements of the role structure of the micro-social system.

The other way in which an institution can be micro is when it is in itself restricted into a very limited geographical area. Consider, for instance, the social structure of some specific village. If this particular social system has certain institutionalized practices specifically its own (perhaps some marriage or burial rites not to be found elsewhere) and which, therefore, do not stretch widely in space, these rituals can legitimately be considered as micro institutional.

10 For the concept of caging see Michael Mann, *The Sources of Social Power, vol. I: A History of Social Power from the Beginning to A.D. 1760*, Cambridge: Cambridge University Press, 1986, pp. 93 ff.

11 The term meso here is introduced in order to stress that the micro–macro distinction does not refer to a dichotomous, either/or situation.

12 To give a striking example: in a volume that has brought together the most important writings on the methodological individualism versus holism debate, the notion of social hierarchy does not appear at all in the subject index. See J. O'Neil (ed.), *Modes of Individualism and Collectivism*, London: Heinemann, 1973.

13 See R. Collins, 'Micro-translation as a theory-building strategy', in K. Knorr-Cetina and A. V. Cicourel (eds), *Advances in Social Theory and Methodology: Towards an Integration of Micro- and Macro-Sociologies*, Boston and London: Routledge & Kegan Paul, 1981. See also R. Collins, 'On the micro-foundations of macro-sociology', *American Journal of Sociology*, vol. 86, 1981.

14 R. Collins, 'Micro-translation as a theory-building strategy', op. cit., pp. 81 ff.

15 R. Collins, 'On the micro-foundations of macro-sociology', op. cit., p. 988.

16 R. Collins, 'Interaction ritual chains, power and property: The micro–macro connection as an empirically-based theoretical problem', in J. Alexander *et al.* (eds), *The Micro–Macro Link*, Berkeley: University of California Press, 1987, p. 195.

17 For a development of this approach, which focuses on the decision-making dimension of organization hierarchies, see J. G. March and H. A. Simon, *Organizations*, New York: John Wiley, 1958; and H. A. Simon, *Administrative Behaviour*, New York: Macmillan, 1961. See also N. Mouzelis, *Organization and Bureaucracy: An Analysis of Modern Theories*, London: Routledge & Kegan Paul, 1975, pp. 123–45.

18 According to Piaget there are two types of social wholes. The one is formed from the aggregation of discrete interactions; the other 'no longer represents the algebraic sum of these interactions but a whole structure analogous to the psychological or physical Gestalt' (my translation). See his *Introduction à l'épistemologie genetique*, vol. III, Paris: Presses Universitaires de France, 1950, p. 210. For a discussion of Piaget's relational sociology, see R. F. Kitchener,

'Holistic structuralism, elementarism, and Piaget's theory of relationalism', *Human Development*, vol. 28, 1985. The concept of configuration or figuration has, of course, been elaborated also in Norbert Elias's historical and developmental sociology (see Chapter 4).

19 See K. Knorr-Cetina, 'The micro social order. Towards a reconceptualisation', in N. C. Fielding (ed.), *Actions and Structure: Research Methods and Social Theory*, London: Sage, 1988, p. 39. See also her 'The micro-sociological challenge to macro-sociology', in K. Knorr-Cetina and A. V. Cicourel (eds), *Advances in Social Theory and Methodology*, op. cit.

20 K. Knorr-Cetina, 'The micro social order', op. cit., pp. 41–4.

21 Ibid., pp. 46–7.

22 The standard macro-sociological critique of micro-sociological approaches is to stress that the latter neglect to take into account the 'larger institutional structures' within which micro phenomena are embedded. I find this critique unsatisfactory on two counts: (a) it implies that institutional structures are macro, and so perpetuates the macro-structure/micro-interaction dichotomy; (b) it does not explain why and precisely how micro sociology fails to link micro and macro – and it therefore cannot suggest detailed ways of how to bridge the existing gap between macro and micro sociology.

23 J. Turner, *A Theory of Social Interaction*, Cambridge: Polity Press, 1990, p. 12.

24 Ibid., p. 14.

25 If I am right about the fact that face-to-face interactions may entail both micro and macro events, and if one follows Turner's advice about keeping (for the moment, at least) micro and macro approaches separate, this would lead to the absurd conclusion that theories about games played at the top of a corporation hierarchy should be developed independently from theories about games played at the bottom of the same hierarchy.

26 Consider for instance the following propositions:
(i) 'The greater the needs for group inclusion among individuals in an interaction, the greater the needs for predictable responses denoting group involvement and activity.'
(ii) 'The level of need for symbolic and material gratification in an interaction is a partial and additive function of the intensity of needs denoting group inclusion and predictability in the responses of others.' (J. Turner, *A Theory of Social Interaction*, op. cit., p. 206).
Statement (i) needs no comment: it is perfectly true but trivial. Statement (ii) is true only in certain conditions, which conditions are not specified. Thus one may have 'needs denoting group inclusion and predictability in the responses of others' without the need for symbolic or material gratification in the interaction. This would be the case of individuals who form a group not for gratifications derived from the actual interaction, but for purely instrumental/strategic reasons (say in order to blow up a bridge in enemy territory).
I think that most of Turner's propositions, once stripped of their positivistic jargon, fall into the category of statements that are either trivial or wrong. Therefore the idea that this type of generalization (once 'tested' and refined) can constitute a solid corpus of knowledge to which other scientists can add new propositions of a cumulative nature is plainly a chimera, a dream which never has and never will come true. The innumerable attempts by positivistically-oriented social scientists at building such 'laws' have led precisely

nowhere. The history of sociology is littered with fruitless efforts to build systems of laws that have ended up only by explaining human activity in a transhistorical, contextless manner. Their overall result is a mosaic of propositional systems that neither connect cumulatively, nor do they tell us anything much about social action we do not know already.

27 Reference to micro events or micro actors (i.e. provision of 'micro foundations'), although necessary, is not enough to avoid reification. Explaining the constitution, reproduction or transformation of institutional structures requires also (or even primarily) reference to macro actors (individual and collective).

28 For the concepts of system and social integration see D. Lockwood, 'Social integration and system integration', in G. K. Zollschan and W. Hirsch (eds), *Explorations in Social Change*, London: Routledge & Kegan Paul, 1964. See also N. Mouzelis, 'System and social integration: A reconsideration of a fundamental distinction', *British Journal of Sociology*, vol. 25, no. 4, Dec. 1974.

29 Another way of establishing the fundamental distinction between system and social integration is to argue that, like *langue* in linguistics, the former refers to a virtual system of rules/normative expectations on the *paradigmatic* level, whereas social integration, like *parole* in linguistics, refers to relations between actors *syntagmatically* placed in time and space.

2 RATIONAL-CHOICE THEORIES: FROM MICRO FOUNDATIONS TO REDUCTIONISM

1 See for instance G. A. Cohen, *Karl Marx's Theory of History: A Defence*, Oxford: Clarendon Press, 1978; J. Elster, *Making Sense of Marx*, Cambridge: Cambridge University Press, 1985; J. E. Roemer (ed.), *Analytic Marxism*, Cambridge: Cambridge University Press, 1986; and his *Free to Lose*, Cambridge, Mass.: Harvard University Press, 1988.

2 See M. Olson, *The Logic of Collective Action*, Cambridge, Mass.: Harvard University Press, 1965; S. Popkin, *The Rational Peasant*, Berkeley: University of California Press, 1979; R. Boudon, 'The individualistic tradition in sociology', in J. Alexander *et al.* (eds), *The Micro–Macro Link*, Berkeley: University of California Press, 1987; and J. H. Coleman, *The Foundations of Social Theory*, Cambridge, Mass.: Harvard University Press, 1990.

3 See for instance A. Giddens, 'Commentary on the debate', *Theory, Culture and Society*, vol. 2, 1982, pp. 527–39.

4 See for instance J. Elster (ed.), *Rational Choice*, Oxford: Blackwell, 1986, Introduction.

5 A. Przeworski advances this argument in his *Capitalism and Social Democracy*, Cambridge: Cambridge University Press, 1986, chs 4 and 5.

6 This is, of course, the kind of logic that underlies most of neo-classical economic theory.

7 I use the concept of figuration in the way in which Norbert Elias has developed it. See Chapter 4.

8 See on this point D. S. King and M. Wickham-Jones, 'Social democracy and rational workers', *British Journal of Political Science*, vol. 20, Oct. 1990.

9 For a discussion of the logico-deductive and the historico-genetic approaches

in Marx's work see C. Luporini, 'Reality and historicity: Economy and dialectics in Marxism', *Economy and Society*, vol. IV. no. 2, May 1975.

10 It is interesting to note here that the same difficulties of integrating the logico-deductive with a more historically- and empirically-oriented approach have been encountered by theories that are lopsided in the opposite direction – theories which, like the 'capital logic' school in Marxism, overemphasize institutional structures at the expense of agency. See for instance J. Holloway and S. Piciotto (eds), *State and Capital: A Marxist Debate*, London: E. Arnold, 1978. Here as well, the main methodology is logico-deductive. It consists of an attempt to derive in armchair fashion the conditions of existence of the capitalist state, the limits of its expanded reproduction, and its fundamental contradictions. As in rational-choice Marxism, frequent pronouncements have pointed out the need for complementing the logico-deductive orientation with a historico-genetic one (see for instance T. Hirsch, 'The state apparatus and social reproduction: Elements of a theory of the bourgeois state', in J. Holloway and S. Piciotto (eds), *State and Capital*, op. cit., pp. 81 ff.), but these pronouncements have remained mere rhetoric. For a critique of the capital-logic school see N. Mouzelis, 'Types of reductionism in Marxist theory', *Telos*, Fall 1980.

11 On p. 5 of his *Foundations of Social Theory*, op. cit., Coleman writes (italics mine):

> No assumption is made that the explanation of systemic behaviour consists of nothing more than individual action and orientations, taken in aggregate. The interaction among individuals is seen to result in *emergent* phenomena at the system level, that is phenomena that were neither intended nor predicted by the individuals.

12 Ibid., Parts IV and V.

13 Ibid., p. 483.

14 Ibid., p. 500.

15 B. Moore, *Social Origins of Dictatorship and Democracy: Lords and Peasants in the Making of the Modern World*, London: Allen Lane, Penguin, 1967; Theda Skocpol, *State and Social Revolution: A Comparative Analysis of France, Russia and China*, London and New York: Cambridge University Press, 1979; Eric Wolf, *Peasant Wars of the Twentieth Century*, London: Faber & Faber, 1971.

16 See J. Coleman, *Foundations of Social Theory*, op. cit., pp. 21 ff.

17 On the 'uniqueness' of the West European city see M. Weber, *The City*, London: Macmillan, 1958.

18 J. Coleman, op. cit., p. 453. See also pp. 170 ff.

19 For an early clear exposition of this thesis see R. B. Braithwaite, *Scientific Explanation*, London: Cambridge University Press, 1964.

20 J. Coleman, op. cit., p. 29

21 Ibid., p. 243.

22 Ibid., p. 32

23 J. Elster, *The Cement of Society: A Study of Social Order*, Cambridge: Cambridge University Press, 1989, p. 15.

24 Ibid., p. 100. Elster qualifies the statement by saying that it somehow 'exaggerates the unreflective character of norm-guided behaviour'. But this qualification is purely decorative; Elster does not keep it seriously in mind when developing his overall theory about norms and interests.

25 By this I mean that Parsons' pattern variables link up systematically and in logically rigorous manner with other features of societal systems (like the adaptation, goal-achievement, integration and latency institutional orders), whereas Coleman's and Elster's concepts of norms and interests do not.

26 See J. Elster, *The Cement of Society*, op. cit., pp. 119–21, 129–30, 134–5, 136–7.

27 The falsity of the norms-versus-interests dichotomy becomes even more blatant with Elster's qualified claim that the orientation to norms tends to be blind and compulsive. If one takes into account the prolonged criticism that interpretative sociologies have launched against Parsons' passive portrayal of role players, as well as what was said already about the role/positional, dispositional and interactional dimensions of all social games, it is quite obvious that actors may and do orient themselves to social norms both in instrumental and non-instrumental ways, both in a 'blind' and a highly reflexive manner.

28 J. Elster, *The Cement of Society*, op. cit., p. 98.

29 The socially constructed character of interests raises of course the perennial question of the possibility of distinguishing 'subjective' from 'objective' interests – which is to say that it raises the issue of false consciousness. I would suggest that the various impasses to which this issue has led owe much to the fact that the debate has been conducted on a predominantly philosophical rather than a sociological/theoretical level.

Given that this is not the place for a detailed examination of the long and complex debates on the notion of objective interest, I shall limit myself to two remarks.

First, one should begin by rejecting the essentialist idea that interests are somehow natural, obvious or preconstituted entities with which an observer can identify unambiguously on the basis of his/her knowledge of evolutionary 'laws' or other such 'scientific insights'.

Second, the rejection of essentialism does not preclude the possibility of distinguishing actual from potential interest construction.

Hypothesize a situation where direct agricultural producers, operating under a quasi-feudal system of ownership and control, in a specific Third-World country, do not perceive any conflict of interests between themselves and their landlords. It is perfectly legitimate for an outside observer to assess the potentiality for the development of alternative (e.g. more conflictual) conceptions of self-interest – given certain trends that, for instance, undermine non-capitalist relations in the countryside. In such a situation the outside observer can perfectly legitimately distinguish actual from potential perceptions of interests. He/she can also – given certain 'objective' developments (like the growth of mass communications, the development of secular and instrumental orientations to work, the proliferation of agrobusinesses, the rise of urban elites demanding agrarian reforms, etc.) – predict a radical change in the agricultural producers' perception of their interests.

Let me give a more specific example. J. M. Paige's *Agrarian Revolution* (New York: Free Press, 1975) shows convincingly how variations in the types of relationship between cultivators and non-cultivators, or in other features of the immediate work environment, lead to different kinds of rural mobilization in the agricultural export sectors of Third-World countries, and therefore to different types of 'interest construction'. In other words, if one replaces the subjective–objective by the actual–potential distinction as far as interest construction is concerned; and if, in addition, one stresses that if potentialities are realized they may take a variety of forms, then one avoids essentialism while retaining a distinction which, in the work of both Marx and other analysts, has been of very great heuristic utility.

I do think that this sociological/theoretical rather than ontological/epistemological way of tackling the subjective–objective interest problem is more satisfactory if one is concerned with conceptual tools useful for empirical research.

3   POST-STRUCTURALISM: THE DEMISE OF BOUNDARIES

1   Given this perspective, I shall not at all deal with postmodern theorists like Alain Tourraine or D. Bell, who focus not so much on the status of modern theory as on the nature of post-industrial societies. There is a certain tendency in the literature to use the term 'post-structuralist' when referring to the former concerns, and 'postmodern' when referring to the latter. Since, however, there is a large conceptual overlapping between the two terms, in this book they are used interchangeably.

2   See J. F. Lyotard, *La condition postmoderne*, Paris: Minuit, 1974.

3   See N. Mouzelis, *Modern Greece: Facets of Underdevelopment*, London: Macmillan, 1978; and his *Politics in the Semi-periphery: Early Parliamentarism and Late Industrialization in the Balkans and Latin America*, London: Macmillan, 1986.

4   See G. Gutting, *Michel Foucault's Archeology of Scientific Reason*, Cambridge: Cambridge University Press, 1986, p. 177.

5   M. Foucault, *The Archeology of Knowledge*, New York: Pantheon, 1972, p. 161.

6   Moreover, his claims about the 'local' character of his statements are directly contradicted by such global generalizations as 'In any given culture, at any given moment, there is always only one episteme that defines the conditions of possibility of all knowledge' (*The Order of Things*, New York: Random House, 1970, p. 168).

7   See on this point G. Gutting, op. cit.

8   See M. Foucault, 'Truth and power', in C. Gordon (ed.), *Power and Knowledge*, Brighton: Harvester Press, 1980, pp. 114 ff. Apart from his total neglect of the vast Anglo-Saxon literature on power, he even neglects Weber who, several decades before Foucault, touched on and developed in great depth theses on modern power very similar to Foucault's. In fact, Weber's emphasis on the growing rationalization of Western societies, the rapid spread of bureaucratic forms of organization not only in public administration but in all spheres of modern life, his portrayal of modern men and women as cogs in huge bureaucratic machines that destroy the soul and create 'mutilated personalities' – all these themes, although unacknowledged, are central to Foucault's work on the spread of surveillance/disciplinary micro technologies in the modern era. In comparable fashion, Weber's ideas on the asceticism, internal loneliness and internally imposed discipline of the Protestant believer is remarkably similar to Foucault's late work on self-formation, asceticism and spirituality (see M. Foucault, *The Use of Reason*, New York: Pantheon, 1985; his *The Care of the Self: History and Sexuality*, vol. 3, New York: Pantheon, 1986; and J.

Bernauer and D. Rasmussen (eds), *The Final Foucault*, Cambridge, Mass.: MIT Press, 1988.

Finally, what is also remarkable is that, if Foucault does not refer to the Anglo-Saxon literature because he is not conversant with it, a lot of his sociologically trained disciples in the U.K. and elsewhere do not refer to it because it is unfashionable to do so. Reminiscent of the 1960s, when Marxist sociologists systematically avoided references to 'bourgeois' works, so a similar divide seems to operate today between conventional and 'post-conventional' social theory.

9   For an early critique of Foucault's notion of power along such lines see N. Poulantzas, *L'Etat, le pouvoir, le socialism*, Paris: Presses Universitaires de France, 1978, pp. 180 ff.

10 See on this point J. Bernauer and D. Rasmussen (eds), *The Final Foucault*, op. cit.

11 M. Foucault, 'The confessions of the flesh', in C. Gordon (ed.), *Power and Knowledge*, op. cit.

12 Moreover, even Foucault's constant efforts to explore the conditions of existence of certain types of knowledge also entails functionalist, quasi-Parsonian connotations. 'Conditions of existence' more often than not operate as 'functional requirements'. Both notions point to necessary but not by themselves sufficient preconditions: i.e. to factors without which the social phenomena studied could not exist or would break down. In neither case does the mere identification of the conditions of existence constitute an adequate explanation of the phenomena under consideration.

To argue, for example, as Foucault does, that the establishment of medical archives in hospitals was one of the conditions of existence of medical knowledge today, tells us nothing about the precise mechanisms that brought this new knowledge about. In a similar fashion Parsons' reference to the four functional requirements (i.e. conditions of existence) that a given social system has to solve in order to survive tells us nothing about the actual processes that constituted, reproduced and have transformed the system.

This is to say that by their very logic, neither conditions of existence nor functional requirements can provide causal explanations. The only difference between the two terms is that the former is preferred by those (like Foucault or Giddens) who use functionalist logic while denying that they are doing so.

13 Consider for instance the following passage:

> I know as well as anyone how 'thankless' such research can be, how irritating it is to approach discourses not by the way of the gentle, silent and intimate consciousness which expresses itself through them, but through *an obscure set of anonymous rules*…. I can understand those who feel this distress. They have doubtless had difficulty enough in recognizing that their history, their economy, their social practices, the language they speak, their ancestral mythology, even fables told them in childhood, obey rules which are not given to their consciousness.
>
> (quoted in G. Burchell, C. Gordon and P. Miller (eds), *The Foucault Effect*, London: Harvester Press, 1991, p. 71, italics in original)

One would think this is Levi-Strauss speaking!

14 For an early work stressing the unavoidable centrality of agency in social causation see R. M. McIver, *Social Causation*, New York: Harper, 1942.

15 In order to show the relevance of the above critique for ongoing debates on the decentring-of-the-subject issue, I shall briefly discuss the spirited defence of Foucault's position on agency as developed by Roy Boyne ('Power-knowledge and social theory: The systematic misrepresentation of contemporary social theory in the work of Anthony Giddens, in C. G. A. Bryant and D. Jary (eds), *Giddens' Theory of Structuration*, London: Routledge, 1991). Boyne, who has written extensively on French post-structuralism, is critical of Giddens' approach to the writings of Foucault. Giddens (quite rightly, I think) points out that post-structuralism in general, and Foucault's work in particular, fails to theorize or underemphasizes agency, and that this creates serious problems for anyone wanting to use structuralist or post-structuralist insights for the analysis of the modern world.

Boyne's reaction to the above is that Giddens has misrepresented Foucault's thought, and in particular failed to grasp the fundamental insights offered by the notion of power-knowledge. In defending Foucault, Boyne points out that all the French theorist argues is that

> the rich and complex workings of our societies are the legacy of historical processes without a sovereign subject (and the case of mental illness is just one of many examples that might have been used to make that point). We are dealing here with the condition of history.
>
> (ibid., p. 54)

Giddens, of course, would have no difficulty in agreeing that there is no 'sovereign subject' behind the complex working of modern societies (his emphasis on unintended consequences is one of the concepts that deals with this situation); but he would point out that post-structuralists in general, and Foucault in particular, conflate the perfectly acceptable notion that history has no sovereign subject, with the totally unacceptable one that history has no knowledgeable human subjects.

To the above Boyne retorts that Foucault's writings do not deny the idea of agency and knowledgeability:

> When Foucault said that there was a moment in the economy of power when it became understood that it was more efficient and profitable to place under surveillance than to punish, he very clearly was not denying the knowledgeable agency of those holders of power who came to see which way the wind of historical change was blowing.
>
> (ibid., p. 60)

But the point is that whenever Foucault talks about agency (as in the example above), this is despite his basic conceptual framework, not because of it. For there is nothing in his concept of power-knowledge that leads one to examine how processes of subjugation are related to micro or macro agents. In what precise ways, for instance, are the micro technologies of power Foucault constantly talks about linked with 'those holders of power who came to see which way the wind of historical change was blowing'? Who were those mysterious holders of power; how were they related to other social actors; what sort of games did they play with each other; what were the unintended consequences of these games? Foucault never raises such questions seriously and systematically – questions that would entail taking historical context and agency much more seriously that he cares to do.

Foucault only shows how micro technologies of power construct subjectivities, he never shows how micro technologies of power are themselves constructed. The fact that the construction of technologies is not altogether intended, and the fact that there is no single 'sovereign' constructor, does not mean that one cannot identify specific interest groups, for instance, whose contribution to such a construction is quite significant. The emphasis by post-structuralism on decentring the subject, on the non-existence of pre-constituted subjects, etc., flatly prevents any questions about agents as not only the products but also the producers of their social world.

16 E. Laclau and C. Mouffe, *Hegemony and Socialist Strategy: Towards a Radical Democratic Politics*, London: Verso, 1985; and E. Laclau, *New Reflections on the Revolution of Our Time*, London: Verso, 1990.

17 J. Baudrillard, *The Mirror of Production*, St Louis: Telos, 1981; *Simulacres et simulation*, Paris: Ed. Galiléo, 1981.

18 See on this point A. Giddens, *The Constitution of Society*, Oxford: Polity Press, 1984, pp. 284 and 374.

19 G. A. Cohen, *Karl Marx's Theory of History: A Defence*, Oxford: Clarendon Press, 1978.

20 A. Giddens, *A Contemporary Critique of Historic Materialism*, London: Macmillan/Berkeley: University of California Press, 1987.

21 It is for this reason, Foucault argues, that in contrast to past struggles against exploitation or political domination, in present-day struggles against subjugation it is impossible to identify the 'enemy'. Disciplinary/surveillance micro technologies, once spread to society as a whole, are not controlled from above by specific elites. The whole process of subjugation operates in a completely impersonal, disembodied manner. It is a process which, despite specific objectives, is 'subjectless'.

22 See for instance E. Laclau and C. Mouffe, *Hegemony and Social Strategy*, op. cit.

23 See D. Lockwood, *Solidarity and Schism: 'The Problem of Disorder' in Durkheimian and Marxist Sociology*, Oxford: Oxford University Press, 1992.

24 When Marxists argue, for instance, that ideological discourses have less causal weight than the material base, this can be translated into a non-essentialist manner as follows. Second-order discourses, let us say on the nature of capitalist property, are more malleable than first-order discourses related to the routine, recurrent reproduction of capitalist relations of production. To be more specific: one can easily distinguish two discursive levels as far as capitalist relations of production are concerned.

Level A (first-order discursive constructs): Millions of working people, in the U.K. say, routinely follow rules about property. By being instantiated these rules are reproduced. In this sense private property institutions are discursively produced and reproduced.

Level B (second-order discursive constructs): Academics, politicians, propagandists, etc. construct second-order discourses about the nature and legitimacy of capitalist relations of production in the U.K.

When Marxists argue that Level A is more fundamental or 'material' than Level

B, what they really mean is that the discursive practices on Level A are more durable, less malleable than those on Level B.

25 As an illustration of the decorative use of Foucault in empirical research I shall consider a relatively recent collective volume entitled *Foucault and Education: Discipline and Knowledge* (ed. by Stephen Ball, London and New York: Routledge, 1990). It is hardly possible to find in this work any contribution which could not be translated into the more conventional terminology of the sociology of education or knowledge, and without any loss of meaning.

Richard Jones, for instance, tries by means of Foucault's genealogical method to explain some interesting homologies between the development of physiology and socio-political arrangements in pre- and post-revolutionary France ('Educational practices and scientific knowledge: A genealogical reinterpretation of the emergence of physiology in post-revolutionary France', in S. Ball (ed.), op. cit.). Following very faithfully Foucault's style of argumentation, he first gives a caricatured picture of the 'sociological method', in order then to establish the specificity and fruitfulness of the Master's 'genealogical' approach. For Richard Jones, sociology tries to explain homologies between disciplines such as physiology and socio-political organization either in neo-Marxist fashion (i.e. in terms of changes in the wider socio-economic environment) or in terms of the 'conscious intentions of the knowing subject' (ibid., p. 100). In the first case one privileges the socio-economic infrastructure, and views biological or physiological discourses as merely the conditions of existence of ideologies based on an organismic model of society. In the second case one ignores the unanticipated consequences of action, the fact, as Foucault has expressed it, that 'people know what they do – but they don't know what what they do does' [sic], (ibid., p. 93).

Having dismissed sociological analysis in such an incredibly superficial manner, Jones proceeds to apply Foucault's genealogical method to the field of physiology. His major argument here is that the development of the educational system in France can throw light on the type of linkages that exist between developments in physiology and the socio-political context of post-Revolutionary France. Given that France, both before and after the Revolution, was forging a national, highly centralized educational system that entailed (among other things) the professionalization of medicine, a variety of educational practices (bureaucratic discipline, hierarchy, formal examinations) became the conditions of existence of a new discourse in physiology, stressing the organization and the 'hierarchical division of labour involving tissues, organs, and organ systems' (ibid., p. 87), as well as new modes of power which, during the *Directoire* administration, can be characterized as bureaucratic corporatism. In other words, given that 'both administrators and physiologists were increasingly receiving their training under the new educational regime' (ibid., p. 95), which was marked by growing centralization, bureaucratization and professionalization, their administrative and scientific discourses were partly shaped or influenced by the new educational disciplinary technologies.

Assuming now that the overall argument is plausible (a very problematic assumption indeed), one should ask why Jones labels his approach genealogical rather than sociological. Why limit the sociological method to Marxist economistic explanations and/or to an approach exclusively preoccupied with actors' intentions? After all, the idea of the unanticipated, unintended consequences of action has been at the centre of sociologists' preoccupations for decades now. Moreover, the exploration of linkages between scientific and extra-scientific discourses and practices has been, from its very inception, the main focus of the sociology of science. In what sense is Jones' analysis different? Why is what he is doing called genealogy rather than sociology of science or knowledge? If it is because Jones is using Foucault's power/knowledge notion, then in this particular case that notion seems entirely decorative – in the sense that Jones could express equally well or better what he had to say without using those terms. In so far as power/knowledge means something more than the banal idea that the two notions are interrelated, in so far as it implies a situation where the knower, via his/her discourses, to a considerable extent shapes the subject matter of her/his knowledge, then power/knowledge is much more relevant to psychiatry and psychoanalysis than to physiology. For theories about the human tissues do not shape or affect them or the organism in the way that psychoanalytic theories affect the construction of the human psyche or libido.

26 K. M. Baker, *Inventing the French Revolution*, Cambridge: Cambridge University Press, 1990.

27 Ibid., p. 24.

28 As Colin Jones has pointed out in an exellent review of Baker's book,

> By providing an account of political change in which social factors find no place save where they were packaged in neat discursive practices, and by concentrating above all on the writings and speeches of a small élite, Baker's approach makes it difficult to include many of the findings of historians working alongside him.
>
> ('The return of the banished bourgeoisie', in
> *Times Literary Supplement*, 29 March 1991, p. 7)

29 See E. Laclau and C. Mouffe, *Hegemony and Social Strategy*, op. cit.

30 For the influence of Althusser on Laclau's early work see E. Laclau, *Politics and Ideology in Marxist Theory*, London: New Left Books, 1977. For a critique of Laclau's structuralism see N. Mouzelis, 'Ideology and class politics: A critique of Ernesto Laclau', *New Left Review*, no. 112, Nov.–Dec. 1978.

31 See on this fundamental point R. Bhaskar, *The Possibility of Naturalism: A Philosophical Critique of the Contemporary Human Science*, Brighton: Harvester Press, 1979, pp. 31 ff.; see also A. Callinicos, *Making History: Agency, Structure and Change in Social Theory*, Cambridge: Polity Press, 1987.

32 See on this point N. Geras, 'Post-Marxism?', *New Left Review*, no. 163, May–June 1987, p. 74; and N. Mouzelis, 'Marxism versus Post-Marxism', *New Left Review*, no. 167, Jan.–Feb. 1988.

33 J. Baudrillard, *La Société de consommation*, Paris, Gallimard, 1970; and his *Pour une critique de l'économie politique du signe*, Paris: Gallimard, 1972.

34 For instance, the sun as a symbol connotes ambivalence, in that it is traditionally regarded as both beneficial and dangerous. This ambivalence is lost in the 'plastic' sun of the holiday advertisements, where the sun is portrayed as a commodity, as an item of unambiguous goodness that can be bought and sold in the market.

35 See J. Baudrillard, *Pour une critique*, op. cit., pp. 110 ff.

36 See on this point D. Kellner, *Jean Baudrillard: From Marxism to Postmodernism and Beyond*, Cambridge: Polity Press, 1989, p. 31.
37 See for instance J. Baudrillard, *The Mirror of Production*, op. cit.; *Simulacres et simulation*, op. cit.; and *L'Echange symbolique et la mort*, Paris: Gallimard, 1976.
38 Quotation taken from D. Kellner, *Jean Baudrillard*, op. cit., p. 63.
39 J. Baudrillard, *De la seduction*, Paris: Denoel-Gouthier, 1979; *Les Stratégies fatales*, Paris: Grasset, 1983.
40 For an analysis of postmodernism in terms of cultural dedifferentiation see Scott Lash, *The Sociology of Postmodernism*, London: Routledge, 1990.
41 For a critique of structuralism and post-structuralism in terms of the 'retreat to the code' see A. Giddens, 'Structuralism, post-structuralism and the production of culture', in A. Giddens and J. Turner (eds), *Social Theory Today*, Cambridge: Polity Press, 1987.
42 On the monistic character of postmodernist/post-structuralist analyses see Stephen Crook, 'The end of radical social theory? Radicalism, modernism and postmodernism', in R. Boyne and A. Rattansi (eds), *Postmodernism in Society*, London: Macmillan, 1990.
43 See D. Kellner, *Jean Baudrillard*, op. cit., p. 203.
44 For the basic differences between theorists of desire and deconstructionists see Scott Lash, *Sociology of Postmodernism*, op. cit.

4 INSTITUTIONAL AND FIGURATIONAL STRUCTURES: PARSONS AND ELIAS

1 On the growing popularity of Elias's work both in the United Kingdom and abroad see S. Mennell, *Norbert Elias: Civilizations and the Human Self-Image*, Oxford: Blackwell, 1989.
2 N. Elias, *The Civilizing Process* (2 vols), Oxford: Blackwell, 1978 and 1982.
3 See particularly vol. 2 of *The Civilizing Process*, op. cit.
4 See E. Dunning and C. Rojek (eds), *Sport and Leisure in the Civilizing Process: Critique and Counter-Critique*, London: Macmillan, 1992, Introduction.
5 For a qualification of this critique see Chapter 5, Section 1.
6 For the distinction between general and specific evolution, see M. D. Sahlins and E. R. Service (eds), *Evolution and Culture*, Ann Arbor, Mich.: University of Michigan Press, 1960.
7 See E. Dunning, P. Murphy and J. Williams, *The Roots of Football Hooliganism*, London: Routledge, 1988.
8 For a similar critique of Elias's approach see Maguire's contribution in E. Dunning and C. Rojek (eds), op. cit.
9 See E. Dunning and K. Sheard, *Barbarians, Gentlemen and Players*, Oxford: Martin Robertson, 1979; and E. Dunning, P. Murphy and J. Williams, *The Roots of Football Hooliganism*, op. cit.
10 Since all commentators stress the fact that Elias's work was long disregarded in the Anglo-Saxon world, it has to be conceded that one of the main reasons for this was his unwillingness to consider seriously anybody else's work, including work directly related to his major concerns. Nothing shows this self-inflicted isolation better than his statement that 'It is more productive if I go on working in the laboratory as I have done before, like a physicist who would go to his

labour every day and do his stint, instead of criticising other physicists' (quoted in E. Dunning and C. Rojek, op. cit., p. 16). Elias was wrong about physicists, of course, but as someone who was his colleague at the University of Leicester I can say that his assessment of his own 'monologic' approach to the discipline is quite correct – hence his critics' entirely justified complaint that he systematically caricatured all rival approaches. Fortunately, his followers do not share Elias's cavalier attitude to the work of others.

11 See for instance N. Elias, *What is Sociology?*, London: Hutchinson, 1978; and his *The Society of Individuals*, Oxford: Blackwell, 1991.
12 See S. Mennell, *Norbert Elias*, op. cit.
13 N. Elias, *Involvement and Detachment*, Oxford: Blackwell, 1987.
14 See on this point his *The Society of Individuals*, op. cit.
15 For a further development of this crucial point see Chapter 5.
16 In linguistics,

> syntagmatic refers to the linear relationship operating at a given level between the elements in a sentence; paradigmatic refers to the relationship between an element at a given point within a sentence and an element with which, syntactically, it is interchangeable.

(*The Fontana Dictionary of Modern Thought*, London: Fontana Books, 1977, p. 620)

17 See A. Giddens, *Central Problems in Social Theory*, London: Macmillan, 1979, p. 66.
18 See Chapter 6, Section 1.
19 See N. Mouzelis, *Post-Marxist Alternatives: The Construction of Social Orders*, London: Macmillan, 1990, pp. 50 ff.
20 D. Lockwood, 'Social integration and system integration' in G. K. Zollschan and W. Hirsch (eds), *Explorations in Social Change*, London: Routledge, 1964, and his *Solidarity and Schism: 'The Problem of Disorder' in Durkheimian and Marxist Sociology*, Oxford: Oxford University Press, 1992.
21 See E. P. Thompson, *The Making of the English Working Class*, London: Allen Lane, Penguin, 1963 and L. Althusser, *For Marx*, London: Allen Lane, 1969. For a comparison of the two approaches see P. Anderson, *Arguments within Marxism*, London: New Left Books, 1980, pp. 38 ff.
22 For a discussion and critique of the material/ideal distinction see Chapter 3, Section 3.

5 ON THE ARTICULATION BETWEEN INSTITUTIONAL AND FIGURATIONAL STRUCTURES: BRINGING PARSONIAN AND MARXIST SOCIOLOGIES CLOSER TOGETHER

1 See for instance T. Parsons, *The Evolution Societies*, Englewood Cliffs, N.J.: Prentice Hall, 1977.
2 See for instance J. C. Alexander and P. Colomy (eds), *Differentiation Theory and Social Change*, New York: Columbia University Press, 1990.
3 Ibid., p. xiii.
4 N. Smelser, *Social Change during the Industrial Revolution: An Application of Theory*

to the Lancashire Cotton Industry 1770–1840, London: Routledge and Kegan Paul, 1962.

5 For a critique of Smelser's work along these lines see E. P. Thompson, *The Making of the English Working Class*, London: Allen Lane, Penguin, 1963, pp. 297 ff. See also P. Anderson, *Arguments within Marxism*, London: New Left Books, 1980, pp. 38 ff.

6 See N. Smelser, 'Evaluating the model of structural differentiation in relation to educational change in the nineteenth century', in J. C. Alexander (ed.), *Neo-Functionalism*, London: Sage, 1985; and his 'The contest between family and schooling in nineteenth century Britain', in J. C. Alexander and P. Colomy (eds), *Differentiation Theory*, op. cit.

7 N. Smelser 'Evaluating the model', op. cit., pp. 168 ff.

8 S. N. Eisenstadt with M. Abitbol, N. Chazan and S. Schachar, 'Modes of structural differentiation, elite structure and cultural visions', in J. C. Alexander and P. Colomy (eds), op. cit., p. 32.

9 See J. C. Alexander, *Action and its Environments*, New York: Columbia University Press, 1988, p. 197.

10 S. N. Eisenstadt with M. Abitbol *et al.*, op. cit., p. 21.

11 F. J. Lechner, 'Fundamentalism and sociocultural revitalization', in J. C. Alexander and P. Colomy (eds), op. cit.

12 P. Colomy, 'Uneven differentiation and incomplete institutionalization: Political change and continuity in the early American nation', in J. C. Alexander and P. Colomy (eds), op. cit.

13 J. C. Alexander has tried to inject more voluntarism into the unit-act by arguing that the dimensions of interpretation, 'strategizing' and invention that various microsociologies have stressed can be linked to Parsons' undertheorized category of 'effort' (effort being for Parsons one of the elements of the action frame of reference – the other being means, ends, norms and conditions). Moreover, Alexander tries to show how the restructured action frame of reference can be linked to culture, society and personality as the three basic environments of action. (See his *Action and its Environments*, op. cit., Chapter 10.) However, what Alexander does not show is how this reformulation affects the AGIL scheme.

14 See T. Parsons, 'On building social systems theory: Some of its functions', in his *Social Systems and the Evolution of Action Theory*, New York: Free Press, 1977, p. 27. For a systematic discussion of the Parsonian notion of collectivity and of collective actors see J. M. Domingue, *Sociological Theory and the Problem of Collective Subjectivity*, Ph.D. thesis, London School of Economics, 1993.

15 T. Parsons and N. Smelser, *Economy and Society*, London: Routledge, 1956, pp. 14–15 and T. Parsons, 'An outline of the social system', in Parsons *et al.* (eds), *Theories of Society*, New York: Free Press, 1960, p. 34.

16 In fact, the notion of collectivity is not so very different from that of the figurational whole, since the latter either portrays decision-making features or has the potential of doing so.

17 By analytic category I mean a concept that concerns aspects of social reality that cannot be distinguished from each other in terms of concrete operations. For instance, one can *concretely* distinguish the production and the sales departments of a formal organization (they may even have separate locations),

but one cannot *concretely* distinguish the political from the economic dimensions of social systems or social games.

18 Marx's concept of forces of production, as most of his other key concepts, have been interpreted in various ways. Here I partly follow G. Cohen's *Karl Marx's Theory of History: A Defence*, Oxford: Clarendon Press, 1978, pp. 28–62. See also N. Mouzelis, *Post-Marxist Alternatives: The Construction of Social Orders*, London: Macmillan, 1990, pp. 50–6.

19 N. Mouzelis, ibid., pp. 56–68.

20 For a development of this point see *ibid.*, pp. 9–20.

21 I use inverted commas (a', i') in order to distinguish the notions of appropriation (a') and ideology (i') from Parsons' adaptation (a) and integration (i) sub-subsystems.

22 See N. Mouzelis, *Post-Marxist Alternatives*, op. cit., p. 47.

23 See on this point D. Lockwood, *Solidarity and Schism*, op. cit., p. 116. See also J. Barbalet, 'Social closure in class analysis: A critique of Parkins', *Sociology*, vol. 16, no. 4, Nov. 1982.

24 See N. Mouzelis, *Post-Marxist Alternatives*, op. cit., pp. 26–31 and 56–68.

25 D. Lockwood, *Solidarity and Schism*, op. cit., p. 379.

26 Finally, given the variety of competing theoretical approaches, initial efforts to grapple with voluntaristic considerations at the more empirical levels will be most fruitful if formulated within existing theoretical frameworks. *Working within the neo-functionalist tradition*, this essay indicates how one specification of structural voluntarism contributes to a more thorough understanding of institutional development. (P. Colomy, 'Strategic groups and political differentiation in the antebellum United States', in J. C. Alexander and P. Colomy, op. cit., p. 224, emphasis mine).

6 THE 'PARTICIPANT–SOCIAL WHOLE' ISSUE: PARSONS, BOURDIEU, GIDDENS

1 These are the terms used by J. Habermas in his *The Theory of Communicative Action, vol. 2: Lifeworld and System: A Critique of Functional Reason*, London: Polity Press, 1967.

2 In Wallerstein's work, for instance, when he focuses on the global capitalist system, the nation-states are participants of a whole that is the world market. See E. Wallerstein, *The Modern World System* (3 vols), New York: Academic Press, 1974, 1980, 1989.

3 For the serious drawbacks of the individual–society distinction see N. Mouzelis, *Back to Sociological Theory: The Construction of Social Orders*, London: Macmillan, 1990.

4 P. Bourdieu, *The Logic of Practice*, Cambridge: Polity Press, 1990, p. 54.

5 See on this point P. Bourdieu and J-.C. Passeron, *Reproduction in Education, Society and Culture*, London: Sage, 1970, p. 205.

6 P. Bourdieu, *The Logic of Practice*, op. cit., p. 52.

7 See L. Boltanski and L. Thévenot, *De la justification: Les économies de la grandeur*, Paris: Gallimard, 1991. See also N. Dodier, 'Action as a combination of "common worlds"', *The Sociological Review*, vol. 41, no. 3, Aug. 1993.

8 For an initial formulation of the threefold distinction see N. Mouzelis, 'The

interaction order and the micro–macro distinction', *Sociological Theory*, vol. 9, no. 2, Nov. 1991.

9 See P. Bourdieu, *Outline of a Theory of Action*, Cambridge: Cambridge University Press, 1977, pp. 80 ff.

10 For the underemphasis of the interactive dimension in Parsons' middle and late period see J. H. Turner, *A Theory of Social Interaction*, Cambridge: Polity Press, 1990.

11 I find this criticism quite justified, as long as it is made clear that Parsons' passive portrayal of actors is not due to any conviction on his part that, as a rule, actors faithfully follow the norms inherent in the roles they play. (He has pointed out repeatedly that the extent of role players' compliance with norms varies from case to case.) Instead, Parsons' passive portrayal of actors was due to his underemphasis of interaction, once he had moved from the analysis of social action to the study of social systems and their long-term evolution.

12 J. K. Campbell, *Honour, Family and Patronage: A Study of Institutions and Moral Values in a Greek Mountain Community*, Oxford: Clarendon Press, 1964. For a sympathetic critique of Campbell's unidimensional model see Papataxiarchis' 'Introduction' to E. Papataxiarchis and T. Paradellis (eds), *Identities and Gender in Modern Greece* (in Greek), Athens: Kastaniotis, 1992.

13 J. Cowan, "Going out for coffee?" Contesting the grounds of gendered pleasures in everyday sociability', in P. Loizos and E. Papataxiarchis (eds), *Contested Identities: Gender and Kinship in Modern Greece*, Princeton, N.J.: Princeton University Press, 1991.

14 See E. Goffman, 'The Interaction Order', *American Sociological Review*, vol. 48, 1983. See also D. Layder, *Understanding Social Theory*, London: Sage, 1994, pp. 155 ff.

15 As I shall argue below, Bourdieu falls into this kind of reductive error by emphasizing the dispositional at the expense of the interactional-situational dimension.

16 P. Bourdieu, *Outline of a Theory of Action*, op. cit., p. 80.

17 To use the seminar example again: my schemata of action while teaching (lively gesticulation, an upright 'self-satisfied' posture, and suchlike) are less hidden to me or to an outside observer than are the types of linkage Levi-Strauss 'reveals' by a structuralist analysis of myths, kinship systems or other institutions. This means that if a Levi-Strauss disciple attempted a structuralist analysis of the seminar game, s/he would have to break up the whole into elementary parts or 'episodes', and then try to discover the links between them that are unsuspected by both the researcher her/himself and the participants.

18 Unlike the hidden codes of Levi-Strauss, which manifest themselves on the level of practice (i.e. on the level of *parole*), *habitus* does not 'just manifest in behaviour, it is an integral part of it (and vice versa)' (R. Jenkins, *Pierre Bourdieu*, London: Routledge, 1991, p. 75).

19 See H. Garfinkel, *Studies in Ethnomethodology*, Cambridge: Polity Press, 1984.

20 Foucault's work as well as Baudrillard's exemplify this type of disposition perfectly. On Foucault's constant preoccupation with 'transgression' see H. L. Dreyfuss and P. Rabinow, *Michel Foucault: Beyond Structuralism and Hermeneutics*, Brighton: Harvester Press, 1982. On Baudrillard's obsession with the new see D. Kellner, *Jean Baudrillard: From Marxism to Postmodernism and Beyond*, Cambridge: Polity Press, 1989.

21 In so far as Bourdieu constantly refers to objective social structures and objective positions, he is obviously implying that certain other dimensions are less objective or non-objective. Consider for example his distinction between positions and stances:

> The field of positions is methodologically inseparable from the field of stances (*prise de position*) i.e. the structured system of practices and expression of agents. Both spaces, that of objective positions and that of stances must be analysed together, treated as 'two translations of the same sentence' as Spinoza put it.
>
> (P. Bourdieu and L. J. D. Wacquant,
> *An Invitation to Reflexive Sociology*,
> Cambridge: Polity Press, 1992, p. 105)

If stances are clearly distinguished from objective positions, and if they refer to the system of practices and expressions of agents – is this not the objective–subjective distinction again, formulated in a more convoluted and confusing manner?

Bourdieu argues in self-defence that his 'transcendence' of the objectivism–subjectivism divide consists in his refusal to see the objective and subjective dimensions in a compartmentalized fashion, and in establishing dialectical linkages between the two. His position is neither new nor consistently adhered to. It is not new because his idea of the compartmentalization of the objective and subjective dimensions of social life in the social sciences is an obvious caricature. He is not consistent in his use of the notion of the dialectical relations between the two because quite often, in strikingly Althusserian fashion, he subordinates agents' practices or 'expressions' to their 'objective' positions:

> A third general property of fields is that they are systems of relations that are independent of the populations which these relations define. When I talk of the intellectual field, I know very well that in this field I will find 'particles' (let me pretend for a moment that we are dealing with a physical field) that are under the sway of forces of attraction, of repulsion, and so on, as in a magnetic field. Having said this, as soon as I speak of a field, my attention fastens on the PRIMACY of this system of objective relations over the particles themselves. And we could say, following the formula of a famous German physicist, that the individual, like the electron, is an Ausgeburt des Feldes: he or she is in a sense an emanation of the field.
>
> (My capitals, ibid., p. 107)

Is this really so very different from Althusser's idea of actors as 'bearers of structures'?

To conclude: not only does Bourdieu reintroduce the subjective–objective distinction, but (like Althusser and Parsons) he also systematically subordinates the former to the latter. From this point of view R. Jenkins (*Pierre Bourdieu*, op. cit., p. 61) is perfectly right when he argues that

> Despite his stated aim of doing so, he has yet, perhaps, to actually transcend the 'rock-bottom antinomy' of objectivism and subjectivism.

22 See on this point R. Jenkins, *Pierre Bourdieu*, op. cit., pp. 81 ff.

23 Bourdieu talks generally about internalization without distinguishing cases where people follow rules for purely external or instrumental reasons, and cases where rules become part of their super-ego or conscience.

24 As already mentioned, Bourdieu systematically peripheralizes or downgrades the interactive-situational aspect of social games:

> What exists in the social world are relations – not interactions between agents or intersubjective ties between individuals, but objective relations which exist 'independently of individual consciousness and will' as Marx said.

> (P. Bourdieu and L. J. D. Wacquant, op. cit., p. 97)

But why do interactions exist less than 'objective' relations? And if the interactions are really and systematically less important, how can one explain the transformation of objective relations between positions? Here we see once more that Bourdieu, instead of transcending objectivism and subjectivism, has simply subordinated the latter to the former – something which is as unhelpful as it is unoriginal.

25 Cf. P. Bourdieu, *The Logic of Practice*, op. cit., p. 292 (my capitals):

> The most profitable strategies are usually those produced, without any calculation, and in the illusion of the most absolute 'sincerity', by a habitus objectively fitted to the objective structures. These strategies WITHOUT STRATEGIC CALCULATION produce an important secondary advantage for those who can scarcely be called their authors: the social approval accruing to apparent disinterestedness.

26 See quotation in R. Harker *et al.* (eds) *An Introduction to the Work of Pierre Bourdieu*, London: Macmillan, 1990, p. 17:

> The idea of strategy, like the orientation of practice, is not conscious or calculated nor is it mechanically determined. It is the intuitive product of 'knowing' the rules of the game.

27 Ibid., p. 17.

28 P. Bourdieu, *In Other Words: Essays towards a Reflexive Sociology*, Stanford: Stanford University Press, 1990, pp. 62–3.

29 Richard Harker makes a distinction between two models one can build on the basis of Bourdieu's work. The 'minimal' model is

structures → *habitus* → practice
$\mathrel{\rule{0pt}{1.3ex}\smash{\underline{}}}$

Harker does not consider this to be 'enough to parry the charges that the theory is merely reproductive' (see 'Bourdieu – Education and Reproduction', in R. Harker *et al.* (eds), *An Introduction to the Work of Pierre Bourdieu*, op. cit., p. 101). To account for historical transformation rather than mere reproduction, one must see practice

> as a dialectical production, continually in the process of reformulation. The reformulation may be almost imperceptible in a slowly changing traditional-type culture, or of major proportion in a revolutionary situation. The latter events would involve a disruption of the habitus-controlled perception of historical circumstances (the destruction of false

consciousness, the overthrow of a ruling hegemony), and a refocussing on a new set of principles (a 'true' consciousness, a counter-hegemonic transformation).

(ibid.)

Therefore the more complex 'reproduction and change' model would look like this:

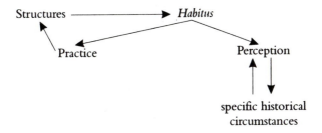

But this merely complicates the issue without solving it. A 'disruption of the habitus-controlled perception of historical circumstances' and the 'refocussing on a new set of principles' may well require calculated strategies – which do not fit into the position–disposition straitjacket.

30 See R. Jenkins, *Pierre Bourdieu*, op. cit.
31 On the notion of decisional premises see H. A. Simon, *Administrative Behaviour*, New York: Macmillan, 1961.
32 C. Wilkes, 'Bourdieu's class', in R. Harker *et al.* (eds), op. cit., p. 130.
33 P. Bourdieu, *Homo Academicus*, Cambridge: Polity Press, 1988, pp. 36 ff.
34 Ibid., pp. 66–7.
35 Quoted in R. Jenkins, *Pierre Bourdieu*, op. cit., p. 67.

> There is no doubt a theory in my work, or, better, a set of thinking tools visible through the results they yield, but it is not built as such ... It is a temporary construct which takes shape for and by empirical work.

36 I shall base my exposition and criticism mainly on Giddens' structuration theory as formulated in his comprehensive work *The Constitution of Society*, Cambridge: Polity Press, 1984.
37 The definition of structure as rules and resources constituting a virtual order creates difficulties when one refers to material resources such as land. A more satisfactory conceptualization might have been to restrict oneself to rules only in the definition of structure, in the sense Giddens uses the term. The notion of resources on the paradigmatic level could then have been covered by pointing out that rules frequently entail the mobilization of resources. This would have been perfectly compatible with Giddens' thesis that

> rules cannot be conceptualized apart from resources, which refer to the modes whereby transformative relations are actually incorporated into the production and reproduction of social practices.
>
> (*The Constitution of Society*, op. cit., p. 18)

Since this stricture is not really central to my main criticism of structuration theory, I shall continue to use the term structure in the way Giddens has defined it.

38 See A. Giddens, *Central Problems in Social Theory*, London: Macmillan, 1979, pp. 66 ff.

39 The notion of 'natural-performative' attitudes, in contrast to theoretical or 'hypothetical-reflective' ones, is used by J. Habermas in his *Theory of Communicative Action*, vol. 1, op. cit., pp. 80–1 and 122–3.

40 For a more extensive discussion of the notions of duality and dualism on the paradigmatic and syntagmatic levels see N. Mouzelis, 'Restructuring structuration theory', *Sociological Review*, vol. 37, no. 4, Nov. 1989.

41 It goes without saying that the same subjects who adopt predominantly natural-performative attitudes *vis-à-vis* rules can also, given a change in their circumstances, shift their orientations to predominantly theoretical or strategic monitoring ones. So in our example, shop-floor workers may themselves become interested in the rules underlying their work arrangements and may try to change them in a way that increases, not necessarily productivity, but perhaps their room for manoeuvre.

It is equally obvious that in all actual situations actors' orientations consist of a mixture of both practical and theoretical orientations, within which mixture the one or other component tends to dominate.

In all cases we are, of course, talking about tendencies rather than 'iron laws'.

42 See A. Giddens, *The Constitution of Society*, op. cit., p. 375.

43 Ibid., p. 288.

44 See D. Lockwood, 'Social integration and system integration', in G. K. Zollschan and W. Hirsch (eds), *Explorations in Social Change*, London: Routledge, 1984. Giddens (quite wrongly, I think) uses the system/social integration distinction differently. See N. Mouzelis, *Back to Sociological Theory*, op. cit., pp. 31–4.

45 A. Giddens, *The Constitution of Society*, op. cit., pp. 376–7.

46 For the concepts of socionalysis and reflexivity, see P. Bourdieu and L. J. D. Wacquant, op. cit., pp. 210–11, 88–9, 181–2.

47 Critics of the agency/structure distinction such as Elias, for instance, argue that those who use such distinctions view the social world as divided into two separate realms: that of agents and that of structures. Against this crude and unjustified critique, I would like to point out that the agency/structure conceptualization – as all concepts in the social sciences – take different meanings according to the theoretical context in which they are embedded. For instance, in order to understand Lockwood's social/system integration conceptualization (which is based on the agency/institutional structure distinction) one has to see it in relation to the author's attempt to identify some basic differences between Marxist and normative functionalist theories of social change (see D. Lockwood, 'Social integration and system integration', op. cit). When this is done, one realizes that Lockwood refers to two aspects of social wholes which, although both very real, can be distinguished analytically rather than concretely. In that sense if Lockwood's theory entails any dualism, it is certainly not an ontological dualism. It is the type of dualism that is unavoidable when one constructs typologies or makes distinctions which – rather than faithfully reflecting the social world – are used as analytic tools for its empirical

investigation. To give another example, the agency/structure distinction allows sociologists to raise interesting questions about the relations between specific agents and the sociocultural contexts within which they operate; questions like what type of constraints/enablements specific institutional and figurational structures create for specific actors, why, in certain contexts, actors' room for manoeuvre is more or less restricted, etc. As M. Archer has correctly pointed out, Giddens' structuration theory, particularly his duality of structure concept, by rejecting the agency/structure distinction, simply cannot raise such crucial questions. (See M. Archer, 'Morphogenesis vs. structuration', *British Journal of Sociology*, vol. 33, 1982 and *Culture and Agency*, Cambridge: Cambridge University Press, 1988. See also D. Layder, *Understanding Social Theory*, London: Sage, 1994, pp. 155–72.)

The same points can be made, of course, when one looks at the micro–macro distinction. Here as well it is quite obvious that the distinction never refers to two ontologically different social realities. Moreover, the meaning of the distinction varies according to the theoretical contexts in which it is found and/or according to whether it refers to figurational or aggregrative wholes. In the case of figurational wholes or games, for instance, the micro/macro conceptualization sensitizes the student to the fact that certain games have consequences which stretch more in time/space than those of other games. To be more specific, the managerial games played at a local branch of a multinational corporation are less 'consequential' than games played at the national or international headquarters. On the other hand, when one refers to aggregative wholes, the micro/macro distinction is equally useful in reminding the student that one can study how social traits are distributed in more or less encompassing social systems. For instance, one can see how income is distributed in a specific locality/village (micro) or how income is distributed on the regional or national levels (more macro level).

Therefore, in the figurational case the micro/macro distinction has to do with power differences between social players. In the aggregative case, it has to do with whether the distributional phenomena that one studies cover a geographically or historically more or less restricted area/era. Needless to say, the abolition of the micro/macro distinction tends to lead to the neglect of the hierarchical and 'onion-like' features of the social world. It leads to a flat, non-hierarchical view of social phenomena and this in turn opens the door to all sorts of crude, reductionist explanations of how societal wholes are constituted and transformed. (See on this point Chapter 3, section 5.)

7 SYNTHESIS AND APPLICATION: A SOCIOLOGICAL RECONSIDERATION OF FUNCTIONALISM

1 In my *Post-Marxist Alternatives: The Construction of Social Orders*, London: Macmillan, 1990, I followed up the criterion of 'direct relevance to empirical research' when assessing the utility of some of the concepts developed (such as the concept of the mode of domination). Here I continue this type of proof in the Appendix.

2 See R. K. Merton, *Social Theory and Social Structure*, Glencoe, Ill.: Social Press, 1963, ch. 1.

3 For an early formulation of this point see N. Mouzelis, 'System and social integration: A reconsideration of a fundamental distinction', *British Journal of Sociology*, vol. 25, no. 4, Dec. 1974.

4 For a discussion of the internalist–externalist distinction see J. Habermas, *The Theory of Communicative Action, vol. 2: Lifeworld and System: A Critique of Functional Reason*, Cambridge: Polity Press, 1967, pp. 117 ff.

5 For such a critique see J. Johnson, C. Dandeker and C. Ashworth, *The Structure of Social Theory: Dilemmas and Strategies*, London: Macmillan, 1984.

6 See on this point J. H. Turner, *A Theory of Social Interaction*, Cambridge: Polity Press, 1990.

7 For an early critique of Althusser's and Poulantzas' class theory and its utility in empirical research see N. Mouzelis, *Modern Greece: Facets of Underdevelopment*, London: Macmillan, 1978, pp. 46 ff.

8 L. Althusser and E. Balibar, *Lire le capital*, vol. II, Paris: Maspero, 1973, p. 146 (my translation).

9 See on this point N. Thrift, 'Bear and mouse or bear and tree? Anthony Giddens' reconstruction of social theory', *Sociology*, vol. 19, no. 4, Nov. 1985. The interminable debates on functionalism have almost exclusively centred on whether teleological explanations are methodologically legitimate or not. Despite the fact that the issue was settled long ago by Merton, it returns with predictable regularity again and again in different forms (see for instance the debate between G. Cohen, J. Berger, C. Offe and A. Giddens in *Theory and Society*, 1982, 11, pp. 453 ff.). However, the real issue about functionalism is not the legitimacy of teleological explanations (they are definitely not legitimate); the real issue is whether or not it is methodologically correct and/or necessary to view social wholes from an 'externalist' perspective: i.e. to ask questions about the necessary but not sufficient conditions of existence of social wholes, as well as questions about whether certain conditions (actual or counterfactual) strengthen or weaken the overall cohesion of such wholes. As far as I am concerned, such questions are perfectly legitimate.

Let me illustrate the above points by referring to Giddens' critique of Merton's contribution to the functionalism issue. Giddens dismisses Merton's analysis by arguing that despite the latter's determination to distinguish teleological from non-teleological functionalist explanations, in the actual examples he provides he falls into the teleology trap. Thus in the famous Hopi rain-dance example that Merton uses, he explains the persistence of this ritual in terms of its latent functional consequences: the rain dance enhances the unity of the group, and it is for this reason that it persists.

I think that Giddens is right when he says:

> To indicate that the Rain dance is 'a source of group unity' shows nothing about why it came into existence in the first place, or why it persists once instituted.
>
> ('Comments on the debate', *Theory and Society* 1982, 11, p. 529)

But what Giddens does not consider is whether or not it is legitimate to ask such functionalist questions as: Does the rain dance enhance group unity? If it does, to what extent does this enhanced unity explain why the dance ritual persists?

It is true that such questions cannot be answered without empirical research. But they are perfectly legitimate functionalist, i.e. externalist/systemic questions. Merton was wrong to give aprioristic answers. He was perfectly right, however, when he distinguished teleological from non-teleological explanations and argued that the latter are legitimate.

Let me take this opportunity to repeat once more that Giddens, when he makes the distinction between institutional analysis and an analysis in terms of strategic conduct (see Chapter 6, Section 2), simply reintroduces the functionalist logic by the back door. For when one brackets actors and focuses on institutions, one unavoidably views social wholes from an 'externalist' perspective. And an externalist perspective is nothing more or less than a functionalist perspective. The very notion of labelling certain institutions 'economic' or 'political' entails a functionalist logic. It entails viewing a set of interrelated norms, not from the point of view of the participant actors but from the point of view of the social whole and its conditions of existence. The only way of eliminating the functionalist logic altogether is by categorically refusing the bracketing of actors that, as Giddens correctly points out, an institutional analysis entails. This is precisely what many interpretatively-oriented micro-sociologists do; but the price they have to pay is that they provide us with extremely one-sided and shortsighted views of the social world. One can easily eliminate functionalist terminology. But, to repeat, one cannot eliminate functionalist logic without paying an unacceptably high price.

10 For an analysis that tends to conflate necessity with actual or sufficient conditions of existence see for instance S. Brunhoff, *Etat et capital*, Grenoble: Presses Universitaires de Grenoble, 1978. For a critique of her approach and more generally of the Marxist logic-of-capital school see N. Mouzelis, *Post-Marxist Alternatives*, op. cit., pp. 164 ff.

11 I do not believe that functionalism can be equated with social or sociological analysis, however broad or flexible the definition of the term. If functionalism is to retain any meaning, it must be viewed as a type of sociological analysis which, in its acceptable form, puts greater emphasis on the social-whole→participant relationship than on its reverse. It is only when the accent is on both that we move from functionalist analysis to sociological analysis *tout court*.

12 Functionalists can also raise historical questions about the long-term transformation of such norms. For instance, N. Smelser examined the long-term differentiation between family (L) and work (A) roles/norms during the English Industrial Revolution (*Social Change in the Industrial Revolution: An Application of Theory to the Lancashire Cotton Industry 1770–1840*, London: Routledge & Kegan Paul, 1962). However, given the peripheralization of collective actors, his account was descriptive rather than explanatory. See Chapter 5.

13 On the connection between causality and agency see the early contribution of M. McIver, *Social Causation*, New York: Harper, 1942.

14 In many concrete situations it is, of course, difficult to distinguish virtual/actual, or paradigmatic/syntagmatic, game rules/actual games. So for example participants in actual games may, while playing (syntagmatic level), think about

some rules of the game not instantiated at that particular moment (paradigmatic level). This is to say that in actual situations the paradigmatic and syntagmatic are frequently inextricably intertwined. However, even in those cases the distinction is useful, since one of the two dimensions will tend to be dominant at any particular moment. In the example above it is the syntagmatic element that dominates, and the paradigmatic element that is peripheral.

15 It may be useful at this point to introduce a further distinction from the positional perspective, between 'ideal' and 'current' norms/expectations/rules. The former tell us how actors are ideally expected to conduct themselves in specific contexts, the latter says what is merely 'acceptable' and what most people tend to follow in practice. (To give an example: the ideal standard for a lecturer is to radically revise his/her lectures every year in the light of new research; the acceptable standard and the more common pattern is minor yearly revision and a radical overhaul at longer intervals.) Note that both 'ideal' and 'current' norms are, on the paradigmatic level, virtual. The only difference is that the latter tend to be actualized more than the former. A similar distinction can be made on the syntagmatic level between what Goffman calls front- and back-stage games. The former refer to actual strategies and interactions that players are willing to perform in public, the latter take place behind the scenes, so to speak.

16 N. Chomsky, *Language and Responsibility*, Brighton: Harvester Press, 1979.

17 The linkage of a 'contemplative' attitude with paradigmatic dualism, and an 'action-oriented' attitude with paradigmatic duality, is being suggested here in tentative, rule-of-thumb fashion.

18 See on this point Chapter 1.

19 See Chapter 6, section 2.

20 Think of the incompatibilities or strains between capitalist industrialization and a traditionally-oriented monarchical government. For specific examples of this type see S. Huntington's classical work *Political Order in Changing Societies*, New Haven and London: Yale University Press, 1968.

21 See Chapter 6, section 2.

22 On the decision-making aspects of formal organizations see H. A. Simon, *Administrative Behaviour*, New York: Macmillan, 1961; and N. Mouzelis, *Organization and Bureaucracy: An Analysis of Modern Theories*, London: Routledge & Kegan Paul, 1975, pp. 123–45.

23 Paradigmatic duality here operates on the normative level. This means that actors are expected to accept rules coming from above in an unquestioning, taken-for-granted manner; or, to put it differently, decisions taken at the top become decision premises delineating the discretionary scope of those below. Whether rank-and-file members actually accept decisions or rules coming from above in a taken-for-granted manner is, of course, an empirical question that varies from one case to another.

24 The attempt to bring Bourdieu's typology of capitals closer together with Parsons' AGIL scheme entails a partial restructuring of the former. This becomes necessary because, irrespective of the AGIL scheme, Bourdieu's distinction between social and symbolic capital seems to me problematic. For Bourdieu, social capital refers to the capacity for mobilizing a network of social relations (kin or otherwise) in pursuit of one's goals (see his *The Logic of Practice*, Cambridge: Polity Press, 1990, p. 35). Symbolic capital, on the other hand,

entails the idea of honour and social prestige (see for instance his *In Other Words: Essays Towards a Reflexive Sociology*, Stanford, Stanford University Press, 1990, p. 22), as well as the idea of misrecognition: the fact that the possession of symbolic capital becomes effective when others misrecognize or do not see at all the material capital that for Bourdieu is at the basis of prestige and honour.

> Symbolic capital, a transformed and thereby disguised form of physical 'economic' capital, produces its proper effect inasmuch, and only inasmuch, as it conceals the fact that it originates in 'material' forms of capital which are also, in the last analysis, the source of its effects.
>
> (*Outline of a Theory of Action*, Cambridge: Cambridge University Press, 1977, p. 185)

I think that the notion of symbolic capital is dubious because honour and concealment do not always go together. For instance, if honour is acquired while fighting in a patriotic war, this does not necessarily entail either the concealment or the possession of other forms of capital (economic or cultural). Moreover, in so far as all forms of capital have a symbolic dimension, to distinguish between symbolic and non-symbolic capital is either wrong or at any rate confusing.

For the purposes of this analysis, therefore, I shall disregard Bourdieu's notion of symbolic capital and retain his notion of social capital. Social capital, as the capacity to mobilize social networks or relations, is usually based on the possession of various types of honour or social prestige (inherited prestige, prestige derived from the achievement of socially valued goals, etc.).

In addition I shall use the term political capital, in order to refer to the capacity for mobilizing resources that are directly or indirectly related to party or state power in differentiated, complex societies.

If one reformulates Bourdieu's notion of different types of capital in the above way, then it is possible to link them with Parsons' AGIL scheme – the adaptation subsystem entailing the notion of economic capital, goal-achievement that of political capital, integration that of social capital, and latency that of cultural capital.

25 See on this point the Conclusion.

26 I think that my reducing Bourdieu's many different types of capital to just four can be justified on both substantive and theoretical grounds. I would suggest that in most complex, differentiated societies it is the struggles over economic wealth, political power, social prestige and cultural distinction that constitute the most important arenas for actors engaging in competitive games. In theoretical terms, the fourfold typology corresponds to Parsons' AGIL scheme, which is a much more rigorous attempt at theorizing the broad institutional spheres of societies than is Bourdieu's half-baked theorization of 'fields'. Of course, the AGIL scheme presents serious weaknesses (as already discussed), but I think they can and must be overcome by some form of restructuring, rather than by the theory being rejected outright.

27 See the biographical example provided in the Appendix.

28 For an analysis and restructuring of Marx's concept of technology see N. Mouzelis, *Post-Marxist Alternatives*, op. cit., pp. 50–6.

29 The situation changes of course when micro actors become organized and constitute collectivities, the decisions of which stretch widely in time and space.

APPENDIX: HIERARCHICAL ASPECTS OF LIFE TRAJECTORIES

1 During the inter-war period, the establishment of a private bank was a relatively easy affair. The Mouzelis brothers, in collaboration with a partner, created the Croco-Mouzelis Bank Ltd, the activities of which extended over the whole of the Phiotis province. The bank ceased to operate when the cotton mills became technologically obsolete and my father moved to Athens.

2 To use Marxist terminology, 'Way I' (i.e. from simple commodity to capitalist production) was much easier in early twentieth-century Greece (that is, before the dominance of industrial capitalism in the 1940s and 1950s) than it is today. For a discussion of when the capitalist mode of production became dominant in Greece, see N. Mouzelis, *Modern Greece: Facets of Underdevelopment*, London: Macmillan, 1978, ch. 1.

3 For regional differences in Greek family structures (in terms of patri-/matrilo-cality, degrees of male dominance, types of inheritance, etc.) see P. Loizos and A. Papataxiarchis (eds), *Contested Identities: Gender and Kinship in Modern Greece*, Princeton, N.J.: Princeton University Press, 1991, pp. 3–29.

4 The Greek word *tzaki* literally means 'hearth', and metaphorically implies 'aristocratic' in the broad rather than the technical sense. *Tzakia* families, whose origins can be traced back to the military chieftains and notables of the pre-independence era, initially derived their authority from the leading role they played during the War of Independence. Given that the landowning avenue became relatively blocked to them, they turned to the professions to preserve and perpetuate their power, and above all to the state itself as politicians, state officials, academics, lawyers and tax farmers. (See G. Mavro-gordatos, *Stillborn Republic*, Berkeley: University of California Press, 1983, p. 123.) These families controlled parliamentary politics in nineteenth-century Greece and lost this control only after the rise of Venizelos' Liberal Party in the post-1909 period. (See N. Mouzelis, *Politics in the Semi-Periphery: Early Parliamentarianism and Late Industrialization in the Balkans and Latin America*, London: Macmillan, 1985, pp. 97 ff.)

5 I was Assistant Lecturer from 1965–1966 and Lecturer in Sociology from 1966–1969.

6 The department was admirably run by Ilya Neustadt, with Norbert Elias as the major intellectual influence.

7 For the typology of capital I use, see Chapter 7, section 3.3

8 The risky move entailed a shift from merely importing Japanese (Mazda) vehicles, to assembling and even producing a large percentage of their parts in Greece.

9 In other words, unlike in poetry or literature, for instance, it is not possible – particularly in the field of sociological theory – to ignore what has been said and written earlier. If one does, one is not taken seriously. Homespun theorizing is definitely looked down upon.

10 Limits here refers to normative expectations – such as, for example, that one should not caricature someone else's work.

11 *Modern Greece*, op. cit., and *Politics in the Semi-Periphery*, op. cit.

12 In addition, as Giddens argues, by routinely, and in a taken-for-granted manner instantiating such rules, my father contributed to their reproduction.

13 My post-adolescent religious preoccupations – the result of guilt, chronic existential anxiety, as well as a deeply felt genuine disposition towards the spiritual – often made me feel I should drop the struggle for accumulation in all four dimensions. Although this tendency was never very strong, it always persisted in the background whenever I reflected on the various rules of the games I was involved in.

One could argue, of course, that a concern with spirituality might simply lead to yet another type of accumulation, that of amassing religious or spiritual capital (Bourdieu does in fact speak of religious capital). To this I would reply that the search for genuine spirituality is radically different from the search for wealth (A), political power (G), social prestige (I) or cultural influence (L); it is less instrumental, more 'expressive'. If spirituality is sought for the purpose of achieving other goals – such as eternal life, peace of mind, mystic experiences – then, unlike in the other four cases, the spiritual capital is destroyed. It is only when the 'beneficial' results of the spiritual game are the genuinely unintended results of an expressive search for the 'divine' (inside or outside oneself) that spiritual 'progress' is possible. Therefore, if one can speak at all of accumulation of spiritual capital, it is an accumulation qualitatively different from that of other types of capital: it is an accumulation that is radically incompatible with any type of instrumentality, however elevated or ethereal it might be. Unlike all other types, spiritual capital disappears once one begins to regard it as something to be hoarded.

14 See on this point P. Loizos and A. Papataxiarchis, op. cit.

15 The Japanese translation of my first book, *Organization and Bureaucracy: An Analysis of Modern Theories*, London: Routledge & Kegan Paul, 1975, has been used as a textbook in courses on business, industrial sociology and the sociology of organizations.

16 See on this point, N. Mouzelis, 'The Future of the LSE: An Alternative View', *LSE Magazine*, Autumn/Winter 1992, section 3.

SELECT BIBLIOGRAPHY

Alexander, J. C. (ed.), *Neo-Functionalism*, London: Sage, 1985.

—— *Action and its Environments*, New York: Columbia University Press, 1988.

—— 'Against historicism/for theory: A reply to Levine', *Sociological Theory*, vol. 7, 1989.

—— and Colomy, P. (eds), *Differentiation Theory and Social Change*, New York: Columbia University Press, 1990.

—— *et al.* (eds), *The Micro–Macro Link*, Berkeley: University of California Press, 1987.

Almond, G. and Verba, S., *The Civic Culture*, Princeton: Princeton University Press, 1963.

Althusser, L., *For Marx*, London: Allen Lane, Penguin, 1969.

—— and Balibar, E., *Lire le capital*, Paris: Maspero, 1973.

Anderson, P., *Arguments within Marxism*, London: New Left Books, 1980.

Archer, M., 'Morphogenesis vs. structuration', *British Journal of Sociology*, vol. 33, 1982.

—— *Culture and Agency*, Cambridge: Cambridge University Press, 1988.

Baker, K., *Inventing the French Revolution*, Cambridge: Cambridge University Press, 1990.

Ball, S. (ed.), *Foucault and Education: Discipline and Knowledge*, London and New York: Routledge, 1990.

Barbalet, J. M., 'Social closure in class analysis: A critique of Parkin', *Sociology*, vol. 16, no. 4, Nov. 1982.

Barber, B., *Science and the Social Order*, New York: Free Press, 1952.

Baudrillard, J., *La Société de consommation*, Paris: Gallimard, 1970.

—— *Pour une critique de l'économie politique du signe*, Paris: Gallimard, 1972.

—— *L'Echange symbolique et la mort*, Paris: Gallimard, 1976.

—— *De la séduction*, Paris: Denoel-Gouthier, 1979.

—— *The Mirror of Production*, St Louis: Telos, 1981.

—— *Simulacres et simulation*, Paris: Ed. Galiléo, 1981.

—— *Les stratégies fatales*, Paris: Grasset, 1983.

Bellah, R. M., *Beyond Belief*, New York: Harper & Row, 1970.

Bernauer, J. and Rasmussen, D. (eds), *The Final Foucault*, Cambridge Mass.: MIT Press, 1988.

Bhaskar, R., *The Possibility of Naturalism: A Philosophical Critique of the Contemporary Human Sciences*, Brighton: Harvester Press, 1979.

Blau, P., 'Microprocesses and macrostructures', in K. S. Cook (ed.), *Social Exchange Theory*, London: Sage, 1987.

Boltanski, L. and Thevenot, C., *De la Justification: Les economies de la grandeur*, Paris: Gallimard, 1991.

Boudon, R., 'The individualistic tradition in sociology', in J. Alexander *et al.* (eds), *The Micro–Macro Link*, Berkeley: University of California Press, 1987.

Bourdieu, P., *Outline of a Theory of Action*, Cambridge: Cambridge University Press, 1977.

—— *Homo Academicus*, Cambridge: Polity Press, 1988.

—— *In Other Words: Essays Towards a Reflexive Sociology*, Stanford: Stanford University Press, 1990.

—— *The Logic of Practice*, Cambridge: Polity Press, 1990.

—— and Passeron, J. C., *Reproduction in Education, Society and Culture*, London: Sage, 1970.

—— and Wacquant, L. J. D., *An Invitation to Reflexive Sociology*, Cambridge: Polity Press, 1992.

Boyne, R., 'Power-knowledge and social theory: The systematic misrepresentation of contemporary social theory in the work of Anthony Giddens', in C. G. A. Bryant and D. Jary (eds), *Giddens' Theory of Structuration*, London: Routledge, 1991.

—— and Rattansi, A. (eds), *Postmodernism and Society*, London: Macmillan, 1990.

Braithwaite, R. B., *Scientific Explanation*, London: Cambridge University Press, 1964.

Brunhoff, S., *Etat et capital*, Grenoble: Presses Universitaires de Grenoble, 1978.

Bryant, C. G. A. and Jary, D. (eds), *Giddens' Theory of Structuration*, London: Routledge, 1991.

Burchell, G., Gordon, C. and Miller, P. (eds), *The Foucault Effect*, London: Harvester Press, 1991.

Callinicos, A., *Making History: Agency, Structure and Change in Social Theory*, Cambridge: Polity Press, 1987.

Campbell, J. K., *Honour, Family, and Patronage: A Study of Institutions and Moral Values in a Greek Mountain Community*, Oxford: Clarendon Press, 1964.

Chomsky, N., *Language and Responsibility*, Brighton: Harvester Press, 1979.

Cohen, G. A., *Karl Marx's Theory of History: A Defence*, Oxford: Clarendon Press, 1978.

—— 'Comments on the Debate', *Theory and Society*, 1982, 11.

Coleman, J. H., *The Foundations of Social Theory*, Cambridge, Mass.: Harvard University Press, 1990.

Collins, R., 'Micro-translation as a theory-building strategy', in K. Knorr-Cetina and A. V. Cicourel (eds), *Advances in Social Theory and Methodology: Towards an Integration of Micro- and Macro-Sociologies*, Boston and London: Routledge & Kegan Paul, 1981.

—— 'On the microfoundations of macrosociology', *American Journal of Sociology*, vol. 86, 1981.

—— *Weberian Sociological Theory*, London: Cambridge University Press, 1986.

—— 'Interaction ritual chains, power and property: The micro–macro connection as an empirically-based theoretical problem', in J. Alexander *et al.* (eds), *The Micro–Macro Link*, Berkeley: University of California Press, 1987.

Colomy, P., 'Uneven differentiation and incomplete institutionalization: Political

change and continuity in the early American nation', in J. C. Alexander and P. Colomy (eds), *Differentiation Theory and Social Change*, New York: Columbia University Press, 1990.
—— 'Strategic groups and political differentiation in the antebellum United States', in J. C. Alexander and P. Colomy (eds), *Differentiation Theory and Social Change*, New York: Columbia University Press, 1990.
—— (ed.) *The Dynamics of Social Systems*, London: Sage, 1992.
Cook, K. S. (ed.), *Social Exchange Theory*, London: Sage, 1987.
Cowan, J., 'Going out for coffee? Contesting the grounds of gendered pleasures in everyday sociability', in P. Loizos and E. Papataxiarchis (eds), *Contested Identities: Gender and Kinship in Modern Greece*, Princeton, N.J.: Princeton University Press, 1991.
Crook, S., 'The end of radical social theory? Radicalism, modernism and postmodernism', in R. Boyne and R. Rattansi (eds), *Postmodernism and Society*, London: Macmillan, 1990.
Deutsch, K., *The Nerves of Government*, New York: Free Press, 1963.
Dodier, N., 'Action as a combination of "common worlds"', *Sociological Review*, vol. 41, no. 3, Aug. 1993.
Domingue, J. D., 'Sociological theory and the problem of collective subjectivity', Ph.D. thesis, London School of Economics, 1993.
Dreyfus, H. L. and Rabinow, P., *Michel Foucault: Beyond Structuralism and Hermeneutics*, Brighton: Harvester Press, 1982.
Dunning, E. and Rojek, C. (eds), *Sport and Leisure in the Civilizing Process: Critique and Counter-Critique*, London: Macmillan, 1992.
—— and Sheard, K., *Barbarians, Gentlemen and Players*, Oxford: Martin Robertson, 1979.
——, Murphy, P. and Williams, J., *The Roots of Football Hooliganism*, London: Routledge, 1988.
Eisenstadt, S. N., *The Political System of Empires*, New York: Free Press, 1963.
—— with Abitbal, M., Chazan, N. and Schahar, A., 'Modes of structural differentiation, elite structure and cultural visions', in J. C. Alexander and P. Colomy (eds), *Differentiation Theory and Social Change*, New York: Columbia University Press, 1990.
Elias, N., *What is Sociology?* London: Hutchinson, 1978.
—— *The Civilizing Process* (2 vols), Oxford: Blackwell, 1978 and 1982.
—— *Involvement and Detachment*, Oxford: Blackwell, 1987.
—— *The Society of Individuals*, Oxford: Blackwell, 1991.
Elster, J., *Making Sense of Marx*, Cambridge: Cambridge University Press, 1985.
—— (ed.), *Rational Choice*, Oxford: Blackwell, 1986.
—— *The Cement of Society: A Study of Social Order*, Cambridge: Cambridge University Press, 1989.
Fielding, N. C. (ed.), *Actions and Structure: Research Methods and Social Theory*, London: Sage, 1988.
Fontana Books, *The Fontana Dictionary of Modern Thought*, London: Fontana Books, 1977.
Foucault, M., *The Order of Things*, New York: Random House, 1970.
—— *The Archaeology of Knowledge*, New York: Pantheon, 1972.
—— 'Truth and power', in C. Gordon (ed.), *Power and Knowledge*, Brighton: Harvester Press, 1980.

—— 'The confessions of the flesh', in C. Gordon (ed.), *Power and Knowledge*, Brighton: Harvester Press, 1980.

—— *The Use of Reason*, New York: Pantheon, 1985.

—— *The Care of the Self: History of Sexuality*, New York: Pantheon, 1986.

Fuchs, S., 'The constitution of emergent interaction order. A comment on Rawls', *Sociological Theory*, vol. 6, 1988.

—— 'Second thoughts on emergent interaction order', *Sociological Theory*, vol. 7, 1989.

Garfinkel, H., *Studies in Ethnomethodology*, Cambridge: Polity Press, 1984.

Geras, N., 'Post-Marxism?', *New Left Review*, no. 163, May–June 1987.

Giddens, A., *Central Problems in Social Theory*, London: Macmillan, 1979.

—— 'Commentary on the debate', *Theory, Culture and Society*, vol. 2, 1982.

—— *The Constitution of Society*, Cambridge: Polity Press, 1984.

—— 'Structuralism, post-structuralism and the production of culture', in A. Giddens and J. Turner (eds), *Social Theory Today*, Cambridge: Polity Press, 1987.

—— and Turner, J. (eds), *Social Theory Today*, Cambridge: Polity Press, 1987.

Goffman, E., 'The interaction order', *American Sociological Review*, vol. 48, 1983.

Gordon C. (ed.), *Power and Knowledge*, Brighton: Harvester Press, 1980.

Gutting, G., *Michel Foucault's Archaeology of Scientific Reason*, Cambridge: Cambridge University Press, 1986.

Habermas, J., *The Theory of Communicative Action, Vol. 1: Reason and the Rationalisation of Society*, London: Heinemann, 1984.

—— *The Theory of Communicative Action, vol. 2: Lifeworld and System: A Critique of Functional Reason*, Cambridge: Polity Press, 1987.

Harker, R. *et al.* (eds), *An Introduction to the Work of Pierre Bourdieu*, London: Macmillan, 1990.

Hirsch, T., 'The state apparatus and social reproduction: Elements of a theory of the bourgeois state', in J. Holloway and S. Piciotto (eds), *State and Capital: A Marxist Debate*, London: E. Arnold, 1978.

Holloway, J. and Piciotto, S. (eds), *State and Capital: A Marxist Debate*, London: E. Arnold, 1978.

Jenkins, R., *Pierre Bourdieu*, London: Routledge, 1991.

Johnson, T., Dandeker, C. and Ashworth, C., *The Structure of Social Theory: Dilemmas and Strategies*, London: Macmillan, 1984.

Jones, C., 'The return of the banished bourgeoisie', *Times Literary Supplement*, 29 March 1991.

Jones, R., 'Educational practices and scientific knowledge: A genealogical reinterpretation of the emergence of physiology in post-revolutionary France', in S. Ball (ed.), *Education, Discipline and Knowledge*, London and New York: Routledge, 1990.

Kellner, D., *Jean Baudrillard: From Marxism to Postmodernism and Beyond*, Cambridge: Polity Press, 1989.

King, D. S. and Wickham-Jones, M., 'Social democracy and rational workers', *British Journal of Political Science*, vol. 20, Oct. 1990.

Kitchener, R. F., 'Holistic structuralism, elementarism and Piaget's theory of rationalism', *Human Development*, vol. 28, 1985.

Knorr-Cetina, K., 'The micro-sociological challenge of macro-sociology: Towards a reconstruction of social theory and methodology', in K. Knorr-Cetina and A. V. Cicourel (eds), *Advances in Social Theory and Methodology: Towards an Integration of Micro- and Macro-Sociologies*, Boston and London: Routledge & Kegan Paul, 1981.

—— 'The micro social order: Towards a reconceptualisation', in N. C. Fielding (ed.), *Actions and Structure: Research Methods and Social Theory*, London: Sage, 1988.

—— and Cicourel, A. V., *Advances in Social Theory and Methodology: Towards an Integration of Micro- and Macro-Sociologies*, Boston and London: Routledge & Kegan Paul, 1981.

Laclau, E., *Politics and Ideology in Marxist Theory*, London: New Left Books, 1977.

—— *New Reflections on the Revolution of Our Time*, London: Verso, 1990.

—— and Mouffe, C., *Hegemony and Social Strategy: Towards a Radical Democratic Politics*, London: Verso, 1985.

Lash, S., *The Sociology of Postmodernism*, London: Routledge, 1990.

Layder, D., *Understanding Social Theory*, London: Sage, 1994.

Lechner, F. J., 'Fundamentalism and sociocultural revitalization', in J. C. Alexander and P. Colomy (eds), *Differentiation Theory and Social Change*, New York: Columbia University Press, 1990.

Levine, D., 'Parsons' structure (and Simmel) revisited', *Sociological Theory*, vol. 7, 1989.

Levy, M., *The Family Revolution in China*, Cambridge, Mass.: Harvard University Press, 1949.

Lipset, S., *The First New Nation*, New York: Doubleday, 1963.

Lockwood, D., 'Social integration and system integration', in G. K. Zollschan and W. Hirsch (eds), *Explorations in Social Change*, London: Routledge, 1964.

—— *Solidarity and Schism: 'The Problem of Disorder' in Durkheimian and Marxist Sociology*, Oxford: Oxford University Press, 1992.

Loizos, P. and Papataxiarchis, E. (eds), *Contested Identities: Gender and Kinship in Modern Greece*, Princeton, N.J.: Princeton University Press, 1991.

Luporini, C., 'Reality and historicity: Economy and dialectics in Marxism', *Economy and Society*, vol. IV, no. 2, May 1975.

Lyotard, J. F., *La Condition postmoderne*, Paris: Minuit, 1974.

McIver, R. M., *Social Causation*, New York: Harper, 1942.

McLleland, D. C., *The Achieving Society*, Princeton, N.J.: Van Nostrand, 1961.

Mann, M., *The Sources of Social Power, vol. 1, A History of Social Power from the Beginning to A.D. 1760*, Cambridge: Cambridge University Press, 1986.

March, J. G. and Simon, H. A., *Organizations*, New York: John Wiley, 1958.

Mavrogordatos, G., *Stillborn Republic: Social Conditions and Party Strategies in Greece 1922–1936*, Berkeley, Los Angeles, London: University of California Press, 1983.

Mennell, S., *Norbert Elias: Civilizations and the Human Self-Image*, Oxford: Blackwell, 1989.

Merton, R. K., *Social Theory and Social Structure*, Glencoe Ill.: Social Press, 1963.

Mills, C. W., *The Sociological Imagination*, New York: Oxford University Press, 1959.

Moore, B., *The Social Origins of Dictatorship and Democracy*, London: Allen Lane, 1967.

Mouzelis, N., 'Silverman on Organizations', *Sociology*, vol. 3, no. 1, Jan. 1969.

—— 'System and social integration: A reconsideration of a fundamental distinction', *British Journal of Sociology*, Dec. 1974.

—— *Organization and Bureaucracy: An Analysis of Modern Theories*, London: Routledge & Kegan Paul, 1975.

—— 'Ideology and class politics: A critique of Ernesto Laclau', *New Left Review*, no. 112, Nov.–Dec. 1978.

—— *Modern Greece: Facets of Underdevelopment*, London: Macmillan, 1978.

—— 'Types of reductionism in Marxist theory', *Telos*, Fall 1980.

—— *Politics in the Semi-Periphery: Early Parliamentarism and Late Industrialization in the Balkans and Latin America*, London: Macmillan, 1985.

—— 'Marxism versus Post-Marxism', *New Left Review*, no. 167, Jan.–Feb. 1988.

—— 'Restructuring structuration theory', *Sociological Review*, Nov. 1989.

—— *Post-Marxist Alternatives: The Construction of Social Orders*, London: Macmillan, 1990.

—— *Back to Sociological Theory: The Construction of Social Orders*, London: Macmillan, 1990.

—— 'The interaction order and the micro–macro distinction', *Sociological Theory*, vol. 9, no. 2, Nov. 1991.

Nadel, S. F., *The Theory of Social Structure*, vol. 1, London: Routledge, 1962.

Olson, M., *The Logic of Collective Action: Public Goods and the Theory of Goods*, Cambridge, Mass.: Harvard University Press, 1965.

O'Neil, J. (ed.), *Modes of Individualism and Collectivism*, London: Heinemann, 1973.

Paige, J. M., *Agrarian Revolution*, New York: Free Press, 1975.

Papataxiarchis, E. and Paradellis, T. (eds), *Identities and Gender in Modern Greece* (in Greek), Athens: Kastaniotis, 1992.

Parsons, T., *The Social System*, London: Routledge, 1951.

—— *The Evolution of Societies*, Englewood Cliffs, N.J.: Prentice Hall, 1977.

—— 'On building social systems theory: Some of its functions', in his *Social Systems and the Evolution of Action Theory*, New York: Free Press, 1977.

—— *Social Systems and the Evolution of Action Theory*, New York: Free Press, 1977.

—— and Smelser, N., *Economy and Society*, London: Routledge & Kegan Paul, 1956.

—— et al. (eds), *Theories of Societies*, New York: Free Press, 1960.

Piaget, J., *Introduction à l'épistemologie genetique*, vol. III, Paris: Presses Universitaires de France, vol. 3, 1950.

Pierce, C. S., *The Collected Papers of Charles Saunders Pierce*, ed. C. Hartshorne and P. Weiss, Cambridge, Mass.: Harvard University Press, 1932–5.

Popkin, S., *The Rational Peasant*, Berkeley: University of California Press, 1979.

Poulantzas, N., *L'Etat, le pouvoir, le socialisme*, Paris: Presses Universitaires de France, 1978.

Przeworkski, A., *Capitalism and Social Democracy*, Cambridge: Cambridge University Press, 1986.

Rawls, A. W., 'The interaction order *sui generis*: Goffman's contribution to social theory', *Sociological Theory*, vol. 5, 1987.

—— 'Interaction vs. interaction order. Reply to Fuchs', *Sociological Theory*, vol. 6, 1988.

Roemer, J. E., *Analytical Foundations of Marxian Economic Theory*, Cambridge: Cambridge University Press, 1986.

—— (ed.), *Analytic Marxism*, Cambridge: Cambridge University Press, 1986.

—— *Free to Lose*, Cambridge, Mass.: Harvard University Press, 1988.

Rogers, E. M., *Modernization among Peasants: The Impact of Communication*, New York: Rinehart & Winston, 1969.

Sahlins, M. D. and Service, E. R. (eds), *Evolution and Culture*, Ann Arbor, Mich.: University of Michigan Press, 1960.

Simon, H. A., *Administrative Behaviour*, New York: Macmillan, 1961.

Skocpol, T., *States and Social Revolutions: A Comparative Analysis of France, Russia and China*, London and New York: Cambridge University Press, 1979.

Smelser, N., *Social Change in the Industrial Revolution: An Application of Theory to the Lancashire Cotton Industry 1770–1840*, London: Routledge & Kegan Paul, 1962.

—— 'Evaluating the model of structural differentiation in relation to educational change in the nineteenth century', in J. C. Alexander (ed.), *Neo-Functionalism*, London: Sage, 1985,

Taylor, M. (ed.), *Rationality and Revolution*, Cambridge: Cambridge University Press, 1988.

Thompson, E. P., *The Making of the English Working Class*, London: Allen Lane, Penguin, 1963.

Thrift, N., 'Bear and mouse or bear and tree? Anthony Giddens' reconstitution of social theory', *Sociology*, vol. 19, no. 4.

Turner, J. J., *A Theory of Social Interaction*, Cambridge: Polity Press, 1990.

Wallerstein, E., *The Modern World System: Capitalist Agriculture and the Origins of the European World Economy in the Sixteenth Century*, New York and London: Academic Press, 1974.

Weber, M., *The City*, London: Macmillan, 1958.

Wilkes, C., 'Bourdieu's class', in R. Harker *et al.* (eds), *An Introduction to the Work of P. Bourdieu*, London: Macmillan, 1990.

Wolf, E., *Peasant Wars of the Twentieth Century*, London: Faber & Faber, 1971.

Zollschan, G. K. and Hirsch, W. (eds), *Explorations in Social Change*, London: Routledge & Kegan Paul, 1964.

INDEX